NEW WOMEN

New Women

Short Stories by Canadian Women

1900–1920

CANADIAN
SHORT
STORY
LIBRARY,
No. 14

Edited by
Sandra Campbell
and Lorraine McMullen

University of Ottawa Press
Ottawa • Paris

Canadian Short Story Library, Series 2
John Moss, General Editor

© University of Ottawa Press, 1991
  Printed and bound in Canada
  ISBN 0-7766-0323-X

Canadian Cataloguing in Publication Data
Main entry under title:
  New women

(The Canadian short story library; 14)
Includes bibliographical references.
ISBN 0-7766-0323-X

  1. Short stories, Canadian (English) — Women
authors. 2. Canadian literature (English) — Women
authors. 3. Canadian literature (English) — 20th
century. I. Campbell, Sandra. II. McMullen, Lorraine,
1926- . III. Series.

PS8327.N49 1991   C813'.010   C91-090043-4
PR9197.33.W65N49 1991

UNIVERSITÉ D'OTTAWA
UNIVERSITY OF OTTAWA

"An Adventure in Youth" by Mary Lowrey Ross
reprinted with the kind permission of Mary Hutton.
"The Quarantine at Alexander Abraham's" by
L. M. Montgomery reprinted with the kind permission
of Marion D. Hebb.

Series design concept: Miriam Bloom
Book design: Marie Tappin
Cover photo courtesy of National Archives Canada
(PA 138853)

For
Sarah Horrall
(1940–1988)

Valued colleague, revered teacher,
respected scholar

CONTENTS

Introduction

Alice Munro, Mavis Gallant, Margaret Atwood, Margaret Laurence. Today, Canadian short fiction writers are among the most esteemed in the world, and the names of women are very much in evidence. It is not always appreciated, however, that these women are writing in a long tradition of Canadian women writers.

Short fiction has always appealed to women, as writers and as readers. Yet, because little short fiction of the nineteenth and early twentieth centuries has been collected, or even catalogued, hundreds of stories lie buried in back issues of newspapers and periodicals, lost to today's readers. This is particularly true of the writings of women, who have tended to have less access to major publishing centres and to publication in book form than their male counterparts. Given the importance of recovering women's writings and the significance of the short story as literary genre and its value as social document, our objective is to make the short fiction of earlier women accessible. This book introduces early twentieth-century women, some of whom have had an enduring reputation — L. M. Montgomery and Nellie McClung, for instance — and some of whom need to be discovered anew. Their stories illustrate ideas these women valorize in their writings, and the complexity and subtlety with which they manipulate the short story, the most protean of literary forms.

By the early years of this century, the short story was enjoying great popularity throughout North America. In the United States, such skilled exponents of the form as Bret Harte, Sarah Orne Jewett and O. Henry had helped establish a public appetite for the genre in all its variety. Canadians — readers and authors alike — shared this enthusiasm for the short story. Writers like Charles G. D. Roberts, Ernest Thompson Seton, E. W. Thomson and Duncan Campbell Scott were well known in the form, Roberts and Seton with animal stories, Thomson and Scott with local colour. Stephen Leacock was becoming an international byword for the comic sketch.

For their part, Canadian women writers were turning their pens to this current — and marketable — means of self-expression. One popular periodical of the day, the *Canadian Magazine*, published over three hundred stories by Canadian women in the two decades represented in this anthology. Many of these stories are conventional, uninspired exercises in the popular modes of the era: tales of historical romance or local colour, "society" love stories, or moralistic melodramas rife with penniless waifs, unexpected bequests and surprise endings (especially on Christmas Eve). But some of the stories published by women at this period are not only entertaining but of particular artistic and/or historical merit. After all, 1900 to 1920 was the era of female campaigns for suffrage and for temperance and of continuing public debate over the "New Woman," who had first evolved in the eighties and nineties with her need for independence and a career. The country itself was becoming, in the words of two leading Canadian historians, "a nation transformed"[1] — increasingly urbanized and industrialized and the object of immigration by many ethnic groups on a scale unprecedented in Canadian history. More women were entering the labour force in a wider variety of jobs.[2] At the close of the period, the country experienced the upheaval, suffering and maturation of the Great War. By 1922, women were to win the right to vote in federal and in provincial elections (except in Quebec).

Given such change, many women were seeing themselves in new ways: they were energetically examining their relations with one another, with men and with society. Some of Canada's best-known female writers spoke out publicly on social issues. Nellie McClung campaigned for temperance and women's suffrage from the perspective of a maternal feminist seeking to bring women's domestic virtues to bear on social ills. Pauline Johnson addressed the treatment of the native peoples. Kit Coleman treated a wide variety of current events and issues in her widely read women's column in the Toronto *Mail*. Like Coleman, many of the well-known female journalists of the period (Jean Blewett, Ethelwyn Wetherald, Mabel Burkholder) also wrote fiction.

This collection makes clear that the short stories of women writers were frequently coloured by the momentous transitions underway in women's status and in society. Women employed the power of the short story form to portray telling incidents or vignettes from life in ways that foreground the aspirations and frustrations of the women of this time. The reader is immediately struck, for example, by the number of stories published at this time in which the female protagonists belong to one of the occupations recently opened to women — doctor, lawyer, manager, journalist, factory worker, secretary — natural subject matter for women writers who themselves experienced at first hand the interplay of personal and professional life.[3]

In fact, the most striking characteristic of these stories is the way in which many of them reflect shifts underway in Canadian society and women's roles, especially vis-à-vis men. In stories like "A Pair of Gray Gloves," "An Adventure in Youth," "The Heir Apparent" and "The Experiences of a Woman Bachelor," the conflict that is at the heart of any effective short story derives from psychological tension within the individual, or dramatic conflict between men and women. The stories address the shifting balance of love, identity and vocation. In "A Pair of Gray Gloves," Kit Coleman's protagonist, a woman journalist, is toiling over a long article about the impossibility of platonic love between men and women as her own love affair is ending. The "old woman" image which concludes that story is echoed in "An Adventure in Youth" by Mary Lowrey Ross. Much of the interest of the latter story centres on Ross's depiction of the sensitive, intelligent, elderly woman narrator, whose involvement in a young girl's romance is ultimately shadowed by her realization that the girl sees her, not as one of "the sisterhood of the rising generation," but as a stereotypical "old dear," a spinster at the margin of life and love. The presentation of youthful romance is thus qualified by ironic contrast. Sara Jeannette Duncan's "The Heir Apparent" sketches the illusions of two older women, both convinced that the niece of one will undoubtedly marry a man of genius, one worthy of her own "spark of genius." Romantic and intellectual aspirations are both treated humorously by Jean Blewett in "The Experiences of a Woman Bachelor."

Blewett presents an exchange of letters between a young baccalaureate and her conventional friend. After college, Eunice Complin's unsuccessful attempts at intellectual, platonic friendships with men are repeatedly interpreted by the men involved as romantic. Blewett's ending, however, in which quest is set aside for marriage, does not resolve the expectations aroused in us by the half-teasing, half-wistful and subversive challenge made to Eunice by her housewife friend at the outset of the story:

> I expect great things from you. What are you going to make of yourself? You surely won't fall in love and marry. Leave all this sweet foolishness to us who know nothing of the delights of brand new womanhood; who can't write books, speak on platforms, box, fence, run, row or analyse our emotions; who hang to our embroidery frames, our smelling salts, our whims — created from the beginning to be in bondage to the sterner sex, and to hug our chains.

In Ethelwyn Wetherald's "Jealousy," the image of the subjugation of wife to husband becomes tragic. A traditional wife-and-mother is unable to deal with her husband's intellectual rapport with a female colleague, a rapport that, through no fault of her own, she is unable to emulate. Wetherald's ending dramatizes the inadequacies of a concept of marriage in which the wife is restricted to the narrow role of "child" or "little girl." For her part, Mazo de la Roche implicitly questions the fitness of a wife's devotion to her husband at all costs. In "Canadian Ida and English Nell," Nell marshalls shrewdness, determination and domestic skills to reclaim her emigrant husband. But the victory is hollow, the "happy ending" ironic. The husband for whom Nell has struggled is not only weak and dishonest: ironically, their reconciliation is cemented by his guilt at once having severely beaten her.

L. M. Montgomery, on the other hand, presents a more optimistic skirmish between the sexes in "The Quarantine at Alexander Abraham's," when a single woman who is contemptuous of men and a misogynistic bachelor move from antagonism to reciprocal concern and support.

By contrast, for the first time in her marriage, the long-suffering Jane Bender of Adeline Teskey's story "The Ram Lamb" finds the will to resist her husband's financial and emotional autocracy. On one level, Jane Bender's situation is a local-colour rendering of the actual problems of farm women. Her lament in a sequel that "I never hed no money I could call my own, an' Jake would give me none o' hisn"[4] could serve as an epigraph to the writings of social historians of the period, who have observed that farm women usually received little or no pay for their labour-intensive work:

> . . . few farm wives received *tangible* recognition. Farmers were notorious for purchasing new equipment for the barn or fields but refusing to buy anything for the house.[5]

The issue of recognition and remuneration for farm wives has endured to our own day, notably in the early 1970s in the legal battle of Irene Murdoch, wife of a Saskatchewan farmer, for an equitable divorce settlement.[6]

Other stories in this volume are also rooted in historical realities of the time. As W. H. New suggests, the "documentary impulse" characteristic of much Canadian literature is very apparent in our short fiction.[7] The magazine that in 1905 published Alice Jones's "At the Harbour's Mouth" reminded its readers that Jones's Julla Perrier is a fictional version of the more than 165,000 Maritime women who left Canada between 1881 and 1921 to seek a livelihood on the eastern seaboard of the United States.[8] Jones involves her character in a conflict between her desire to return to Nova Scotia to marry for love and her sense of obligation for the debts of her Boston dressmaking business, a dilemma between labour and love that is resolved only by an unexpected windfall. The "liquor question" so hotly debated early in the century underlies Isabel Ecclestone Mackay's "The Despair of Sandy MacIntosh"; it also enters into Nellie McClung's "The Live Wire."

In "The Assimilation of Christina," Jean McIlwraith's central character is a familiar figure of the day: an immigrant domestic servant from the British Isles. Although set in the United States, Edith Eaton's "Mrs. Spring Fragrance" draws on widespread discrimination against Orientals and cultural conflict within the Chinese immigrant community that its author, a Eurasian, experienced in both Canada and the United States. As "Sui Sin Far," Eaton wrote sympathetically of the difficulties of Chinese and Eurasian families, especially women, in North America. For her part, Eaton's sister Winnifred Babcock Reeve ("Onoto Watanna") wrote about Japanese characters, against whom prejudice was considerably less virulent in North America in the early years of the century. "Miss Lily and Miss Chrysanthemum" is one example of her popular fiction on this theme.

In fact, "problem fiction" which foregrounded social or religious questions had great appeal at this time, as the popularity in Canada and elsewhere of English novelist Marie Corelli and Canadian novelist Ralph Connor indicates.[9] Women writers recognized that the short story form was well suited to the portrayal of a single aspect of such questions. Labour unrest animates "The Heart of Kerry" by Mabel Burkholder, who also wrote a novel on the subject.[10] Nellie McClung's "The Live Wire" lampoons the venality and vanity of the all-male political world, an arena she was determined to transform through female suffrage. "Munitions!," like many of J. Georgina Sime's stories, shows her keen understanding of the social conditions of women of the period, particularly working-class women. Through Bertha, the protagonist of her sketch, Sime conveys the situation and state of mind that prompted thousands of young women to forsake domestic service for munitions work at the time of the Great War. Bertha exults in her greater social and sexual freedom, but Sime's story also captures the fatigue and exploitation experienced by plant workers. The story draws on the situation as it actually existed in the munitions industry:

> . . . by 1917 over 35,000 women in Ontario and
> Quebec were producing shells for the Allies.
> Although the munitions manufacturers paid
> wages well above those earned by women in tra-
> ditional occupations, female munitions workers
> in 1917 earned only 50–83 percent of what their
> male co-workers earned. In addition, the wartime

emergency was used to justify extremely long hours (13–14 hours a day) and deplorable working conditions.[11]

The experience of the Great War, particularly as it affected the home front, colours many of the stories by Canadian women after 1914. Of the war's "turmoil of echoing misery" Sime recalled that, "though we [women] were far from the scene of conflict, the facts of death and destruction were brought home to Canadian women in the cities of the Dominion."[12] In "An Adventure in Youth," Mary Lowrey Ross incorporates the spiritual questioning and the attitudes to military service generated by the horrendous casualty lists of the Western Front. Most war stories by women at this time do not reject the war, but they do acknowledge its terrible toll in physical suffering and spiritual malaise.[13] Such stories often end with a mitigation of suffering or even a miraculous "happy ending." Such is the case with "An Adventure in Youth." Here, while the romance ends happily and the heroic soldier returns to battle, the anguish and suffering of war is displaced to the woman narrator's own sense of loss and marginality.

Women were not simply writing direct or refracted social commentary in short stories, however. To encompass the scope of women's short fiction in the period 1900 to 1920, we ought to consider the importance of the wilderness, sometimes thought of as a male topic. Stories of the wilderness — whether Jack London's tales of Alaska, the northern fiction of D. C. Scott and Gilbert Parker, or the animal stories of Charles G. D. Roberts and Ernest Thompson Seton — abounded in the literature of the time. The elemental struggle for survival, be it that of man or beast, is central to such fiction by the very nature of the setting.[14] The portrayal of the wilderness as a testing ground for the human psyche had a special appeal for some women writers, notably, in this text, Susan Jones and Marjorie Pickthall. J. G. Sime crystallized this appeal in her memoir of the Laurentian bush at the time of the Great War:

But up from that soil on which my feet rested and out of that circumambient air, so it felt to me, came something else — a sense of the possession of that land by something earlier than any of us. Was it the Indian I was thinking of? Was it something even more primitive than that? Was this land we were camping on not meant for us, and was it still held by forces that none of us would be able to control? . . . Canada is a strange land. Once you leave the cities and go even a few hours away you feel the power of its earth. The people are nothing . . . [they] grow faint against that insistent earth.[15]

In such an uncompromising environment, the stories of Jones and Pickthall suggest, a divided self will perish. In Pickthall's "On Ile de Paradis," the wilderness is a "step-mother to the ignorant," testing individuals to the utmost:

Brains fail so easily, so easily, in the wilds. It is all perfectly simple, perfectly explicable, perfectly horrible.

The Reverend Antoine, whose resourcefulness, iron will and steadfast faith prevail over his fears and conflicts, survives when stranded on the ironically named Ile de Paradis, but the tenderfoot he finds there has been reduced to "less than a beast" in the wilds: he is a doomed being, incapable of speech, whose "soul must be somewhere wandering in the woods, looking for its lost house." At the outset of Susan Jones's "The Frenchwoman's Son" the protagonist survives a trek across dangerous, alien Long Swamp, instinctively sustained by skills which, he later discovers, are the legacy of his native father. After he rejects the aboriginal part of his heritage, he dies "as a white man" in the Long Swamp, doomed by the confusion and inner conflict his denial has precipitated.

Other stories celebrate the prowess of the native Indian. In "The Assimilation of Christina" by Jean McIlwraith, the young Scottish servant Christina initially senses what Joe, the young Ojibway, represents. His dignity and self-sufficiency within nature are contrasted with the crudeness of the urban worker:

Motormen, plumbers, electric light men, with
their cheap slang and clumsy gallantries, were
part of the semi-civilisation that had kept up the
heartache for old Scotland. Here, at last, was the
free, untrammeled America of her dreams. To be
no hireling, but to fish and hunt directly for his
living — that seemed the fitting way for a man to
live.

But, before resolving to marry Joe, Christina must overcome
her own prejudices — those of white society — which lead
her to treat him as an inferior. White attitudes towards the
Indian are also at the centre of Pauline Johnson's "The
Haunting Thaw." Of Mohawk ancestry and the daughter of
a chief, Johnson saw herself as an advocate for her people in
art as well as in life. The Indian sled driver of "The
Haunting Thaw" is portrayed as the proud equal of both the
wilderness and the Scots trader. (Like Pickthall and Susan
Jones, Johnson underlines the degree of skill and self-knowledge needed to sustain oneself in the wilderness.) The
story's stress on the ability and autonomy of this native partner in the fur trade forms an interesting contrast to another
story of the fur trade published in the same year, 1907. In
"Expiation" by Duncan Campbell Scott, a white trader rec-
ognizes the pride and prowess of his Indian partner only
after he has destroyed both qualities.[16] In Scott's "Expiation,"
unlike "The Haunting Thaw," the Indian is a secondary
character whose virtues are used as a foil for the central character's folly; the former is devalued and destroyed beyond
hope of recompense.

The stories in this collection illustrate the variety
of writing styles of the time. Local-colour writing continued
to be widely popular early in the century; Adeline Teskey,
L. M. Montgomery, Nellie McClung, Jean McIlwraith,
Isabel Ecclestone Mackay, Alice Jones and Mazo de la Roche
provide the flavour and sometimes the speech of specific
locales. Marjorie Pickthall, Susan Jones and Pauline Johnson
all use landscape to create haunting atmosphere, thus giving
their stories a tincture of romance. The contrived twists of
plot frequent in the fiction of the early twentieth century can
be found in Alice Jones's "At the Harbour's Mouth" and

Mabel Burkholder's "The Heart of Kerry," among others. In other modes, Sara Jeannette Duncan writes with a complexity and irony that owe something to Henry James, while Georgina Sime's prose strives for Flaubertian precision and irony.[17] Some writers have a gift for characterization. The peppery Miss Peter MacNicol of "The Quarantine at Alexander Abraham's" is a strong-willed woman in L. M. Montgomery's deft comic style, one whose belated venture into matrimony will clearly mellow but not subjugate her. Nellie McClung's "The Live Wire" opens with the lively dialogue of the young Pearlie Watson, the female hero of three of McClung's most popular books — *Sowing Seeds in Danny* (1908), *The Second Chance* (1910) and *Purple Springs* (1922). Pearlie, a child in this story, grows up intelligent, articulate, intrepid and a proponent of temperance and women's suffrage. Jean McIlwraith's Christina has real individuality, as does de la Roche's bumptious Nell.

Handling of voice and perspective becomes more sophisticated in these stories. Duncan makes deft use of first-person narration in "The Heir Apparent" to shade the ironies of three women's estimations of a young man's abilities. Through the use of the epistolary form, Jean Blewett successfully juggles two perspectives in "The Experiences of a Woman Bachelor." In "Mrs. Spring Fragrance," Edith Eaton manipulates the omniscient point of view to present — in a lighter vein than in many of her stories — a conflict of Chinese and New World values which affects relations between husband and wife. By use of monologue in "Frieda's Engagement" and "Gifts," Madge Macbeth gives immediacy to her satiric portrayal of a selfish and malicious young woman of fashion. The incessant "I" of the monologue enmeshes the reader in the woman's narcissism and lays bare her shortcomings as an individual. The "I" of Ross's first-person narrative in "An Adventure in Youth" functions differently. The sensibility of the narrator is an ironic and affecting filter for a tale of young love: the use of the first person makes the story more intimate and poignant in tone. By contrast, the effect of third-person narration in Georgina Sime's "Munitions!" is to distance the reader somewhat from the characters, disposing one to focus not so much on individuals as on the social realities of the lives of domestics and factory workers and on the consciousness engendered by such experience. Moreover, the use of the sketch form by Sime, the epistolary form by Blewett, and the monologue form by Macbeth gives their stories the aura of social documentary.

It is noteworthy that Sime's story touches on a young woman's awakening sexuality in a way rarely found in Canadian stories of this period. In "Munitions!," Sime describes Bertha's sexual arousal after an incident on the factory floor:

> There was the Factory — the Factory, with its coarse, strong, beckoning life — its noise — its dirt — its men.
>
> Its men! And suddenly into Bertha Martin's cheek a wave of colour surged. Yesterday — was it yesterday? — that man had caught her strong, round arm as she was passing him — and held it.
>
> Her breath came short. She felt a throbbing. She stopped smiling — and her eyes grew large.

In Canada, such material in a short story — even treated with the restraint of Sime — was found at this period only in stories that, like hers, were published in book form. Undoubtedly because Mrs. Grundy might be a reader, magazines like *Saturday Night*, *Maclean's* and *Canadian Magazine* were circumspect in their choice of stories. That is to say, not until after World War I did *Canadian Magazine*, to take one example, occasionally publish stories that treated such topics as adultery and divorce as a reality of contemporary life.[18] But the emphasis even in these magazine stories tended to be on the social disruption and individual disillusionment attendant on such things; moreover, physical passion was still definitely offstage. It was largely left to "Munitions!" and other stories of Sime's 1919 volume *Sister Woman* to treat such topics as divorce, extra-marital sex, illegitimacy and prostitution with greater candour and complexity than could be found in Canadian magazines.[19] The magazines themselves acknowledged this. When *Sister Woman* was published in London and Toronto,[20] Peter Donovan's review in *Saturday Night* coyly referred to the unusual subject matter:

> Clerks, munitions workers, charwomen — the author knows them all and writes of them gracefully and sympathetically, especially of those whose histories are rather unconventional, let us say.[21]

As John Moss has observed, it was not until the mid-twenties that "sexual relations came into the open in Canadian letters" with Martha Ostenso's *Wild Geese* (1925), Frederick Philip Grove's *Settlers of the Marsh* (1925) and Mazo de la Roche's *Jalna* (1927).[22]

Sime's story bears mention in another respect. Adeline Teskey's "A Common Man and His Wife: The Ram Lamb" (1901) and Sime's "Munitions!" (1919) frame the time span of this anthology. The differences in tone and treatment in the two stories are a microcosm of changes taking place in women and in the genre. For her part, Teskey deals with a farm woman in a story that is unmistakably a Canadian variant of the "kailyard" school of fiction with its "double specification of work and worship"[23] — in a sequel, the industrious Jane Bender selflessly uses her prize money to aid a missionary in India, winning her husband to the cause.[24] The tone of the story is homespun and familiar. As a writer, Teskey embraced the rural, the small town and the devout, and in some of her stories looked back to pioneer days.[25] By contrast, Sime's story treats a type of the female industrial worker in an urban context. A marked social and feminist awareness quite unlike Teskey's pervades Sime's prose: the style and effect are very different. Sime's story, unlike Teskey's, anticipates in some respects the Depression stories of Dorothy Livesay, Mary Quayle Innis and others.[26]

As we have seen, many of the twenty stories of this collection have as backdrop (vivid in some stories, dim in others) the social change of the period 1900–1920, change that left few women untouched or indifferent, women writers of fiction — with its responsiveness to social mores — least of all. For women, 1900 marked not only the numerals of a new century but also another landmark publication by the National Council of Women of a federally funded report, *Women of Canada: Their Life and Work* — "the first national portrait of Canadian women." The two decades to 1920 saw changes in all areas this report addressed — changes in, to cite *Canadian Women: A History*, "women's group activities and problems in the legal and political realms, the professions, in trades and industries, education, literature, the arts, the churches, charitable and reform work, and social life"[27] in addition to changes in individual lives. Change did not stop in 1920, of course. Far from it. But once the Great War and its immediate aftermath were past, women, society and literature were launched on a new era with its own changes and characteristics.

Canada's small population (about seven million in 1914) and smaller literary world in the period 1900–1920 are reflected in the bonds of friendship and/or collegiality among her women writers. As women, located as they were at the edge of a group — writers — itself marginalized in Canadian society, women writers looked to one another for support. For example, Kit Coleman, Mabel Burkholder (Coleman's biographer) and Jean Blewett, among others, were members of the pioneering Canadian Women's Press Club. Isabel Ecclestone Mackay was a friend to Pauline Johnson and Marjorie Pickthall when the latter two moved to Vancouver. Through their early success as journalists in the eighties and nineties, Kit Coleman and Sara Jeannette Duncan inspired other women writers, while L. M. Montgomery and Nellie McClung were icons of success early in this century. Family ties bound sisters Winnifred Reeve and Edith Eaton, and sisters-in-law and cousins Alice and Susan Jones. Home towns linked Sara Jeannette Duncan, Mary Lowrey Ross and Pauline Johnson (Brantford) and Jean McIlwraith and Mabel Burkholder (Hamilton). The isolation of women writers was beginning to lift as each found literary voice in an era of change.

This anthology is rooted in two decades whose literature is a crucible of change, and the currents that swirl in the stories — feminism, realism, local colour, romance, melodrama, social problems — coalesce in an intriguing way. Many of the stories are focused on the inner lives of the protagonists (usually women). Inner life takes primacy over outer action: here we have the beginnings of a shift in emphasis characteristic of the modern short story. The moment is ripe to look at these earlier, more pioneering decades — to make available to the present-day reader for the first time a substantial number of short stories published by Canada's leading women writers between 1900 and 1920.[28]

Accordingly, we called this anthology "New Women" in response to the currents of social change and feminism implicit in many of these stories. Although many of our authors were by no means new women in the strict sense of the term coined for strong-minded, non-conformist women by English novelist George Gissing in his *Odd Women* (1893), none of them was untouched — if only in reaction — by the debate over women's place in society, so prominent in the Western world in the late nineteenth and early twentieth centuries. The title also suggests the need to consider anew the work of women writers of the past. We need to reassess these women writers with a better understanding of their sensibility and milieu — and of ours.

As editors of this anthology, we have been fortunate in the generous assistance and advice of many people in its preparation. To the following, our thanks for their interest, support and expertise: Marilyn Barber, Thora Brown, Warwick Caverhill, Gwen Davies, Douglas Daymond, Misao Dean, John Dunn, Barbara Freeman, Carole Gerson, Deborah Gorham, Mollie Hutton, Marjory Lang, Gerald Lynch, Carrie MacMillan, Duncan McDowall, W. H. New, Mary O'Brien, Jeremy Palin, Mary Rubio, Frank Tierney, R. B. Tuer, Elizabeth Waterston and Jane Watt. Marie McKinnon typed the manuscript with speed and efficiency.

We are grateful to Marcel Hamelin, former Dean, Faculty of Arts, University of Ottawa, for the research grant that made this project possible. Lorraine McMullen's research on Canadian women's fiction is also supported by the Social Sciences and Humanities Research Council of Canada.

INTRODUCTION

Notes

1   See R. C. Brown and Ramsay Cook, *Canada 1896–1921: A Nation Transformed* (Toronto: McClelland and Stewart, 1974).

2   To wit: between 1901 and 1911, the female paid labour force increased by fifty percent. By 1921, only eleven percent of working women were in domestic service, whereas nearly half of working women had been domestic servants just thirty years earlier. In the first two decades of this century, the industrial, retail and clerical sectors began to be a major source of employment for women, albeit one with difficult working conditions and low wages. Over seventeen percent of Canadian women over the age of fifteen were in the paid labour force by 1921. See Alison Prentice, Paula Bourne, Gail Cuthbert Grant, Beth Light, Wendy Mitchinson and Naomi Black, *Canadian Women: A History* (Toronto: Harcourt Brace Jovanovich, 1988), 113–141, 220.

3   For example, Jean Blewett, "Dr. Dorothy Treherne: An Easter Love Story," *Canadian Magazine* 20 (April 1903): 558–564, about a woman physician; a woman journalist figures in Ethel Seymour's "Valuable Space," *Canadian Magazine* 39 (Oct. 1912): 502–516; a woman manager's judgement is vindicated in Hilda Ridley, "The Harder Way," *Canadian Magazine* 40 (Nov. 1912): 59–62. All these stories valorize women's professional competence — quest — as well as romance.

4   Adeline Teskey, "A Common Man and His Wife: How Jane Spent the Prize Money," *Where the Sugar Maple Grows: Idylls of a Canadian Village* (Toronto: Musson, 1901), 75.

5   See Prentice *et al.*, 118, 398–399.

6   *Ibid.*

7   W. H. New, *Dreams of Speech and Violence: The Art of the Short Story in Canada and New Zealand* (Toronto: University of Toronto Press, 1987), 21.

8   Prentice *et al.*, 125.

9   See Mary Vipond, "Best Sellers in English Canada 1899–1918: An Overview," *Journal of Canadian Fiction* 24 (1979): 96–119.

10   Mabel Burkholder, *The Course of Impatience Carningham* (Toronto: Musson, 1912).

11   Prentice *et al.*, 139.

12   J. G. Sime, *In a Canadian Shack* (Toronto: Macmillan, 1937), 122.

13   Some examples — Jean Blewett, "Love Pays the Score" and "The Little Refugee," *Heart Stories* (Toronto: Warwick, 1919) (published in aid of the Imperial Order of the Daughters of the Empire [IODE]), are dream-come-true tales of war wounds and war losses healed. In Mazo de la Roche's "The Comrade," *Canadian Magazine* 48 (Dec. 1916): 148–151, an other-worldly Christ figure helps a soldier at the front to save a mother and child. Isabel Ecclestone Mackay's "The Curtain," *Canadian Magazine* 48 (Dec. 1916): 89–99, deals with a soldier's recovery from shell shock after a traumatic incident at the Front. Nellie McClung's "Men and Money," *Maclean's* 32 (Nov. 1919): 15–17, 99–100, underlines the sacrifices of parents whose sons went to war, never to return, in contrast to the selfish materialism of others who sacrificed nothing.

14   Peter Schmitt, "Wilderness Novels in the Progressive Era," *Journal of Popular Culture* 111, 1 (1969): 76–77.

15   J. G. Sime, *In a Canadian Shack*, 219.

16   D. C. Scott's "Expiation" was first published as "The Recompense," *Munsey's Magazine* 38 (1907): 25–28; Pauline Johnson's "The Haunting Thaw" appeared in *Canadian Magazine* 29 (May 1907): 20–22.

17   Desmond Pacey, "Fiction 1920–1940," *Literary History of Canada*, 1965 ed., 675.

18   For example, Beatrice Redpath, "Out of Reach," *Canadian Magazine* 53 (Oct. 1919): 464–472; Mary Heaton Vorse, "At Tristan," *Canadian Magazine* 55 (Sept. 1920): 399–406; Helen N. Brooks, "With the Tide," *Canadian Magazine* 55 (Oct. 1920): 484–494. Daringly, *Canadian Bookman* reprinted Sime's "An Irregular Union" about extra-marital love, taken from *Sister Woman*, in April 1920 (pp. 59–60).

19   London: Grant Richards, 1919.

20   The book was also issued under the imprint of the firm of S. B. Gundy, Toronto.

21   "Tom Folio" (Peter Donovan), review of *Sister Woman*, by J. G. Sime, *Saturday Night*, 28 Feb. 1920: 9.

22   John Moss, *Sex and Violence in the Canadian Novel* (Toronto: McClelland and Stewart, 1977), 13.

23   Elizabeth Waterston, "Canadian Cabbage, Canadian Rose" (1973), rpt. *Twentieth Century Essays on Confederation Literature*, ed. Lorraine McMullen (Ottawa: Tecumseh, 1976), 96.

24   Teskey, "How Jane Spent the Prize Money," *Where the Sugar Maple Grows*.

25   Teskey, *Candlelight Days* (London: Cassell, 1913).

26   A selection of these stories is available in *Voices of Discord: Canadian Short Stories from the 1930s*, ed. Donna Phillips (Toronto: New Hogtown, 1979).

27   Prentice *et al.*, 189.

28   For example, Rosemary Sullivan's *Stories by Canadian Women* (Toronto: Oxford, 1984) and W. H. New's *Canadian Short Fiction: from myth to modern* (Scarborough: Prentice-Hall, 1986) each contains one story by a woman for this period, while Margaret Atwood and Robert Weaver's *The Oxford Book of Canadian Short Stories* (Toronto: Oxford, 1986) contains none.

Adeline M. Teskey (c.1855–1924)

A Common Man and His Wife: The Ram Lamb (1901)

This story appeared in 1901, as the nature of the country was shifting from largely agrarian to industrial, from two cultures to multiculturalism. In this period, no writer gave more affectionate voice to the values of the devout and the bucolic — that Canadian version of "kailyard" fiction that Elizabeth Waterston has so vividly described for us — than Adeline Margaret Teskey. Born in Appleton (near Almonte), Ontario, of Irish, German and English descent (groups warmly depicted in her fiction), she was the daughter of Elizabeth Kerfoot and Thomas Appleton Teskey, members of the pioneering families of the area. Teskey was educated at Genesee College, Lima, New York and at Boston art schools. She taught art for a time at Alma Ladies' College in St. Thomas. Teskey lived for many years in the family home in Welland on the Niagara peninsula; about 1904 she moved to Toronto where she died on 21 March 1924.

Her short fiction appeared in a variety of Canadian and American periodicals. Her novels include *The Yellow Pearl* (1911), the story of an orphan girl of Chinese–American parentage taken to live with her racist aunt and uncle, and *Candlelight Days* (1913), which fictionalizes actual incidents of pioneer life in the Niagara area and elsewhere. Other works present simple Christian morals.

"A Common Man and His Wife: The Ram Lamb" is taken from Teskey's best-known book, *Where the Sugar Maple Grows* (1901), a collection of twenty-two stories set in and around the "typical Canadian village" of Mapleton, an imaginative version of Welland. Sketches and stories of Mapleton life are narrated in a manner similar to that of Sarah Orne Jewett's *The Country of the Painted Firs* (1896). In Teskey's story cycle, the narrator is a townswoman who travels widely but returns annually to her "summer home in law-abiding Canada, where righteousness seemed to have the upper hand, as to a Sabbath rest. . . ." In the stories, the faith of ordinary people (especially women) and their steadfastness in suffering are valorized. "The Ram Lamb" has two sequel stories: "How Jane Spent the Prize Money" and "The Effect Upon Jake," in which Jane selflessly sends her prize money to a missionary friend in India, where it is used to support an Indian child-widow; her flint-hearted husband is so moved by this action that he too donates funds for the orphan in India. He at last appreciates the virtues of his wife. The hard lot of women and the economic thralldom of farm wives provide a subtext in all three stories. Jane herself says in "How Jane Spent the Prize Money": "I never before hed any [money] really my own to give, — not even the widow's mite — married women don't seem to hev no mite." She is well aware that "women hev it hard enough enywhere."

Stephen Leacock may have read *Where the Sugar Maple Grows* before writing his popular *Sunshine Sketches of a Little Town* (1912). There is a parallel in narrative mode and to some extent in tone: a devout Methodist, Teskey shares Leacock's humour but not his irreverence or sly debunking of religion. The short story cycle continues to be popular with Canadian writers, for example Mavis Gallant and Alice Munro.

⌒

Suggested Reading

"Adeline M. Teskey," Welland *Evening Tribune*, 25 March 1924: 5.

Campbell, Sandra. "Change and the Kailyard: The Fiction of Adeline M. Teskey," *Canadian Literature* No. 127 (Winter 1990): 189–193.

Teskey, Adeline M. *Where the Sugar Maple Grows* (Toronto: Musson, 1901).

———. *Candlelight Days* (London: Cassell, 1913).

Waterston, Elizabeth. "Canadian Cabbage, Canadian Rose" (1973), rpt. *Twentieth Century Essays on Confederation Literature*, ed. Lorraine McMullen (Ottawa: Tecumseh, 1976), 93–101.

A Common Man and His Wife: The Ram Lamb

Adeline M. Teskey

"That there thing ain't good fer nothin'," growled Jake Bender, giving a prod with his heavy boot at the apparently lifeless body of a lamb stretched on the half-frozen ground. Then picking up a clod, he threw it at the mother sheep hovering concernedly near her helpless offspring.

The remark was addressed to his wife Jane, who was standing near with a shawl over her head and around her shoulders, she was out milking. She made no response, but as her husband disappeared into the barn "shooing" the reluctant old sheep ahead of him, she caught up the forlorn little body in her strong arms, wrapped her shabby shawl tenderly about it and set off for the farmhouse.

Her appearance as she strode across the corner of the stubble-field taking the shortest cut home, could hardly have been more commonplace. She bent forward as she walked; her skirt was short, to "git quit o' the mud;" her cow-hide boots, their leather laces tied in a clumsy bow-knot at the top of each, showed plainly beneath the short skirt, and her faded shawl, whose ends enfolded the shivering lamb, was drawn tightly around a thin, weather-beaten face, and yet, at the moment, she was performing the work of an angel — if angels are ministering spirits.

Her husband, on coming out of the barn and seeing that the lamb had disappeared, cast an angry look after her, muttering:

"There she be agin, wastin' her time over that there half-dead lamb, which ain't no good fer nothin'. *I* oughter know! She be always a-coddlin' over some lame hen or sick chicken, or — or somethin'!"

While she, as she looked down at the lamb in her arms with a great tenderness in her eyes, murmured:

"He be gettin' harder an' harder every day. . . . If I had only tuk Silas Marner. *He'd* a had a kind heart," and a sigh for the lover she had rejected years before, when she gave the preference to Jake Bender, broke from her thin lips.

Jake Bender had a mighty good opinion of himself. He thought he was always right, and had asserted this infallibility for so long that he had almost brought his meek, self-effaced wife to think so too. But on this occasion she had allowed her heart to get the better of her head.

She kept on with the lamb to the house, and there laid it gently upon a piece of old carpet placed behind the big wood-stove where the heat would fall generously upon its numbed body. Then warming some of the milk which had just been brought in from the barn, she managed to coax a few spoonfuls of it down the creature's throat.

When Jake, who had been out to the "sugar-bush" visiting the sap-troughs, came in he cast a contemptuous look at the lamb behind the stove, saying,

"That there thing ain't good fer nothin'; *I* oughter know."

And he would have given it another cruel prod with the toe of his big boot if Jane had not anticipated him and protected it with her hand.

After a few hours of warmth and judiciously-administered nourishment the lamb was persuaded to open its eyes on the world again. By noon it could raise its head, and when night came it could actually stand on its feet. Two or three days later Jane considered it well enough to be returned to the old sheep.

But, strange to relate, the maternal instincts of the latter seemed to have taken flight, and she refused to own

ADELINE M. TESKEY

her offspring. So the lamb was thrown back upon the tender mercies of its benefactor.

Jane, nothing loth, brought it to the house, and despite the constant protest and scorn of Jake, continued her daily ministration to its wants.

It grew in vigor and beauty daily, and when it was two months old Jane christened it "Dandy."

Jake, not having succeeded in stopping his wife in her work of mercy and love, and hating to be thwarted, then threatened to kill Dandy, as good spring lamb was bringing a high price in the market.

Jane, aghast at the proposition, for the lamb had now become a real pet, and fearing lest her husband would carry his threat into execution some morning before she was up, hunted out an old padlock, fastened with it the door of the small pen in which Dandy was kept, and carried the key on a piece of twine suspended around her neck.

That summer, by happy chance, the prize list of Canada's great industrial fair fell into Jane's hands, and she was aimlessly looking through it when her eyes alighted on the following entry: "Best Ram Lamb, fifteen dollars."

At once she conceived the idea of taking Dandy to the fair. There surely could not be a finer lamb than he, why, therefore, should he not win the fifteen dollars? She would tell Jake nothing about it, but would forthwith begin to save up money from the sale of her butter and eggs to pay the necessary expenses. She afterwards confided to a neighbor that she made cider apple-sauce, and "made it extry good a-purpose," and Jake and the hired man ate it with relish in lieu of the butter, suspecting nothing of her plans, but thereby leaving her more of her excellent butter to sell.

As the day of the fair drew near Jake, one evening when he was at a neighbor's house, heard a whisper of what his wife intended doing, although Jane had breathed it to nobody save one woman "in a secret." He cogitated about it as he walked home along the quiet country road.

"She won't do it when the time comes," he said positively, after a prolonged meditation, addressing the "snake fence" which divided his fields from the highway. "She's too skeery. She never went anywhere by herself in her life, let alone a great tearin' city like Toronto, an' I won't go with her. I'll be slivered if I will!"

And a noise issued from his mouth which was intended for a laugh of triumph, but suggested the "crackling of thorns under a pot" more than anything else.

"She ain't a-goin' to come it over me that that there lamb is good fer ennythin'. I said onct for all *that there lamb ain't good for nothin'*, an' I oughter know."

But he waited in vain for his wife to ask him to go.

It was with no slight quaking of heart that Jane Bender began to make preparations to take the lamb to the Fair herself, yet she was buoyed up all the time by the determination to let Jake see that Dandy was good for something.

Dandy was occasionally a little obstreperous, as all pet animals of the male sex are apt to be, and although a kind neighbor offered to take him along with his sheep, Jane was obliged to go herself, and lead him by a cord, for not a step would he budge for any one else, and so it came about that on the afternoon of the last day of entry she had the high satisfaction of seeing him, proud and haughty, standing within one of the pens on the fair ground.

He was certainly a beauty, and she did not see how the judges could fail to realize it. She had washed him to almost spotless whiteness, and tied a blue ribbon around his neck.

He was a saucy, petted fellow, and had a trick of holding up his head, and looking fearlessly at the people, that gave him quite an air of superiority over the other sheep, which huddled close in groups, looking frightened and drooping.

The sheep had to be in on the third of September, but were not judged until the seventh.

Jane spent every intervening day on the fair-ground, most of the time looking after Dandy. Her nights she passed with "Almiry" Jones, a niece who lived in the city. She carried her lunch with her, and sat on some retired seat in the grounds timid and "scareful," and munched the bread-and-butter Almiry gave her, with some of her own homemade cheese. And while she was eating, the kind neighbor, when attending to his own sheep, gave a bite and sup to Dandy.

On the fateful seventh Jane kept close beside Dandy's pen until the Judges, bedecked with badges, fussy and important, made their appearance, and then she shrank away to a secluded corner to await their verdict in a tremble of anxiety and hope.

Once and again she nervously peeped around the corner to see if the men whose judgment meant so much to her had gone, but they were still before the sheep pens talking busily.

"If they don't give Dandy the prize I'll not take him back to the farm," she whispered to herself. "Jake will have him killed for sure, and he'll never let me hear the last of it neither."

After what seemed to her an unconscionable delay, but was in reality only a few minutes, the Judges passed on, and the moment they had disappeared, Jane, with white set face, quivering lips and beating heart, darted out of her concealment.

Oh! the ineffable joy of it! What mattered all her silent, patient endurance of Jake's rude ridicule, her harrowing dread that he would put into execution his threat of converting the beloved Dandy into meat for the market? For there, pendant to the blue ribbon, and showing bravely against the snowy fleece, swung the big red ticket which signified First Prize.

Jane Bender was not a woman of the school who take pride in a cynical suppression of emotion. She did not care a jot who might see her and be moved to laughter, as with amazing agility for her years she clambered into the pen, and, dropping on her knees, hugged Dandy to her heart, her thin gray locks loosened by the sudden exertion, falling over his shapely head as she murmured proudly:

"I allus knowed it, Dandy."

The following day there arrived at the Mapleton

post-office a post card the writing upon which plainly indicated a pathetic unfamiliarity with the use of the pen. This was the message it bore:

MISTER JACOB BENDER,
"Dandy's tuk the First Prize.
"JANE BENDER."

∽

Where the Sugar Maple Grows (Toronto: Musson, 1901), 61–69.

Winnifred Reeve
(Onoto Watanna) (1877–1954)

MISS LILY AND MISS CHRYSANTHEMUM (1903)

Sister of Edith Eaton (see page 227), Winnifred was born after their Chinese mother and English father had come to Montreal. She began her career at seventeen as a reporter for a Jamaican newspaper, and shortly moved to Chicago, then New York. There she married journalist Bertrand Whitcomb Babcock and, later, businessman Francis Fournier Reeve. Her semi-autobiographical *Me* (1917) describes her early years as a freelance writer. Reeve moved with her husband to Alberta, where they were involved in ranching and later in oil. Between 1924 and 1931 she edited and wrote Hollywood movie scripts. Her last years were spent in Calgary, where she wrote two novels set in the Canadian West.

A popular and successful writer, Reeve published hundreds of stories in periodicals, including *Scribner's*, *Atlantic Monthly*, *Century*, *Harper's* and *Saturday Evening Post* in the United States and the *Idler* and London *Strand* in England. As a successful writer, she numbered among her friends Edith Wharton, Anita Loos, Mark Twain and, on her move to the Canadian West, Nellie McClung.

Aware that prejudice against the Chinese was strong in Canada and the United States in the late nineteenth and early twentieth centuries while the Japanese were viewed as remotely exotic, Winnifred took a Japanese pseudonym and Japanese–English persona. Most of her stories and novels are well-crafted romances of Japanese or Eurasian women with English or American men. She established her name with her second novel, *A Japanese Nightingale* (1901), which tells of the romance between a young Eurasian woman brought up in the Japanese culture and an American settled temporarily in Japan. Woven into the simply told tale of the meeting of two cultures is some description of Japanese mores. The novel sold over 200,000 copies, was translated into at least six languages, and was produced as a play and as a movie. Unlike Puccini's great success, the opera *Madame Butterfly* (1904) (which, incidentally, was based on John Bolasco's London play *Madam Butterfly* [1900], itself rooted in turn in a supposedly true story published in an English periodical in 1900), Reeve's romance ends happily. Like Puccini, Winnifred Eaton exploited current popular interest in the mystery and exoticism of Japan, and continued to do so in her fiction with immense success for another twenty years.

"Miss Lily and Miss Chrysanthemum: The Love Story of Two Japanese Girls in Chicago" is characteristic of Winnifred Eaton's fiction. The meeting in Chicago of two young Eurasian sisters, one brought up in Japan by her Japanese mother, the other in America by her father, provides the basis for a contrast of occidental and oriental cultures. The gentle, childlike Chrysanthemum, who joins her sister in America on her mother's death, is completely dependent on Lily, a teacher, to whom she refers as "little mother." A simple love story ends happily, although almost frustrated by cultural misunderstandings. Shifting the narrative perspective between Lily and her suitor allows the author to show misunderstandings realistically and to present the childishly innocent Chrysanthemum with sympathy and gentleness, as her loving sister and a friend, outsiders to her culture, see her. The attractive Lily suggests the ideal blending of the best of both cultures — Japanese gentleness, charm, and reserve with American independence and generosity of spirit.

⌒

Suggested Reading

Ling, Amy. "Winnifred Eaton: Ethnic Chameleon and Popular Success," MELUS 2 (Fall 1984): 5–15.

Reeve, Winnifred Eaton Babcock. *A Japanese Nightingale* (1901).

Miss Lily and Miss Chrysanthemum: The Love Story of Two Japanese Girls in Chicago

Winnifred Reeve (Onoto Watanna)

Yuri (which is "Lily" in English) and Kiku (which is "Chrysanthemum") met in one of the noisy and crowded railway stations in Chicago. They were sisters, half Japanese and half English; but neither could understand one word the other spoke, for Yuri had been taken by her English father, who had been long since dead, from Japan when a little bit of a girl, and had lived most of her life in England and afterward in America, so that she had forgotten her mother tongue; while Kiku had stayed with the little mother in Japan, whose recent death had left her so lonely that she had come all the way to America to join her sister, of whom she had only the dimmest memory. For in this double orphanage, thousands and thousands of miles apart, the two had felt strangely drawn to each other.

They were very much alike in appearance, only Yuri looked older and perhaps sadder than Kiku, who really was the younger by two years, and who was fairly beaming with excitement. She chatted away in Japanese to Yuri, forgetting that Yuri would not understand her, and turning half apologetically to be interpreted by the kind English lady who had known her very well in Japan and had brought her to her sister.

"Your sister is pleased to be with you," she said to Yuri.

The girl flushed with pleasure and put her arm affectionately about Kiku. "And I am so glad to have her with me." Then she added, "But I would rather have gone home to her."

∽

Six months passed rapidly, and Kiku had learned to speak English brokenly. The two little strangers boarded together on the South Side. They had an east room which overlooked Lake Michigan. Each morning as Yuri rose softly from the bed, so as not to awaken Kiku, she would throw open the green shutters, and resting her elbows on the sill, look dreamily out across the lake, letting the cool breeze fan her, and watching with eager eyes the sun rise. In those early hours, before Kiku had awakened, Yuri would make great plans for their future. She thought of how much she could save out of her salary (for she was employed as a teacher in one of the public schools in Chicago), so that she and Kiku might return together to Japan. She knew it would take some years before she would have sufficient to take them both back, for Kiku's pretended cheeriness had not deceived her, and the pitiful quivering of the girl's lips told of her homesickness.

Yuri had looked forward for years to the time when she should have enough to take her to Japan. Perhaps she loved even more dearly than Kiku the home that she could not remember. She had almost lived on the hope of going there; but now a new difficulty stood in her way — Kiku had had only enough money wherewith to bring her to America, and was entirely dependent now on her sister, whose salary had only recently been sufficient to lay any aside. Moreover, Kiku was pining for her home, and Yuri knew that when the little fund in the bank should have grown large enough to permit of the trip, it must be Kiku, and not she, who would go. Kiku was nineteen years old; Yuri, though only two years older, felt as a mother to her

WINNIFRED REEVE

little foreign sister. A love wonderful in its strength, devotion and unselfishness had sprung up between these two. Kiku loved Yuri with a pride in her that was pathetic in its confidence, but Yuri's love partook of the supreme and tender love of a good mother.

"Oh, Kiku," she would say, before starting out in the morning, "you must be careful when you go out not to go far, for I don't want my little Yap to lose herself," and Kiku would say with her pretty English lisp, "Ess, liddle mozzer."

∽

Walter Palmer was a young lawyer who boarded in the same house as Yuri and Kiku. He had been in love with Yuri-San for many days, but the girl had known nothing of this. Her life had been a hard one, and the struggle she had had in order to put herself through college and support herself at the same time had occupied all her thought, so that she had paid but little attention to the amusements and distractions that occupy the minds of most girls of that age. She was an extremely pretty girl, with dark, shy eyes, shiny black hair, and sweet, tender mouth. She had never mixed with companions of her age, on account of the strange antipathy the English had shown to her in her childhood, because of her nationality; which prejudice, however, they had long outgrown. Yet it had had a rude effect on her life, making her supersensitive. It was not that she distrusted and doubted the sincerity of all whom she met, but she sought to save herself the little cuts and pains which had seemed but her birthright. From the time when the little schoolmates at the public school had called her "nigger," "Chinee," and other names, which to the Western mind at that time meant the essence of opprobrium, Yuri had distrusted, not them, but herself. That she was inferior to them she never for one moment thought, but that she was different from them, and one whom it would be impossible for them to understand, she firmly believed; hence her strange love for the home she had never known. Holding herself aloof from all whom she met, she had lived a lonely, isolated life ever since her father's death.

So Walter Palmer found little opportunity to speak to her, and it was only in the mornings or evenings as she went to and from work and passed him in the hall, on the stairway or on the doorstep, that the young man had the chance to see her and get a shy glance of recognition, and the girl little knew that he would loiter sometimes around the halls and places where he knew she must pass, for half an hour at a time, simply for the sake of seeing her. He was much in love, and often as he sat in the dreary law office, with his work piled high around him, there would rise before him a picture of a young girl, with a strange, half-foreign proud face, and he would forget the musty law-books, and the confessions or accusations of his numerous clients.

Although scarcely past his thirtieth year he had already made quite a name for himself, so that his practice was extensive, and he had become recognized as one of the first young lawyers of Chicago. He had known Yuri for six months, and during all that time had been unable to speak to her because of the girl's reticence and reserve.

∽

Then Kiku had arrived. She was a wonder to all the other lodgers in the house. She was more Oriental-looking than her sister, but perhaps her chief beauty lay in her animation and bright spirits. She would dress in a style peculiarly her own, half Japanese and half American, and there was something fascinating in the manner in which she would twist a sash about her waist and tie it in a large fantastic bow at the back, as though in imitation of the Japanese obi. And because she was lonely all day while Yuri was at the school Kiku roved about the house and soon made the acquaintance of all the other lodgers, none of whom Yuri had known during all her stay at the house. So it happened one day when Yuri returned home that she found the little room deserted and Kiku nowhere in sight.

WINNIFRED REEVE

Yuri was uneasy, as it was after four o'clock, and Kiku had promised her not to venture out alone after that hour. While she sat wondering in distress what had become of Kiku, the sound of laughing voices floated up from the lower hall, mingled with which were the familiar, half-halting lisps of her sister's. She opened her door, and walking to the head of the stairs looked down at the gay group below. A pitiful tremor flickered across her face as she realized that these people had suddenly come between her and her sister, and that Kiku should not find her sufficient; for Yuri had all the subdued half-jealous passion of a Japanese girl, even if subdued by enforced unselfishness. As Kiku saw her at the top of the stairs she only jerked her little chin saucily and motioned her to descend. At the same time, a young man who had laughingly placed his hand on Kiku's shoulder raised his head, and saw Yuri with the pained embarrassment and surprise on her face. In a flash his hand had dropped and he was seconding her sister's invitation to her to join them, and with half-unwilling, half-hesitating step Yuri descended.

The next morning when Yuri went to the school Walter Palmer walked with her, and the next morning, and each morning after that, he waited for the girl. Mostly they talked of Kiku, and of her future, because it was on this subject that Yuri was most intensely interested, and Palmer would have praised her sister if but for the sake of seeing Yuri's eyes shine with pleasure.

"It would do her a world of good," he said one day, "to take her out on the lake. Can we not go some evening?"

The girl looked at him half hesitatingly. Then she said impetuously: "Yes; I believe I can trust her with you;" adding deprecatingly, "she is such a little thing, and a stranger to your ways; please be careful with her."

"But you will come, too," said the young man eagerly.

"Oh, no," she answered, smiling; "I cannot spare the time. There is so much to do when I return in the evening; and besides, I am studying the Japanese language, and I shall make no headway if I do not persevere."

Palmer swallowed a huge lump of disappointment.

It was a beautiful moonlight night when he took Kiku on the lake, and perhaps its stillness and beauty set the girl thinking; for as they pushed out from the shore she raised her little brown face to him and said in her strangely frank and confiding manner: "What is this 'lofe' of which they speak in America?"

Palmer started sharply, and looked at the girl's innocent, questioning face without replying for some time. Then he said: "That is a leading question, Kiku-San. There are many of us here in America who ask the same question. 'What is this — love?'" He smiled half tenderly at the girl's wondering eyes.

"Ess?" she answered, her voice raised questioningly, "but we do not 'lofe' like that in Japan," speaking as though he had explained to her the meaning of the word. It seemed to please her, and she repeated softly, "Lofe — lofe — it is very queer, but we have no meaning for the liddle word in my home. Tell me the meaning," she persisted.

Palmer turned his eyes reluctantly from hers, which were fastened on his face. He stopped rowing and leaned on his oars.

"I must be stupid, Kiku-San, but I cannot analyze the word any more than you can, though — I — I think I know what it is."

Kiku stirred restlessly. He could not fathom what was going on in her little head, or what had caused her to put the question to him. He had been thrown a great deal in her company of late, and often in the evenings Yuri had left them together while she prosecuted her studies, and Palmer knew that Kiku had more than a common liking for him.

They were both silent for a time; then Kiku said softly: "If you do not know what this lofe means, how then can you be 'in lofe' with me?"

Palmer was mute, and his face had grown an ashy gray in the moonlight.

"I," he said, "I love you?" And then, "How can you

know — how can you think that?"

"They tell me," said the girl calmly; and she added shyly, "They tell me — that you — that you — lofe me," and her voice lingered softly on the last words.

"Who told you that?" asked the man harshly, his voice sounding strange even to his own ears.

"The pritty American ladies at the house," she said. "Is it true?" There was a certain stubbornness in her voice, mingled with wonder and half-pleased vanity.

_◇_

"You must not ask such questions," he said evasively.

The girl's persistency fascinated him, and there was something tender and winning in her innocence. He could see her face distinctly in the pale light, and the moon's soft rays touched it gently, and seemed to spread a halo around the shiny, dark little head. Her eyes were luminous, and in spite of her innocence there was a hesitancy and pitiful faltering in them and about the soft little mouth. Her face in its mixed beauty intoxicated the man. He could not remove his eyes from it. He forgot Yuri. He thought only of the girl sitting opposite to him, with the sweet face softened with the questioning that her innocent soul could not solve. With a sudden fierceness he reached over and caught her little soft hands in his, whispering huskily:

"What makes you look like that, Kiku-San?" (San is the equivalent in Japanese for Miss, and is sometimes used as an endearing expression.)

Kiku did not attempt to withdraw her hands from his, but let them rest there in silent contentment. And thus they sat hand in hand, the boat drifting with the tide, and the moonbeams deepening, and enwrapping them with a silence and mystery that was replete with delight.

Then her soft little voice broke the silence that had fallen between them, and her eyes fell on their clasped hands. "And is _this_ lofe?" she asked softly.

Palmer looked at her with eyes that took note of every outline of her face and form, and he was silent.

Suddenly the girl raised her head and pointed toward the city.

"See," she said, "how far are we — so far! This must be lofe. We have no fear, though so far away from all life." Then she seemed to recall herself.

"My sister, Yuri-San, she will expect us. Surely had we better return."

As she spoke her sister's name the man suddenly shivered, and a cloud of agony flickered across his face. He seemed as one who had been asleep and but rudely awakened. His hands dropped hastily from hers, and he seized the oars in silence.

⁓

It was past one when they reached the house. Yuri was sitting up waiting for Kiku. The room was in darkness, and she sat at the window looking out across the lake with her head on her arms.

"Is it you, Kiku?"

"Ess, liddle mozzer," said the other, and put her arms softly about her sister, sinking on the window-sill beside her.

"You are tired," said Yuri with concern; "we must not sit up any longer, little sis." She began helping her undress, but Kiku stayed the busy hands, and, holding them tightly in her own, clung with a sudden tenderness and almost with terror to her sister.

"Is *this* lofe?" she said wistfully.

"Love, love?" asked Yuri, shivering a trifle. "Why, little sis, what a great big question that is! Of course it is love, and such love as never was perhaps between two sisters."

Her voice was quite hushed as she kissed the upturned, questioning face. Kiku's restlessness puzzled her.

"I fear you have been out too long," she said gravely; "come, sister will undress you."

Kiku shook her head. "No!" she said almost fretfully, "Kiku does not wish to go to bed yet. Kiku wants to hear about this — lofe."

Yuri laughed, the easy, good-natured laugh of an American-bred girl.

"Why, you absurd little goosie; what can I tell you, save that this is 'lofe,' as you call it?" And she bent down and kissed Kiku on the lips.

Kiku shook her head impatiently.

"But *he* did not do that," she said with puzzled eyes.

"*He*! What do you mean?" said Yuri with a sudden fear at her heart. "Who did not do that? — and what — what — oh, Kiku — what is it, little sis?"

Her quick questioning excited Kiku.

"*He*," she said with a sudden scorn at Yuri for not knowing who "He" should mean. "Why, the pritty American gentleman. See, he *lofe* me, and he do *only* this" — and once more she caught Yuri's hands in hers and pressed them with a strange passion.

"He — he — did — that?" Yuri said with slow indignation. And then both were silent.

෭

When Yuri started out the next morning she was alone. It was the first time since she had known Palmer that he had failed to accompany her. The girl's face was troubled, and there were shadows under her eyes which bespoke the sleepless night she had passed.

She was thinking of Kiku. She realized with a sad tenderness that Kiku, being such a stranger to Western ways, must ever be misunderstood by those about her. Her great love for her sister made her sensitive on her account, and it was with apprehension and a good deal of bitterness that she thought of Palmer.

She had never admitted, even to herself, that she loved him; yet, as she felt the sudden wave of helpless agony that swept over her whenever she thought of him, and of how stunned she had been at Kiku's half confession, its truth came home to her with a brutal pain. All her life she had been forced to battle for herself; was she strong enough now, she asked herself, to take up her sister's burdens also? That Kiku was as dear as, if not dearer than, the other to her she told herself repeatedly, calling up a pitiful resentment against the man.

She left the school early that day. Although ignorant of her mother tongue, yet she had many friends among the Japanese. She could not have told what impelled her to go to them, but feeling helpless in this new pain that had come to her she sought them out, and tried in their unfamiliar companionship to forget her own unhappy associates. When she returned home that evening a young chemist of great wealth, named Nishimura, accompanied her.

As they came to the front of the house two figures sitting together on the front steps rose. One ran down to meet them. It was Kiku-San, with shy, shiny eyes, and the one who stood back and looked at Yuri, with a sudden blinding agony before his eyes, was Walter Palmer.

Yuri was smiling bravely. She introduced Nishimura to Palmer, and then turning to Kiku made some gay remarks about her ruffled hair. Though she spoke to Palmer she did not once look him in the face. With arms entwined about each other the two girls mounted the stairs to their room.

Then Kiku began to speak breathlessly: "And I know what this lofe is," she said triumphantly. Yuri turned her face away, and Kiku continued. "I — lofe — him," she said slowly. "I lofe the pritty American gentleman. I dream of him in the night, I think of him all day, and I am very sad. Then he comes home very early, and he speaks to me about this lofe. He say it is nothing. That it is foolish to talk about it — that it is not good. Then I laugh at him, and I say: 'No, then I not believe, for I know this lofe — for I lofe you — and you lofe me, and because of this we would be contradict.'" She laughed happily as she ended.

"What did he say then, Kiku?" said Yuri quietly.

"He laughed and he frowned, but he say nothing."

"And what else did you tell him, Kiku?"

"Oh! I talk much," said Kiku saucily. "For this lofe is so strange. I talk, talk, talk, and he keep still and listen. I tell him I want to be with him largely."

Two months later Palmer joined Yuri as she walked to her work. It was the first time in many, many days. There was a large vacant field that Yuri would cross to make a shorter cut to the school, and it was generally here that they would separate, he taking the cars for the downtown part of the city. But this morning he started to cross the field with her, though a silence, eloquent in its sadness, had been between them from the start.

Palmer's eyes had been on the girl's face almost from the beginning, but she turned from him, and her abruptness amounted to rudeness, and was meant to be noticed.

Palmer stopped in the middle of the field and broke the strained silence.

"I cannot stand it," he said brokenly.

Yuri turned on him with a wild swiftness.

"*You* cannot stand it," she said witheringly. "*You* — you. What have you to say about it? Can't you see, don't you know — it will *kill* her if — if you are not kinder to her. And then — you tell *me* you cannot stand it. What is it you cannot stand? What has she done to you?" She stopped, her indignation choking her.

This was the first time the subject had been broached between them.

The young man's shoulders drooped.

"Don't look like that, Yuri," he said, thinking more of the girl herself than what she had said. "Don't hate me. I tell you I don't deserve it. What can I do? What have I done? I could not help it."

Her anger had died out. Her eyes softened a trifle.

"Then you will make it all right, won't you?" she said wistfully. "You will tell her — you will tell her — poor little Kiku, that you are not offended with her, and you *won't* try to keep away from her. She is such a little thing, and she does not understand people like we are. It is cruel not to be kind to her."

"What can I do?" he asked, his teeth grating against each other with pain. "Surely *you* ought to understand? You know how it all came about, and you cannot blame me altogether. She was such a child, and I tried to discourage her, but I couldn't bear to hurt her."

"You — couldn't — bear — to hurt her," said Yuri slowly. "Am I to understand from that that you never really loved, never really cared for my little sister?"

The man was mute.

"And you let her believe it!" — her voice rose in its pain — "you let her believe that, and then you come to me — you come to me, and pretend you are sorry — that you cannot understand — that — that — Oh! I hate you — you are contemptible — a brute — a — a coward."

She turned to leave him, but he stood in front of her and burst out passionately: "You *shall* not leave me like this, Yuri. Yuri, turn your face to me. Let me look into your eyes. They accuse me so — and I — I have no words for myself. I do not know what to say — but, Yuri — I would not lose — your — your — regard for anything in the world. You will understand and perhaps you will forgive when I tell you, Yuri, dear little Yuri — it is *you* I love — I love *you*! How then could I care for any one else in the world? Can you understand now why I have had to evade even your little sister, whom I — I — cared for only because she was *your* little sister?"

The girl's face was white and drawn.

With a sudden agony she turned and ran blindly from him, scarcely knowing where she went, but wishing to get farther and farther away from him: to forget everything — the hideous pain of living, and the feeling almost of exultation that the knowledge of his love gave her.

Kiku was in a high fever when Yuri returned. She called constantly for her sister, and pitifully begged to be taken home to Japan. Yuri could not understand her well, for in her illness she spoke always in the soft accents of her mother tongue. But she knew what the girl was crying for and would whisper back softly, "Yes, I know; yes, I know, little sis, you want to go home, and you shall go home."

Two more months, and Kiku, clad in a soft, clinging kimono, was on her way home. The girl's face was sadder and more subdued than when, hardly a year before, she had come to America. Her heart bounded with gladness as she thought of Nippon, and because she was scarcely more than a child her thoughts were more with her destination than with the man who had taught her the meaning of the Western "lofe."

And alone in the little room Yuri was crying over the little Japanese relics and remembrances that her sister had left behind, and almost wondering whether the one year so full of laughter and tears in which Kiku-San had been with her were not all a strange dream. Of Palmer she would not think. His white face haunted her constantly, and she hated herself because the bitterness she had conjured up against him was slowly passing away, to be replaced with a feeling of pain and yearning and longing that the girl could not comprehend. She tried to assure herself that she would have all her heart could desire when, after her marriage to Nishimura, she was once more in the sunny land which she had dreamed of since her childhood's days, and on which all her hopes for the future had been built. She knew Palmer had been sick. When she met him she dared not look at him for fear of finding him changed.

Once as the winter months advanced, and Yuri's little cold hand tried in vain to turn the latchkey in the door, a firm hand closed over hers, and taking the key from her, deftly turned the lock. Then as they stood in the little porch alone together, he said with such piercing tenderness in his voice that the girl's defiant eyes filled with tears:

"Yuri, dear, cruel little Yuri."

She did not answer him for a moment; then she raised her head and looked at him. He was smiling, and it angered her. "You must not laugh at me," she said as childishly as Kiku might have done. Suddenly she thought of Nishimura, and she tried to steady her voice.

"See," she said, "I am to be married next month to —

Mr. Nishimura."

The man's face suddenly changed, and its ashy misery appealed to her. With a sudden passion she pulled the little ring from her finger and forced it into his hand.

"No, no!" she said frantically as he turned from her. "I won't! I can't — I — I ——" But Palmer's hand had closed tightly over hers and the little ring, and he was drawing her into his arms with a glory over his face that only "lofe" could have reflected.

⤫

Ladies' Home Journal 20 (Aug. 1903): 11–12.

Kathleen "Kit" Coleman (1856–1915)

A PAIR OF GRAY GLOVES (1903)

As a pioneering woman journalist from 1890 until her death in 1915, Kathleen "Kit" Coleman was a household word in Canada. Because of the research of journalists Robin Rowland and Barbara Freeman, we now know that the same play of wit, creativity and intelligence that characterized her journalism also coloured her account of her own life. She was born Catherine Ferguson in 1856 at Castleblakeney, Ireland, to Mary Burke and Patrick Ferguson, a minor landowner. After attending a Roman Catholic convent school, and a finishing school in Belgium (an experience that evidently broadened her intellectual outlook beyond that of a conventional Irish Catholic gentlewoman of the era), she was married in 1876 to a prosperous merchant, Thomas Willis. After the death of an infant daughter and Willis's death in 1883, Catherine — or Kathleen as she was now called — was left without means of support. She went first to London to seek employment, and in 1884 came to Canada.

Here she recast her past, calling herself Kathleen Blake Willis and giving her age as twenty. While working as a secretary, she married E. J. Watkins. The result was three years in Winnipeg, from where her husband operated — rather unsuccessfully — as a commercial traveller. The apparently unhappy marriage produced two children, and Kathleen Watkins returned to Toronto with her children about 1888, faced again with the need to earn a living. She began to make her way as a journalist. The drudgery of newspaper work depicted in "A Pair of Gray Gloves" is echoed in "Her Home Coming," another of her stories.

Her first publication was a story, "The Organ Grinder," appearing in *Saturday Night* in 1889. She continued to write occasional fiction throughout her career. Her *Saturday Night* work brought her to the attention of the Toronto *Mail*; by October 1889 she was producing the "Woman's Kingdom," the Saturday woman's page, under the byline "Kit."

Coleman's style was pungent, her opinions lively, and her topics wide-ranging. She became a mainstay of the paper. Restless and adventurous, she broke ground in other areas of reporting: in 1892, for example, she went to London and wrote a series of articles about the London of Dickens and Jack the Ripper. Her greatest coup came in 1898 when she successfully wangled newspaper and official permission to go to Cuba to cover the Spanish–American War — the first accredited woman war correspondent. That year, she married Theodore Coleman and moved to Copper Cliff, Ontario, where he worked as a mine doctor. She continued her popular column by mail, and even commented therein on the pollution from the Sudbury-area mines. The couple moved to Hamilton in 1904, the year in which Kit Coleman became the first president of the Canadian Women's Press Club. Kit left what was now the *Mail and Empire* in 1911 in favour of successful syndication; she had been asked to take on additional assignments without increment, a move typical of the poor financial rewards for newspaper work most keenly felt by female journalists of the day. "Kit's Column" was a successful feature of many newspapers until her death in 1915.

Coleman opposed female suffrage, once with the riposte that a pretty dress would always be more important to women than the vote. She was ambivalent about the thralldom of grand passion for women and firmly believed that work was crucial. She told her readers:

> No woman capable of doing higher work should consent to become a man's drudge, at any man's bidding. I am not a stickler for women's rights but I am for women's pluck and independence. . . . Most women of today are capable of independence and are no more slaves of love than men are. The saying about love being but an incident in a man's life while it is a woman's whole existence is today utter rubbish.

In "A Pair of Gray Gloves," her fictional journalist, Marah Tennard — and it is no accident that the name "Marah" suggests "bitterness" — finishes her gruelling and, under the circumstances, ironic feature assignment on platonic love between the sexes despite the anguish caused by the termination of her own love affair. The imagery of the story is particularly significant. The setting for Marah's labours — the high, isolated, arid room with its bleak, blurred perspective — suggests the achievement and the frustrations of her career and personal situation. Coleman thus cleverly utilizes the symbolism of space, so important in women's writing. The imagery of death and decay and the symbolism of the doeskin gloves as emblems of Marah's sexuality give the story its impact. While quest is sustained at great cost, the toll exacted by romance is heavy. In other Coleman stories, women successfully strive for material self-sufficiency but their men are cruelly inadequate and/or unavailable.

∽

Suggested Reading

Coleman, Kathleen. "The Red Cross Nurse: A Tale of Majuba Hill," *Canadian Magazine* 15 (Dec. 1899): 183–188.

Freeman, Barbara. *Kit's Kingdom: The Journalism of Kathleen Blake Coleman* (Ottawa: Carleton, 1989).

Rowland, Robin. "Kit's Secret," *Content* 90 (Nov. 1978): 30–31.

A PAIR OF GRAY GLOVES
Kathleen "Kit" Coleman

"The sweetest joy, the wildest woe is love."
— BAILEY, *FESTUS*.[1]

She was leaning back in her chair very tired. The day was a hot one, and the room, the highest in a tall building, was stuffy and close. It was a bare-looking room, furnished with a mean desk, a chair or two and a piece of matting. There were no blinds on the tall windows, which were covered with dust and looked over a long and narrow court up which at intervals waggons lumbered to the side-doors of warehouses. The woman walked wearily to the windows and looked out. Far below the sun shone on a heap of lumber that lay along the wall, and a gray cat picked her way among the planks. Dirty papers swirled and eddied in the hot wind. A woman with a mop and pail crossed the yard and entered an opposite building. Presently she reappeared standing on the sill of a window and sending the mop up and down the dusty panes. The other woman watched her at her work, and a faint envy was expressed in her eyes. "I wish I were she," she said tiredly. "How she must sleep at night! Oh! to be really tired, really worn out, the way women are who wash and scrub and

---

[1] *Festus* (1839), a long philosophical poem by P. J. Bailey (1816–1902), immensely popular in its time, is a Faustian tale, told in blank verse dialogue in many scenes.

work with their hands, and have no time for hoping and fearing. Oh! to be dog-tired. What a sleep I would have." Then she laughed. "And she, if she looks up, will be envying me here idling at the window," she said. She looked back at her desk, at the disorder of loose sheets covered with narrow writing which lay about the floor, at the little stack of white, blank pages. "I must get back to it," she murmured, stepping to her swing chair and resting a moment against its uneasy back. A bell rang. "Five o'clock," she cried out aloud, "and that article on Platonic Love to be finished by seven. What on earth made Plato start a theory of his own when love is the same to-day as it was in the garden of Eden." She sat down and dipped her pen into the ink-pot. She thought quietly for a moment, then began to write —

"Platonic love is not possible between men and women who have brains and sex — "

A short, hard step coming sturdily along the passage stopped her. Her office door was half of muffed glass, and she heard distinctly. She threw the pen from her and listened. It was a long passage, and her room was the last in the row. Her face flushed slowly, and into her eyes there came a deeper, clearer light; but she never stirred. The footfall halted, and there was a second's wait.

Then came a rap, quick, sharp, decisive.

The woman rose slowly, walked to the door and unlocked it.

"Come in," she said gently, and the man entered.

He looked perturbed. He was a tall, sunburnt man of about thirty-five, with massive shoulders and a great, gaunt frame, indicating immense strength. His head was peculiar; narrow at its base, it widened out above the ears, attaining generous proportions. A noble forehead, square, and with great temples, rose above eyes that were gray-blue in colour and shrewd in expression. The face was narrow at the chin, falling into a perfect oval, which was enhanced by the short brown beard that he wore trimmed down to a point. His nose and mouth were nondescript. A great shrewdness, combined with much intellectual force, and some acquired cynicism, brooded in face and head. He had a peculiar, but undoubted, attractiveness. At heart there seemed to be much that was tender and graceful. This he had done his best to hide under an affectation that could only be called disagreeable. He rather liked the title of disagreeable man. He had a knack of saying disagreeable things in a nice way. This piqued women. And when you excite women to the degree of piquancy they become dangerous. Women ran after David Strang. They professed to abhor him — they secretly adored him, and played their prettiest tricks for his benefit. He remained unmoved. He found it amusing.

The woman to whose office he came this hot July day had long ago fathomed, or thought she fathomed, his complex nature. She had certainly carefully hidden the clay feet of her god, enveloping them in draperies of purple and gold, and denying their existence to her own soul. But this was after she had found the tender places in his deep nature. At first she had seen the clay feet; gradually her imagination — which was royal — had covered them, and a film had grown over the eyes of her soul, a silver film, through which he loomed gracious and tender. For a long time she had been growing in upon herself. A great restlessness consumed her. Then came a feeling abroad for sympathy. This gathered around her work. For a time she wrote brilliantly, pouring her soul out in quaint imagery. All the human nature in her, and the spiritual, cried aloud. Her work satisfied for a time, but hers was a stormy soul, given to recklessness and feeling the need of a personal, a human love. Love was a great trinity, she argued. There should be the intellectual, the spiritual, and also the carnal, or rather the human love. (Should the craving that demands protection, caringness, closeness, tenderness, be marred by a name so suggestive of grossness as carnal?)

She used to envy the old ladies whom she saw carefully cloaked and guarded by their old husbands on steamboats or trains. They brought an atmosphere of home with them. She had had a mere glimpse of home in her childish days. Since, it had been a forlorn sort of life, drifting from one "lodgings" to another; living in trunks, making no friends, shrinking from publicity. "Home, Sweet Home" always made her soul shed tears. So did Christmas-time, and the barrel-organ when it played "Ta-ra-ra-boom-de-ay." Her brother used to whistle that decayed London refrain all day long, one time; but he never would again, for he was stopped suddenly one day by that in his throat which the doctors had called diphtheria, and he drifted out on tides eternal, long, long ago.

As to herself, this woman is not to be described, beyond saying that she was past her first youth, and of that sort of attractiveness which people vaguely term fascination, or magnetism, or psychic force. She was not at all beautiful, yet was far from being ugly or commonplace. Passion and grief were both stamped heavily on her face. There was a story in all her attitude. She was one of those women who, while strong as steel, have a look of fragility that is at times very attractive. A certain waxiness of colour, a deepening shadow about the great eyes, and a growing slenderness of figure, gave this impression. As the man stepped inside the door, which closed quietly upon him, he bent and raised the woman's hand to his lips reverently. A reverence brooded in his eyes, as he looked into her face. When, without a word, he lightly stroked the thick tangle of brown hair that gathered about her forehead, she stood quiet, only smiling at him.

"You must go in a minute," she said, and her voice was exquisite — soft, deep and very tender. "I have a wretched paper to get out before seven o'clock — on love — platonics — and I feel as stupid as an owl — in fact quite woolly. Do you believe in platonic love? Is there such a thing?"

His face grew moody. He walked quickly to a chair and sat down heavily.

"I believe there is," he said — he had a harsh, deep voice — "and what's more, I believe it's the safest kind of love." He pulled at his gloves savagely.

"Oh, indeed!" she said, mocking him playfully, "since when did you come to have an opinion as to love's safeness?"

"Since this long time," he answered sharply. "You yourself taught me. You always said love brought suffering — that it was a thing to be avoided — " He rose and walked to the window, then turned restlessly and strode up and down the room with hands thrust deep in his pockets.

The woman watched him quietly. He was in a mood and she would humour it.

"Look at this," she said, pulling a volume from under a pile of papers. "It's the last *Yellow Book*, and there is an appreciation of Yvette Guilbert in it that will delight you."[2]

"Yvette Guilbert." He stopped his quick walking and looked fixedly at her, "you are very like her — that tall, slender thing all in white, with those long, expressive, black-gloved arms. An ugly woman. *Jolie laide*, as they say in Paris, but the sort of woman who gets to a man's head and intoxicates him. Ah, you women!" He crossed to the chair again, sitting, leaned his arms on the desk and his head against them.

The woman moved to him softly. A great light was in her eyes, a mother-light, serene and holy. She laid a gentle hand on his bright, thick hair.

"Don't!" he cried harshly. Then, in a half whisper, "Help me, Marah."

The woman started back. Her face grew gray with a sudden pallor, bluish shadows crept about her lips. "Help you!" she cried, gaily, for his face was hidden — "How can I help you?"

"Help me to give you up."

A silence fell about the room. Down in the street an organ was grinding out "Paradise Alley." She wondered why it brought her a memory of a crowded race-meet and a sweet girl-face framed in red hair that looked into hers,

---

[2] *Yellow Book*: *avant-garde* London quarterly, known for its publication of aesthetes like Oscar Wilde and Aubrey Beardsley. Yvette Guilbert (1867–1944), a French singer, was known for her risqué songs of Parisian low-life and her trademark black gloves.

while a voice sang to the measure. The flies buzzed heavily. A spider dipped from the roof on his slender thread, touched her hair, then ran nimbly up again.

Then the woman called Marah spoke. Her voice was full of laughter. "Is that all?" she asked gaily, "what a to-do about nothing! Why, of course I'll help you. Are you going to tell me such a light thing as this has so completely upset you? *You*, a man of iron?"

He lifted his face and looked at her. The cynic's smile crept about his eyes. The pallor had been swept from her cheeks by a vivid flush. Her eyes burned.

"If I thought you'd take it so lightly," he said grimly, "I'd have spared myself some suffering. Egad, one never understands women. They are about as constant as the winds."

"Maybe they are," she said, cheerily, as his head dropped upon his arms again, "and maybe that is one of our compensations, for we have to suffer much — but never mind these things. Tell me why you have come to this mind. Have I — " her voice broke for the first time, "have I offended you in any way by any solecism? I know how fastidious, how particular you are."

He shrank a little, knowing her for the perfect gentlewoman she was; it shamed him to be thought caddish and unappreciative.

"Not that, not that at all," he said in a muffled voice, "Oh, can't you see? Didn't you see? Won't you help me, Marah?"

I think it was then that her heart broke. Something surely snapped in her being and went from her forever. But still she smiled. It was a stiff smile, as if the muscles had set that way and she could not change them. She still spoke heartily, though her voice took tenderer tones.

"Didn't you know that I only want your happiness," she said, slowly and gently, "and indeed," this quite stoutly, "I was getting a little tired myself. There is so much work in the world that there is not much time left for love. I shall write the article on platonics from a different and more healthy point of view," she added a trifle bitterly.

He said not a word.

In the silence another foot pattered along the passage. There came a knock on the glass door, and the woman walked slowly to it. A boy stood waiting.

"Any copy ready?" he asked hurriedly, "Mr. Brock sent me for some. Said you had an editorial or sumfin'."

"It will be ready in an hour or so, Jim," said the woman, speaking softly. "I'll talk to Mr. Brock down the tube. Don't you come back, you'll only interrupt me. Mr. Brock will give final directions about it."

She walked to the tube and whistled.

"Is that Mr. Brock? Mr. Brock, would you mind putting Mr. Todd or Bert Lisle on to my work to-night? I feel done up with a headache, and I'd like to go home?"

"H'm well, I'll see what I can do, Miss Tennard, but if you could manage that special I'd be glad. We're short-handed just now, you know. Lisle is out west on that murder case, and Todd's on the law courts. Never mind your assignments, but get out that article if you can. Wish you'd told me you were ill sooner, and I'd have kept one of the boys in. Hope you'll be all right to-morrow."

"Thanks — I'll do the best I can," the voice took a weary tone. The woman walked over towards the man. He still sat with his head leaning on his arms. He might have fallen asleep for all sign of life there was about him.

"David," her voice was exquisitely gentle, "didn't you know that I would help, David? Why, it's nothing, I always expected it. I know your nature, know how easily you tire, what vagaries your fancy takes. Poor David! Nice old David! I'll make it as easy for you as I can."

Her voice broke a little, and a great faintness came upon her. She could hardly see him when he lifted his face and laid his head against her breast. Then she recovered. Her heart leaped against his ear.

"I am a brute," he muttered, "but, Marah, how could I go on with it when I found I was caring for her. She is so young, so fresh and guileless and sweet. I hated to take her hand and look into her clear eyes. I —— ."

"I know," said the woman, brooding above him softly,

"I know it all, David. Intuitively, maybe, but very surely. Will you go now," she added, wearily, "just go without saying anything more. Come to my little house to-night, and we will talk things over, only go, now. I'm going to try to get this special through. They are short-handed below and the work must be done."

She talked so cheerily that the man rose and looked at her amazed. She stood before him in her gray linen gown, a tall and slender creature, beautiful for the moment by reason of the shining light that lay in her deep eyes, and the wild crimson of her cheeks, and the dying sunlight that shifted through her deep brown hair, glorifying it. All the faintness had left her, and she was strangely strong.

The man held out his arms. She shook her head, still smiling stiffly. "Now, David," she said, "how foolish! Why keep this up? I know you like me and ——."

"Never so tenderly," his voice took a curiously soft cadence, "never so tenderly as now in this moment of parting. Oh, my girl!" he struck out and tramped up and down the room, "why is it that I tire so easily? Why is it that those I love deepest and most tenderly pall on me when I am much with them? Will it be this way with *her*?"

She looked at him. The thought that he was a cad slid into her mind. She beat it back stoutly, for she was made of loyal clay. "Because of your immense vanity," she answered, looking steadfastly at him, "because of the unrest of your soul, the fickleness of your fancy, the vagaries of an imagination that would lead you to insanity were you not saved by the magnificent judgment and will-power in that splendid head. Unfortunate man that you are! from my soul I pity you! I pity this other woman, I pity myself for having loved you. You are a poor thing, after all," she cried, her nature leaping to its full altitude above his, "a poor flimsy, tawdry creature! a half-souled man. Ah, go away, go away!"

She walked to the window and set her face against the pane. The glory of the dying day encompassed her slender figure, brightened her brown hair. He stood looking at her. A red flush had come to his sun-burnt cheeks. His eyes glistened.

"Say what you like to me, Marah," he spoke, "but say a kindly good-bye."

"Won't you go?" Her entreating voice was fast breaking.

"Not until you say good-bye, Marah," he said softly.

The woman turned and fled to him. He opened wide his arms and caught her. All the poor soul of her broke into sighs and sobs and wild crying, as she leaned against his breast for the last time — for always.

"Good-bye, David, my David, 'naebody's mon but mine,' — that's what I used to call you, David — my strong sweetheart, my own big man! Good-bye, David. I was very fond of you, David."

So she whispered against his breast.

His eyes lost their brightness. "I'll be coming back, Marah," he said, "I'll be coming back."

But she said, "Good-bye, David," — and "Poor David!" and at last, lifting her poor blurred face — "Kiss me, good-bye, as if you were kissing little old Marah in her coffin."

Then she pushed him from the room.

∽

At ten minutes to six Johnny Dillon, the elevator boy, knocked upon her door — after his custom — to tell her he was making his last trip. A faint voice called out cheerily enough, "Don't wait for me, Johnny, I'm working late to-night."

"All right." The footsteps clattered away. She heard the "cage," as she used to call it, clap doors and go rushing down, the printers shouting to one another, and whistling and laughing as they left work. Then, as she settled to her writing, a pair of gray gloves caught her eye. She took them up and looked at them, turning them softly in her fingers.

"Nice hands David has," she murmured, "and nice gloves. Always those soft gray ones. I don't think I ever saw David in any other but gray doeskin gloves."

Then broke a wild cry, "David gone! David gone out of my life for ever! Oh, heavens!"

Marah sat back in her chair. A dreadful look had crept into her face. It was wax-white, and again those bluish shadows lurked around her lips. Her fingers fastened about the gray gloves. Then she smiled, and slowly drew them over her little thin hands.

The sun died out of the room.

∽

Some hours later, a woman crept down the steep, dark stairs that led to the street. At the foot of the last step, below the bunch of lights that threw a radiance over the entrance, a little man was standing looking intently at the figure that was so slowly descending.

"Why, it's you, Miss Tennard," said the night editor. "I didn't know you. I thought it was an old woman."

∽

Canadian Magazine 22 (Dec. 1903): 121–125.

Susan Jones (S. Carleton) (1864?–1926)

THE FRENCHWOMAN'S SON (1904)

Fiction writer Susan Morrow Jones was born and educated in Halifax, Nova Scotia, the daughter of Helen Stairs and Robert Morrow, prominent Haligonians. Described by her contemporaries as bright, vivacious and attractive, she married her cousin, Guy Carleton Jones, brother of the writer Alice Jones (see page 109). Dr. Jones was to have a controversial career as Director-General of the Canadian Army Medical Services at the time of World War I. The couple lived at this time at "Birkenfels," a spacious home in Rockcliffe Park, an upper-class Ottawa suburb. Susan Jones died in 1926.

Susan Jones won a short story contest sponsored by the New York *Herald* in 1903, and contributed fiction to *Atlantic Monthly*, *Smart Set* and *Lippincot's Magazine*. She employed pseudonyms: "The Frenchwoman's Son" and four stories in a similar vein appeared in *Atlantic Monthly* under the name "S. Carleton." Current research, by Carole Gerson and others, indicates that novels ascribed to Susan Jones under the pseudonym "Helen Milicete" may have been written by her sister Helen Morrow Paske Duffus. Works by "Carleton-Milicete" may have been the result of collaboration between the two. Works currently attributed to Susan Jones include *The Micmac* (1904) and *The La Chance Mine Mystery* (1920).

"The Frenchwoman's Son" is typical of the tales Susan Jones wrote early in the century: stories with a haunting, exotic wilderness setting and a focus on states of mind, stories not unlike Marjorie Pickthall's "On Ile de Paradis" (see page 159) and Pauline Johnson's "The Haunting Thaw" (see page 172). In her tale, Jones depicts the inner conflicts of a "half-breed" who denies his native heritage. Jones's treatment of this theme also has affinities with Duncan Campbell Scott's poems of cultural conflict, such as "The Half-Breed Girl" and some of his Northern stories, for example "Spirit River."

"The Frenchwoman's Son" is the reverse of the initiation story, in which a central character's painful initiation into self-knowledge brings greater growth. In this story, the protagonist, whose several names reflect his fractured identity, denies self-knowledge and perishes as a result. The motif of unresolved forces culminates in the final image of the story — the prized flowered fabric so coveted and so fatal, which remains something forever half-made, as inchoate as the lovers. Like Pickthall and Johnson, Jones presents the wilderness as a psychic force in the destiny of the protagonist.

◆

Suggested Reading

Gerson, Carole. "Restoring Helen Morrow Paske Duffus (1868?–1936)," *Canadian Notes and Queries* 40 (Autumn 1988/Spring 1989): 10–11.

Jones, Susan ("S. Carleton"). "The Lame Priest," *Atlantic Monthly* 88 (Dec. 1901): 760–769.

——. "The Sound of the Axe," *Atlantic Monthly* 90 (Oct. 1902): 454–465.

——. "The Tall Man," *Atlantic Monthly* 99 (Jan. 1907): 36–44.

THE FRENCHWOMAN'S SON

Susan Jones (S. Carleton)

It was the year of the coarse April that the Frenchwoman's son took to the woods. He had no reason, except that with the spring he had become abruptly aware that since his mother's death his house was intolerable, and that he could farm no longer on the small holding that had been hers. It was beyond him to dig, and plant potatoes, and raise two lean pigs to be killed in the fall. He left Bear Cove without ostentation, and his absence found it indifferent; he had never been an ornament, nor precisely a reproach; but neither was he missed. The priest was the only soul in the parish who stood an instant at the shut door of the silent, forlorn house, and even he said nothing. As for his thoughts, they were more in tune with the ceaseless rain than with the battering west wind that was driving the ice off the shore and lifting up the dull winter grass. But he had been too cold all winter, and too much given to fasting that the poor of his flock might eat, to have much of the spring in his blood. And the fact remained; the Frenchwoman's son was gone.

He had made inland of a rough, gray morning, and his method of traveling was the method of the otter, who never sleeps two nights in the same place; and for a fortnight he rioted in it. He sang to himself as he toiled over the wet, treeless barrens; laughed when he just got out with his life from the sucking soil of the Long Swamp, which was not a thoroughfare; was exultant when he came at last to the woods where the trees were a man's girth round. He had turned his back on the sea for good and all; on the gray swelter of the spring tides; on the winter-thickened waves that ran sullen, too cold to break; on the miserable village that dragged a living out of the bitter water and the sour, brackish land. He was free. He did not even mind the icy rain, nor the wicked gales that blew all that month, though down on the shore he had left they would have been another matter. He was where he belonged; and he accepted the rough weather as placidly as did the just come robins that sang all round him, no more at home than he. Things he had never known came to him spontaneously. He built and lit his fires of wet wood without any trouble to speak of, though he had scarcely made a fire out-of-doors in his life; and the camp that he began to build one morning by the head waters of the lonely Sou'west was done in a way which was not that of the shore settlements, nor of any shelter he had ever seen. But it had a form of its own, and it pleased him; also it shed water like a loon's back, and when he was inside it the roar and lash of the spring storms might be sounding like a mighty organ in the great hemlocks overhead, and the rain sluicing on the open spaces, but he was in his house.

"It is," he said to himself thoughtfully, "a camp with long walls." The words pleased him, and sounded familiar; which was absurd, because in all his twenty years he had never heard of anything but shingled houses.

He had no plans about life; it was merely a thing that had been thoroughly distasteful, and was become an insistent, ever-present pleasure and excitement; and when one morning the sun at last came out clear and scorching he sat on a drying deadfall and basked in it, and smelt the spring out of the soggy ground. He never thought at all of Bear Cove, nor even of the priest; and he had been fond of the priest. His mother had been on curiously equal terms with the smooth-faced old man. She had never been a common woman, no matter what else she had been in the years she cast behind her when she arrived in the ugly little English-speaking settlement and bought Jim Miller's house.

"The Frenchwoman," the village called her, all but

the priest; who, perhaps, was sorry for her, for he was kind to her and the boy, and unoffended by her wild moods and flinging tongue. But she had been dead for a year now, and there was no tombstone over her till Sandy Brine had time to cut one. Father Gillespie had not hurried him. There was in his mind a discrepancy between his answers to her dying instructions as to a truthful inscription over her grave, and those regarding her son. But the son had cut away the knot of both promises by his absolute unconsciousness that there was any to cut. Whereby he sat and whistled on his sunny perch, and mocked a song sparrow till it suddenly flew away. The boy sniffed the air quite as suddenly, and swung round his long legs till he faced the east.

An Indian was standing close beside him. He looked young, but it was not then the Frenchwoman's son could tell an Indian's age. Anyhow, he was not thinking of it. He sat angry and very still; and the man greeted him eagerly with a long-drawn "Well?"

"What do you want?" he asked roughly. He had been thoroughly startled, for he had not heard a sound of footsteps. "Do you live here?"

"Want you." The man regarded him from under the thatch of stiff hair that stuck out from his hat. "Your name John — John Noel?" He said Noo-el, with the soft Indian o.

The boy stared. "Yes — But I don't use that name! Ba'tiste, I use."

"That all same," said the visitor blandly. "Ba'tiste your mother call you; your father John. You his son, so we come."

"Whose son?" snapped John Ba'tiste; he had never heard mention of his father, nor been particularly concerned about him.

The Indian took off his hat. "The Old Man's."

It was Greek to the hearer, to whom an old man was an old man; he never dreamed that the words and the act were a shibboleth of respect for an Indian esteemed next to a chief.

"What old man?" he asked contemptuously; the thing had nothing to do with him if his name were John ten times over.

"He tell me you come some day" — the question was placidly ignored — "so we come. Long time ago that — fifteen year — we don' know! But he say you come all same as him."

"You could n't know I was here!"

"We come see," quietly; "every year we come. Old Man my friend; he say, 'We die. You be good friend my son. Some time he come to the Sou'west, where he was born at. You be help to my son.'"

The listener got down from his log and spoke with rage. "I was born at Mirimichi; and I don't know who you are, but you never knew my father. He's been dead for years, and he never needed Indians for friends. Where d'ye live? Because you'd better go back there."

The Indian turned away with an ugly dignity. "Old Man good man to me, he say you all same; very well. You say not so; very well too. We go."

"Oh, stop. Do you live round here? That's what I want to know." If he had neighbors he would tramp at once.

"No one live here. No Indian come but me." He waved his hand around him. "We come not one time more. Your house, your place," he observed finally; and the Frenchwoman's son affirmed it with an oath.

Yet his curiosity was awake in him, and he turned a volley of questions on his visitor; but the man walked away untouched by the demands fired at him. The Frenchwoman's son never knew what made him care, but he made a dash after him and held out his hand.

The Indian seized it, his whole face changing, till it was another man who smiled.

"We bring things," he cried; "flour, all what you say! You good friend; we give you this. Every year we bring it here, like Old Man say. He say: 'Good friend to you, you give it; bad friend, you go 'way!'" He fumbled in his coat and brought out a letter.

The Frenchwoman's son stared at it. Old, tattered, dirty, and written in characters and a language he did not know, it could not belong to him. But he took it. And then a lordly thought struck him.

"Come in and have something to eat." Houses still meant eating to him, and his house was his pride.

The Indian laughed. "We got plenty meat! We kill caribou two days back. You got plenty meat?"

"Yes." John Ba'tiste was savage again. It had seemed to him that he was doing great things by living alone in the wilderness, and here was a low person who considered it a storehouse. "Well," he nodded offendedly, "good-by; if you don't want anything to eat!"

"Adiou," returned the man, and laughed again. He was gone into the bushes while the Frenchwoman's son stood staring stupidly, and wondering where he had heard people say adieu with that twist to it before, till suddenly there came back to him his mother's daily cry at him: "Will you speak like a pig and an outcast? Whistle your u, I tell you; shape your mouth! I will not have you 'adiou' like an outcast." It was funny, and he laughed. Through the laugh a voice came to him suddenly.

"Bimeby you hungry; then we come," it remarked.

The Frenchwoman's son swore at it, and retired to his house. He glanced contemptuously at the extraordinary letter which was meant for somebody else, and was going to burn it; only his fire was out; and then he applied himself once more to the joys of doing nothing, and not caring what time it was; he had had to care in the village. Yet daylight of the next morning found him pulling the letter out of a crack in his wall, and staring at it. What if it were for him, after all? But the queer words were nothing that he could make out, and only made him angry; he put it away again, and was suddenly aware that he was lonely, and afraid; something had taken the heart out of him. He had no pleasure any more in his house, nor in his prowls over the country. He took to sitting at his door, beside a senseless anxiety. Every now and then he took out the crazy letter that was not meant for him, and all he got from it was a biting anger that he could not read the thing. It grew to be an obsession; he woke to it in the long mornings, could not eat for the memory of it lying in its chink; time and again tried to burn it, and never did. He let his food give out, because every day he meant to leave his camp and the letter in it; but he never started, and he knew it was because he had taken a terror of meeting more men who should speak to him of his father. It was like sitting alone in the dark and fearing a dead man at his elbow, and about as sensible. If he had been in his white-washed house by the shore he would have sickened, but the woods he had loved kept him whole. They were kind to him, even while he was hardly conscious of them. The black birch twigs that he chewed, just to be chewing, took his bodily fever out of him; the nameless sweetness in the wind of midnight made him drowsy; a hundred things helped him even while he was careless of all but his own haunting misery, till one May morning he woke to find himself lying hungry at his door with a man between him and the sunshine.

It was the Indian back again, and a queer pain jolted the boy's heart, till he could not think of a word to say. He saw that the man carried a heavy load, and that there must be things to eat in it, but his real thought was that now he could get at that letter. He swayed on his feet as he stood up.

The man looked at him curiously. "We bring things," he said, "we cook; bimeby we talk. You call us Sabiel."

He flung down his pack, and the Frenchwoman's son sat and glared. He had not eaten fresh meat all that winter, — it was not an article of diet in Bear Cove, — and the smell of it made him forget even the letter. As he ate, the strong food went to his head like drink, till he sat happy in the sun, and, basking, lit his last fill of tobacco, or meant to. The match died in his fingers as he spilled half his pipeful in his palm and held it out to Sabiel, who shook his head.

"Bâpkusedumeí!" said he, bringing out a dirty clay.

The Frenchwoman's son started. Somewhere, long and long ago, he had heard that word time and again. He

SUSAN JONES

swore to himself in French, and Sabiel smiled uncomprehendingly: —

"We say, we light our pipe!"

"I know that," snapped the boy, "though I don't see how you do;" and through his angry puzzle a queer phrase came to him. "Menuagaí tamôwayau!" said he, very slowly and falteringly; and sat back lax and sick. The Indian had handed him a fig of tobacco, and gabbled something in a jargon of which at least two words were familiar even if he had not translated the last one as he pointed to the camp, — "pembtek, a house with long walls."

"What are you talking?" screeched the Frenchwoman's son; "what kind of language?"

"Indian," placidly. "Your father's talk."

"Indian! Do you mean my father was an Indian?" He hardly knew he said it, and he did not listen to the answer. He was seeing, as from a long way off, his mother making a fire on the ground; seeing himself, a little boy, playing with a burning stick, and an Indian man laughing where he sat beside him; and the man had been his father. He knew it as he knew he sat now cheek by jowl with another Indian and understood his tongue. "But my father was a Frenchman!" He found his voice without commanding it, and even in the making of the words, remembered they had never been said to him; he had only taken them for granted. But he kept on speaking. "I don't believe you."

Sabiel returned three slow sentences. They broke the defenses the boy was trying to make in his mind, because he knew them to be true; and the gist of them checked his heart. He was a half-breed; just a half-breed. He knew now why there had been days when his mother hated him, knew why the priest had set him down to books and the choir-singing as soon as he began to take to the wind-swept woods over the village. He had never been meant to know; and he saw how easy it had been to keep him ignorant. They never had Indians round Bear Cove, never thought of them; his mother's French blood had been enough to carry a darker skin and eyes than his. Half of his soul rose up in a dreadful revolt, and half of it in a wilder exaltation of freedom. He sat and stammered questions at the man on the other side of the fire, and finally got out what was last in his mind as it had been first. The letter: he wanted it read to him.

When he had heard it his eyes were different. He got up and lit his pipe as if he had never thrown it away from him; and after a long time he spoke, with a laugh that was not a boy's laugh.

"While I choose to be a white man, I will be a white man!" he said, and cast away salvation; for in the woods he was one thing, and out of them another. He took the Indian letter he could not read for himself from where it lay on the ground, and threw it on the fire, and on top of it he tossed the red head handkerchief that had been his mother's. The old paper blazed, and the common silk smouldered writhingly, but he did not look at them; neither of the two should ever call to him any more. He would be a white man now, and make a new name for himself.

But he never did it, his world being a jealous world which did its own christening. There were not ten people who ever knew him as John Noel, and they were unimportant, chief among them being a despised squatter called Welsh, to whose retired abode he was in the habit of repairing when he was tired of being the white man whom his intimates addressed as Frenchy. As for his official name, it was no new one; though when it cropped up in a lawless country it stood for a hundred things. Well-off people shook at the mention of it, but to the poor and desolate it was another matter. When Sabean the outlaw was finally caught and caged there were scores of prayers going up that the Frenchwoman's son might not be caught too. Sabean had been the terror of two counties, and, having the poor on his side, had robbed with impunity; there was not a man anxious for his capture but his victims and the sheriff, and every one but they knew he was only the tool of the Frenchwoman's son. If there were darker things they were only whispered of; the Frenchwoman's son had found a world full of friends by the simple process of placidly, and at once, cracking down on his enemies. There was always, or nearly always, a smack of righteous vengeance in his sins.

When McManus's mill was burned just as he was bringing down his season's cut, well-informed people did not consider it an accident, though not one of them said so; and the Frenchwoman's son was unostentatiously elsewhere on important business, so that the law did not seek him any more than public gossip named him. It was well for McManus that he had no insurance, or his friends would have said he fired his mill himself. As it was they smiled crookedly, and remarked that the attention drawn to the working of his lumber business was worse than the fire; — whereat he swore impotently, and cast about for vengeance, which was not forthcoming; and was so unpleasant to Fanny, his housekeeper, that she ran away of a dark night with his foreman, and he had to do his own cooking, which did not cool him. He began to talk of sending for his only daughter, who had been banished to her uncle Welsh's with the advent of Fanny; but it was a radical measure, and he put it off.

The Frenchwoman's son heard nothing of these last matters because he had gone out to Welsh's on the Long Swamp to make love to Welsh's niece.

In the northern woods the spring comes up in scarlet, leaf and shrub and blossom, with white drifts of Indian pear flower flung across a blood-red world. He had seen the red of it often enough, but it was the first year in his life he had noticed the white, or thought of the priest at Secret Lake in connection with a woman; and he had known a few as tall as Welsh's niece, and not so ragged. In the intervals of his variegated life he had watched her growing up, cast off, half starved, and lonely, till his heart was soft within him.

Welsh was a kind man when he was not drunk, but his shack was too convenient a place to bestow an inconvenient child. In front of it stretched a lake, and close behind it the Long Swamp, which was not as pretty as it looked. It was not called a quicksand; but it was not crossed, even in winter. A few Indians had tried it. Persons having business afterwards on the other side went round; and there grew up about it an ugly tradition with an Indian name. It looked an innocently sleeping waste; but it had its times, which were not seasons, for waking. In the dead calm of an August noon the Frenchwoman's son had seen its bay bushes sway as with wind, bow, and spring backwards with the passage of things he could not see; had heard out of it the crying that might have been the crying of a hurt loon, or the frantic screech of a man who tries to keep death off him by shrieking to the living. To a stray trapper hearing it meant to wipe the sweat from his face, if he knew any Indian words. But the Frenchwoman's son was a white man determinedly, and had put away all fear of ghost-calling; it was merely a shamefaced care for the child that sent him to Welsh's to see her after an absence of a year. He found her a woman. Also absolutely and astoundingly beautiful in an old flannel shirt of Welsh's, and a skirt made of flour sacks.

At the sight of her he stood dumb for the first time in his pleasantly irresponsible life. Then, as she ran to him and put her hands on his, he was suddenly aware that the spring was scarlet, and the whiteness of the pear blossoms the whiteness of Mary McManus's face and throat above her unspeakable clothes. It was not till he had spoken about the priest at Secret Lake that he kissed her.

He was not known by sight in that district, so that when he went to McManus and announced he was going to marry his daughter it was annoying to be shown the door — profanely. McManus's mill happened to burn down the night John Noel went back to his courting. His plans were not changed, merely hurried, but back at Welsh's by the Long Swamp they bade fair to be destroyed. Mary McManus had waked to the desire of clothes.

"But," said he, very tenderly and without laughter, "I will buy you clothes for the wedding. Your father says" — he had never lost his mother's shrug — "there will be no wedding; and he says other things, too."

"You saw Fanny!" She spoke without looking at him.

"Yes." For once his mind was slow.

"Then," very low, "*I'll* have a dress with roses on it;

and a pair of shoes! I never had a pair of shoes since I come here."

"I can buy them." He smiled into her eyes, but they did not answer him.

"No; I'll make him! I'm his daughter; and Fanny has silk dresses."

The Frenchwoman's son sat down on the spring flowers, and looked across the nameless color of the Long Swamp.

"Then it will be a long time to the wedding," he said, softly considering, "when he takes you home and I have to steal you out of his house in the dark. It is spring now, and there are a great many things to do where I live — in spring! There is the loon to watch, — on her nest." Something in his slow voice flooded her slim throat scarlet.

"When I cook for you in your house you shall buy me clothes," she retorted passionately.

The Frenchwoman's son was not used to complex emotions. He sat silent, because he was provoked and grieved and proud of her all at once. He knew that the sooner he and she were off to the priest and the Sou'west the better, for many reasons. But she was extremely beautiful, and very white.

"You go 'way and get me some paper," she ordered suddenly, "and I'll send him in a letter." With his first word of love to her she had changed from the little girl who had openly adored him all her life at Welsh's to a woman who dominated him body and soul. "You learned me to write; I'll write to him."

"When we've been to the priest," he said calmly; and she flung round on him.

"I can't — in these," she sobbed. Her shame had caught her at her heart as she looked at her rags and her bare legs. "Why, there's people, and — I can't. And Welsh has n't any money, and I want a — cotton dress — with roses on it."

The Frenchwoman's son took her in a strong arm and comforted her with more confidence in himself than in McManus.

"You shall have the dress with roses on it. I will bring the paper and you shall write; but it will take two days. Will that do?"

"What's that?" she said, without answering. "Don't you hear some one calling?" She twisted away from him, and stood listening.

"No!" And on the heel of it he did hear. It was only the old cry he was used to disbelieving in that floated over the loneliness, and he laughed. "That? It's only a bird in the swamp! You've often heard it."

"Never that way. There," — every line of her was rigid, — "it's coming again! It — it sounds like as if it was calling me. I — oh, I'm afraid!"

"There's no harm in it. Why," — he moved to her serenely as he remembered, — "I went through the swamp once, when I was a boy. It's a very good way to go if you know the path."

"There's no path!"

"I know one;" and over his comfortable voice the call came close and mocking.

"Welsh says," she clutched him, whispering, "that's lost people's ghosts; and they only call when they're hungry! I — don't it sound like my name?" and he felt the fear in her.

"It's only a bird," he said softly. "Do I look as if I were afraid of it? If it were your name I would be afraid."

McManus's daughter looked at him, and at five-and-twenty the Frenchwoman's son was a beautiful sight. There was no half-breed about him except the straight sling of his walk and the dark clearness of the cheek bent down to her; and there was that in his eyes that made her safe and happy and miserable all at once. If she had not caught sight of her own incredible skirt she would have clung to him, and begged him to take her away then and there. But she had remembered the cotton dress, and her father's money; and Fanny in silk. And perhaps the sudden terror that cut the quiet air was only a bird! What he said was gospel.

"There's nothing you'd be afraid of, except me!" she

said, with the insolence of a woman to the man she adores. "Get me the paper an' a pencil."

It was Welsh who took in the letter, half from honest affection for his niece, and half for the chance of getting thoroughly drunk on some one else's whiskey. If he did it was not on McManus's. Mary was no diplomatist, especially in the written word.

"I take my pen in hand to tel you I am going to be married to mister Noel if you don't send me some mony to get a dress I wil come down to the vilage and tel how you tret me I wil come in Welsh's old shirt and the flower sak I hav for a petticoat that is al the dress I hav and show them Mary at Welsh's."

Perfectly sober, and a day before his time, the messenger returned, and sheepishly confronted his niece and Noel.

"He says," he announced sourly, "that you're to come home right to once, and he'll flour-sack you! — and his mill's burnt down, and the talk is that the Frenchwoman's son done it. And Fanny's run off with Jake Perry, and you're to go home to-morrow. And so I guess you two'd better git married and gone, and tell him afterwards; for he won't give you nothing, and he's wanting of you home."

"He can want," said McManus's daughter blackly. "Did n't he send me nothing?"

"Just that word, honey; and you ain't but seventeen; he can git you. I — I ain't a man to fight," with sudden shrillness, "and that letter made him dump me right out on the road!"

She stood up straight and looked at him. "I'll never go home, and I'll have my clothes; and I'm glad his mill's burnt, and I love the Frenchwoman's son for doing it, and I'm glad Fanny's run away; and I hate dad," she said, as emotionless as though she repeated a lesson.

Noel looked sharply from Welsh to the girl. "What's that about the Frenchwoman's son?"

"Some say it was him had a grudge again McManus. Labrador said so; he only said so; they don't know who done it. I ain't never seen the man, but he's got a hard reputation, and Labrador thinks it was him. But when I wanted to know why, he soured on me; and he said he'd kill me if I opened my mouth on it to McManus."

"He certainly would," returned Mr. Noel placidly; and having been hand in glove with Frank Labrador, perhaps he knew.

"The Frenchwoman's son ain't bad if Labrador likes him," said Mary unexpectedly. "I love him, anyhow!"

"Yes" — began Noel stupidly, and stopped. She did not know any more than Welsh did, and perhaps he had never realized it before. But it was time to get away from the Long Swamp and take his wife with him. "I am sorry about that burning," he observed slowly. "It was a pity; and foolish. But he is not altogether a bad man, the Frenchwoman's son."

"Well, there's no handling McManus till he finds out who burnt his mill!" muttered Welsh. He was suddenly tired of the subject. "He ain't heard of the Frenchwoman's son, and he ain't likely to. You git away and git married, honey! Noel, he'll git you a dress."

Mary made no answer; the Frenchwoman's son saw there was no handling her, either. He stood and whistled a thoughtful tune, and she swung round on him.

"Who's the Frenchwoman's son?" she demanded.

"Just a man." He said it between two bars of the tune that covered his thoughts.

"Is he in the village?"

He shook his head.

"Can dad catch him?"

The whistle stopped abruptly in a scornful smile. "Not if he'd seen him fire the mill!"

"Do you think he did it?"

"Oh yes," carelessly. "But he had his reasons!" He looked at her with amusement. "He has never done things without his reasons."

"They say he's a hard-living man," Welsh objected casually.

"That's a lie," slowly. "And if he was he's done with it. And catch him" — he laughed superbly. "When they can catch the screaming in the swamp!" He flung back at it with a free gesture of his head and shoulders, and McManus's daughter drew a breath and set her teeth on it. There could not be in all the world a man like him! She would go with him to the priest in a dress with roses on it, in spite of her father. She listened without objecting while he and Welsh arranged for the wedding in three days' time, but when she turned away to the house she sat thinking, instead of getting supper. Noel had departed to interview the priest, and, incidentally, the proprietor of the only shop at Secret Lake. In three days he would be back for the wedding; and the dress with roses on it was no nearer. Nothing would take Welsh back to McManus, and she had no other messenger. But when in the white dawn Welsh arose and unexpectedly went fishing, his niece leaped from her bed and cast on her casual garments. Even as his back disappeared in the thin spring bushes she was down at the lake shore, and the last sound of his going was covered by another sound: the plunging rush of a canoe launched and sprung into with one and the same movement. Frank Labrador, coming up half an hour later on business of his own, saw the shack deserted except for the blue jays making faces at him from the rooftree, and went half-heartedly away.

It was sunrise of the next day when the girl came back, to find the place still empty. She was tired, and she went to sleep, but once and again a horrible clamor in the swamp roused her till she went out to listen; when she came back for the second time she barred the door uneasily, and dressed herself. Her skin crept on her as she crouched down by the window and watched the empty glittering lake the long, silent morning, wishing impatiently that Welsh would come back; if she had had even a dog to speak to it would have lightened the senseless dread that was on her. And at the thought, leaning out and shading her eyes, she forgot it. A canoe had shot round the point and was at the landing. There was one man in it, — a dirty messenger with a parcel.

When she raced down and dragged it out of his hand

she saw her shoes, her stockings, and her wedding gown. Her father had been as good as his word, though he had sent the things by a stranger, instead of by Labrador as she had asked him. With a low laugh she plumped down on her knees and fondled the common print with roses on it; when she looked up to ask the man who had brought it if he wanted his dinner, he had gone away, and in the still air the rustling from the swamp was loud. For a moment her chill fear rushed back on her, but she would not heed it. She was back at the house, kneeling on the floor, feverishly putting the scissors into her wedding gown.

The Frenchwoman's son, coming unexpectedly to the door in the late afternoon, stood thunderstruck. Mary had sprung to her feet at the sight of him, transfigured; her face a pale flame, her eyes shining, her triumphant mouth scarlet. He let fall the things he had painfully procured for her as he stared.

"I got it!" she cried, and flung herself at him, her arms warm round his throat; "I made him. I've shoes and stockings and white cotton and a dress with roses on it. And it's nearly done, and I'll marry you to-morrow!"

"How did you get them?" He laughed because he was proud of her, and had never seen her so beautiful. "Tell me! How?"

"I went down," — simply, — "and waited at the portage, and sent a boy with notes on the paper you gave me. I asked him if he would give me the dress if I told him who fired his mill, and he sent back 'Yes.' So I told him it was the Frenchwoman's son, and he sent back to say 'it was cheap at a cotton gown, and he'd send it right away.' And he did. And you said he could n't catch the Frenchwoman's son!"

Life, color, and expression were all wiped off her listener's face.

"The Frenchwoman's son!" he repeated like a parrot. "But — and you told him?" His ready tongue had failed him.

"You said he could n't catch him, any more than the ghost-calling in the swamp." She stood back, a little anxious. "He — he can't, can he?"

"Not then! Now" — He took her with both hands, and held her at his arms' length, and the feel of his hands frightened her, like the strangeness in his voice. "Did n't you know Labrador was here looking for me? That he found me last night, and told me a man from Sabean's had seen me when I fooled over to speak to your father, and told him it was me you were going to marry; me, the Frenchwoman's son! And now" — The familiar shrug did not match the sound in his voice. "Well — I should have told you. But I could n't trust Welsh."

"You ain't French." She smiled disdainfully; but as she saw what was in his face her legs shook under her, and she shrieked at him, "Do you mean it? Did I do — that?"

"My mother was a Frenchwoman," he said heavily; he had no desire to swear, even to be angry with her; the thing had gone too deep. "But I've been coming here for so long I forgot you could n't know." He glanced through the open door to get the time from the westering sun, and saw, instead, that the young scarlet was gone from the world; it was old, green, usual, — and the thought made his voice rough. "Come, we'll get out of this!" If he left her behind he would lose her, and once at the head waters of the Sou'west, it would be a better man than McManus who should lay a claw on him. But his heart felt numb as he stooped to gather up the poor finery that had betrayed him.

As he bent, the girl's miserable eyes fell on the window.

"Keep down," she whispered thickly. "There's a boat! There's — it's dad, and another man!"

The Frenchwoman's son heard her without surprise. He did not even glance out, but as he stepped softly back into the shadow of the room he looked at her with a curious trick of the eyes that made them seem all pupil, and showed the whites above and below the iris.

"That is the sheriff," he said evenly, "with your father. What would you like me to do? For I burned the mill because your father was cruel to you, and I disliked him." He kept his strange gaze on her, standing motionless.

McManus's daughter sobbed wordlessly as she sprang at him and ran him out the back door.

"There's the swamp; you ain't afraid of it," — anguish and hate had killed her own terror of the place; "hide! What's an old mill? Hide!"

"You'd be afraid in it!" he said uneasily; and she laughed fiercely over her sobbing.

"That would n't make me stay. Hurry; stoop down!"

There was dead silence abroad now. Through it the two slipped safely across Welsh's inadequate clearing, into the thin green of its fringe of alders; and between them and the heavy screen of the swamp maples something moved. It was the man from Sabean's, the dirty messenger of the morning; and the Frenchwoman's son cut off his shout in the middle. But the half cry had done it. McManus was hot foot round the house with the sheriff after him, and Noel was dragging the girl through the binding maples, down into the bay bushes that stretched breast-high between green abysses and runnels of fathomless black water. When they reached his path they could drop and lie hidden, for not a man would dare follow them; but for now they must be cat-footed over the deadly green that spurted to their every step. There was cover enough, and he put her behind him, without daring to take his eyes from the quaking ground under his feet.

"Walk in my steps," he ordered, wondering if the next few yards would bear them; and his heart stopped as she screamed, —

"My dress — my dress with roses on it!" Even as he wheeled to clutch her she had broken away from him and was running, leaping helter-skelter back to the house, with no heed to the careful way she had come.

The Frenchwoman's son stood up straight in the afternoon light, his black head a clear mark against the young sun-filtered green of the thicket he was making for.

"Lie down!" he yelled, "lie down!"

He did not hear any answer. It was McManus who had fired, and the sheriff, who was half-hearted about the whole business, had been slow in knocking up his gun.

Mary McManus had lain down in a very pretty patch of quaking grass. The Frenchwoman's son knew she was dead as she crumpled forwards, but he was a white man who had been going to marry a white girl. He went back for her. He was heedless of the sheriff's calling; he knew a path through the swamp, and he must carry her to it that he might bury her out in the clean ground of the Sou'west. But the weight across his shoulder had somehow confused him; and the dead girl's hair kept brushing over his eyes, so that in the waving shadow of it he saw another shadow moving before him. To the dull anguish of his haste the very bushes were malignant; they kept him back, springing in his face with blow after blow, as though he followed too close a trail. But he was a white man, and he fought through them, making blindly for the sinking sun. It was on the edge of a bottomless black channel that he stumbled, and fell.

No sound came back out of the swamp; that which had been unquiet was perhaps fed; but in Welsh's house a light air crept through the open back door and fluttered the dress with roses on it that lay half made on the floor.

&

Atlantic Monthly 93 (April 1904): 449–459.

Sara Jeannette Duncan (1861–1922)

THE HEIR APPARENT (1905)

Sara Jeannette Duncan was the foremost pioneering woman in Canadian journalism in the 1880s. In the nineties, she became a fiction writer known in Canada, England and India, her three homes.

Christened Sarah Janet, she was the eldest of ten children of Janet Bell and Charles D. Duncan, a Scottish-born merchant established in Brantford. She was educated at Brantford Collegiate, the Ladies' College and the County Model School for teachers, as well as at Toronto Normal School, where she earned a teaching certificate in 1882. She taught briefly in her home town. As early as 1880, a childhood desire to become a writer prompted her to publish short pieces in magazines and journals. She began her journalism career on a local paper, then wrote for the Toronto *Globe*, the London (Ontario) *Advertiser* and the Washington *Post*. In 1886 at the *Globe*, she became Canada's first full-time female editorial writer. In 1887 she moved to the Montreal *Star*, becoming one of two women members of the Parliamentary Press Gallery; she also contributed to the *Week*. "Garth Grafton" was often her pseudonym. "Careers, if possible," this pioneering newswoman wrote in the *Globe* on 12 November 1886, "and independence anyway, we must all have, as musicians, artists, writers, teachers, lawyers, doctors, ministers, or something."

Duncan's first book, *A Social Departure: How Orthodocia and I Went round the World by Ourselves* (1890), a lively account of her round-the-world trip with fellow journalist Lily Lewis, is based on articles sent to the *Star*. Duncan spent her second year abroad in London, where her novel was published. In the fall of 1890, she returned to Calcutta to marry English-born Everard Cotes, then a museum official, whom she had met on her travels. She remained in India for twenty-five years, working in journalism with her husband and travelling frequently to Canada and to England, where she spent her last years. Duncan published twenty-two books, set variously in Canada, England, India and the United States. Best known today is her Canadian novel *The Imperialist* (1904) about religious and political small-town Canada. The theme of the new woman animates *A Daughter of Today* (1894). She published one volume of stories, *The Pool in the Desert* (1903). Duncan later became interested in theatre and, though none of her plays was really successful, some had brief runs, several in London's West End. She survived a bout with tuberculosis early in the century, an experience she chronicled in *On the Other Side of the Latch* (1901). She died in Ashton, Surrey, in 1922.

"The Heir Apparent," a little-known Duncan story, is characteristic of much of Duncan's fiction in its sophisticated, ironic style, subtle narrative method, and its juxtaposition of Canadian, American and British sensibilities. The story inverts one of her favourite fictional themes: how a bright young man and woman grapple with their elders' expectations — in this case, however, they strive to be ordinary, not exceptional. Ida Chamier has many fellows among Duncan's independent heroines, and the Canadian narrator and her elderly American friend are naive and romantic. Readers tempted to emphasize the story's clever political allegory — and elements in the story, such as Ida's rendition of "The Maple Leaf Forever," promote such a reading — will note that American Ida and English Randal focus primarily and ultimately not on Canada, the ostensible object of their visit, but on each other. In a style that owes much to Henry James, Duncan pokes elliptical fun at the Atlantic triangle, at intellectual conceptions of the new woman, at heredity, phrenology, and the fond and foolish view of the young by the old, a theme treated quite differently in Mary Lowrey Ross's "An Adventure in Youth."

⌒

Suggested Reading
Duncan, Sara Jeannette. *A Daughter of Today* (1894) (Ottawa: Tecumseh, 1988).
——. *The Pool in the Desert* (1903) (Markham: Penguin Canada, 1984).
——. *The Imperialist* (1904) (Ottawa: Tecumseh, 1988).

———. *Sara Jeannette Duncan: Selected Journalism*, ed. Thomas Tausky (Ottawa: Tecumseh, 1978).

Fowler, Marian. *Redney* (Toronto: Anansi, 1983).

Tausky, Thomas. *Sara Jeannette Duncan: Novelist of Empire* (Port Credit: P. D. Meany, 1980).

The Heir Apparent

Sara Jeannette Duncan

"I like the shape of his head," Miss Garratt said. We were talking of Randal Cope, and there was more than approval in Miss Garratt's words; there was barely suppressed enthusiasm. We three — Miss Garratt, her niece Ida Chamier, and I — were sitting on the veranda of a private hotel in Toronto. Randal Cope was just visible in the smoking-room; his head, indeed, with a pipe attached, was the salient feature of the window. It was a night of warm June; the maple-trees hung heavily in their clustering sprays around the house. The air held an expanded sense that the day had been got through with, and we sat sharing it with all the city, watching the electric cars flash up and down.

"I like the shape of his head," said Miss Garratt.

"It is a head," I responded, "plainly made to carry a great deal."

Ida looked languidly round at the silhouette in the window. "If it carries its own traditions — " she began.

"It will have enough to do?" I suggested. "Oh, well, we expect more than that."

"*Yes* indeed," explained Ida's aunt, with that agreeable Southern enunciation that runs the two words into one emphasis. "We expect, don't we, an immense amount?"

It was partly, no doubt, due to the enervating atmosphere that Miss Garratt stopped short of the catalogue of what we did expect; but none of us, of course, would have been able to make it with confidence and facility. The immense amount that we expected was naturally almost as vague as it was vivid; there were so many possibilities, all of them dramatic in the sense of leaping achievement, and never so much as a sign, as yet, to tell us which way to look. Without other indication the gaze upon Randal Cope enthusiastically travelled back to the chivalric statesman who was his grandfather, and to Mrs. Robert Cope, who was his mother. Either of them by himself or herself would have been an antecedent to build upon, but both! Charles Randal, whose personality had stood even with his power in every capital of Europe, whose moral standards still shone plain above politics: classicist, dialectician, all but artist — and to this great shade his daughter, who was simply in the world of the ideal and its numbered symbols alone a force and a current — here was a Valhalla for a nursery! It contained, so unusually, both the general and the particular. There was not an eye in the great republic so neighboring to us on Miss Lucas's veranda that would not light with a kind of proprietorship in his doctrines at the name of Charles Randal; his was one of those rare circles that widen across the Atlantic and strike effectively upon its still half-hostile farther shore. And to those smaller, more peculiar groups who propose to themselves initiation, what priestess ever stood, with one finger on the curtain and another on her lip, more honored in her function than Margaret Cope? Verily we left our shoes outside. Poet and essayist she was, moulding life with her hands; delicate truth she sounded upon a chord lifted and mystic. Critic and scholar, she measured the world from a height; but in her verse she walked among us and saw all our sad horizons, and beyond.

So that this young man had merely to write his name to make a double appeal, to the heart and to the imagination. He seemed to be aware of this, for he wrote the whole of it and suffered himself to be introduced by the whole of it — "Mr. Randal Cope." On the other hand, he wrote it badly, with cramped carefulness, and he was awkward in acknowledging the eager salutations which the world had for him. We of the boundless expectations had such things to go upon — that he came into a room magnificently and went out of it almost sideways; that he had an immense distinction of appearance, which he wore like a tiresome necessary diadem; that he had taken, at Oxford, a degree even more brilliant than his grandfather's — a reflection which gave us an instant's thrill of sympathy with Oxford upon the high ground of prophecy. These were simple threads, but we found at Miss Lucas's that they could be woven into patterns of quite extraordinary complexity. It is satisfying to think that if he had known we were weaving them he could not have retired himself more completely from the field of observation. We saw him before us every day, and to the fact that his splendid head was the ornament of a commanding person we could add that he was rather slovenly in his dress, with an opulent taste in neckties. There was also the general understanding that he was "out here" on an imperialistic mission for one of the leading English magazines. That was all we knew, all we seemed likely to know, and it was so little that one could understand its constituting, for Miss Garratt, a grievance.

We felt the weight of trifles when, a moment or two later, Mr. Cope joined us on the veranda. His hesitation in the French window from the drawing-room was so palpable, his decision in our favor so obvious, that we could not help apprehending that he did nothing lightly. He sat down beside us — not quite beside us, but near enough to form a communicable part of our group — I speak for Miss Garratt and myself; Ida barely lifted her eyelids. Miss Garratt and I were conscious of excitement; I am afraid in our attitudes of alert encouragement we betrayed it; Miss Garratt even twisted her chair a little to bring Mr. Cope's within an arc of welcome. And it was Miss Garratt naturally who addressed him.

"Well, Mr. Cope," said she, "and what do you think of this *al fresco* life?"

The young man looked at her with distant deference. "This — ?"

"Oh, this emancipation all about you, this sitting on

SARA JEANNETTE DUNCAN

verandas in the public of the moon, these airs of the forest in the city streets. But no; I shouldn't ask. These impressions are precisely — aren't they? — what you've come so far to dig out of yourself. They are, of course, valuable, and you keep them, or you ought to keep them, locked up. But you can at least tell us if you don't think it very hot."

It seems absurd to say that Miss Garratt's speech had the force of an assault upon a citadel. Its object seemed literally to gather himself into himself; he visibly receded, shrank into some fastness, from which he still looked out, startled, troubled, and insecure.

"I do indeed find it hot. But — but very delightful also — Miss Garratt."

There was a peculiar charm in his hesitation before uttering her name, and the way his voice dropped in saying it. Certainly deference was his personal note, his note of intercourse. One's imagination flew to his mother and his grandfather — my imagination and Miss Garratt's. And Ida looked up.

"One mustn't press, I know," Miss Garratt went on. "All the same, it would be fascinating to compare notes — what you see with what we see. We too have brought virgin imaginations to this part of the empire; we haven't been here before, either. And we come from Mississippi."

Mr. Cope looked at her seriously and hesitated, seeming to revolve many replies. One saw a young man in a rather rigid attitude of attention, with eyes in which expression struggled to be born, pulling — as if that would help — at his mustache. One noticed a hand of extraordinary shapeliness — the modern, beautifully nervous kind; a hand, one thought, to grasp its inheritance.

"I suppose," he said, finally, "it is even warmer in Mississippi — just now."

"It is quite impossibly warm there," Miss Garratt replied, and I saw her make, and arrest, a movement toward the lorgnette that hung in the folds of her dress. Ida, where she sat, on the edge of the veranda, made half a movement of her head toward her aunt, in which Miss Garratt might have detected something like protest.

"Have you been penetrated by our national anthem, Mr. Cope?" I inquired.

"'The maple leaf, our emblem dear,
The maple leaf forever.'

In two or three hundred years it will gather sentiment enough to turn it into music. Meanwhile these are all maples, round the house, all that aren't chestnuts."

Mr. Cope started slightly in my direction, as if toward a new emergency. "I have not seen it, I am afraid," he said. His gravity really rendered him culpable. "I must look it up at once."

"I know two more lines," Ida suddenly declared, "if you would like to hear them."

"May I?"

She swung round on the palm of one hand and lifted the clear oval of her face in the shadows.

"'God save the King, and Heaven bless
The maple leaf forever!'"

she sang, with enthusiasm and submission. It was a simple, gay, impersonal note she sounded, with a touch of extravagance, half mocking, in which her young Americanism must needs declare itself; and it took absolutely no account, except the most adventitious, of Mr. Randal Cope as her listener. It was then that I saw, for the first time, his wonderful flash and smile. It was one thing, the sudden happy torch that lightened and deepened in his eyes and the way his upper lip lifted and turned down at the corners, — a demonstration so vivid, a sign so plain, that one threw with a delightful impulse a votive flower to Margaret Cope in the moonlight.

"The maple seems — doesn't it? — to have more leaves than rhymes," he said to Ida, drawing himself back as it were for the effort, which came from him at once audacious and shy, with the oddest effect of old-fashioned prankishness in the way he went on smiling at her from under his eyebrows, very courteous and conceding. It must have been thus, we thought, that he had seen his grandfather address ladies when he was very young.

I suppose Ida Chamier found something to say, but there is no doubt that she looked back at him, felt the release in him, took the smile from his eyes. This one saw in a swift instant pass straight into the soul of her, whence she gave as quickly something back to him that also sped on a smile. It happened then, just then — the story; and a moment's silence followed it, while the moon moved thoughtfully to a better point of view. Presently Ida sprang up and put on her hat. She was going to post a letter, she said, and she would like to go herself, — thanks. When Randal Cope stepped, rather awkwardly, along the wooden walk by her side, Miss Garratt and I exchanged glances which confessed, startled and contrite, our hateful presence where the moon should have been the only one. Then we saw that he went but to open the gate, and felt relief. He closed the gate, indeed, with quite a contrasting deliberateness, and came slowly back to the house, reaching his rooms by another door.

I looked with more interest than ever at Ida's photograph that night. Her aunt had given it to me; when Miss Garratt became fond of anybody she gave her Ida's photograph. It was a fortunate portrait; it yielded Miss Chamier's personality as well as her beauty; it suggested her fastidiousness as well as her grace, and was as true to her easy distinction as it could not help being to her charming clothes. No doubt, as Miss Garratt said, she was immensely clever — I glanced again at the sonnet the elder lady had lent me — no doubt she shared her aunt's passionate interest in human forms of genius. If one did not see the critical worshipping eye, it was, Miss Garratt declared, because in the arrogance of youth she hid her fire, which nevertheless burned fiercely, and nowhere with more ardent dedication, I had been assured, than upon the altar of Margaret Cope.

"You *must* find it," Miss Garratt charged me a week later. "You must. It's too maddening."

What Miss Garratt so peremptorily demanded that I should find ought by now, we both vaguely felt, to be a matter of daily quiet evidence, — the vision and the power, to put it concisely, that with such brilliant confidence we had predicated of him. And it was not; oh, assuredly it was not. How clever we were, how stimulating, how adventurous! How we danced before him with lutes into the realm of the imagination, always, alas! to look back and see him seated upon the verge, with a pipe! Everything worth reading he had read, everybody worth meeting he had met — the latter invariably at his mother's, at lunch, — but his consciousness seemed a deep receptive pool into which these things simply disappeared, leaving an untroubled surface. Now and then at the lifting of an eyelid one caught a reflection; it was always true and just, and sometimes it was charming. It gave one vividly the idea that this life upon which he had been able to draw so largely had contributed very really to a fund, somewhere stored up in him, of right thinking and exquisite taste. But the depths were black and the indication most inadequate. We could both point to half a dozen men who abounded in the testimony we sought without producing a tenth of the belief we had already.

"With her," said Miss Garratt, "it would be so entirely a matter of that."

We were convinced that it would. "That" was especially and peremptorily what Ida Chamier would require, and require not in hypothesis, but in demonstration. Nothing else in a mate would claim her, Miss Garratt declared; she knew Ida; and she cited Teddy Farnham with his millions, and Arthur Rennick with his political future, as if their rejected addresses might illustrate her point, but were by no means necessary to prove it. Miss Garratt's own idea was very clear. Ida had a spark of genius. I had long since learned its family history. Another spark might bring it to a flame. There was something sacred about such a trust, primarily reposed in Ida and secondarily in her aunt, and though hitherto Miss Garratt had been content to interpret her share of it in the duty of vestal virgin fanning at the altar, the advent of Randal Cope had widened both her solicitude and her responsibility.

"Did I tell you he had written her some verses?"

SARA JEANNETTE DUNCAN

Gussie went on, with dejection.

"No!" I said. "How did you know?"

"Oh, she showed them to me. She well might — they were *in Latin*!"

"Good heavens!"

"She said they were very good, very witty. She knows, you know. But when she translated them I couldn't see the wit."

"One never can, in translations," I soothed her. "It's a matter of the use of the gerund, or the conjunction *ut*. They probably *were* good."

"Oh, I dare say — I mean, of course they were. How could he produce anything that wasn't? He simply radiates quality," she went on, looking at me anxiously; "and for fibre, hear him speak — look at his hands."

"You're not trying to convince *me*!" I protested. "But here she comes. Shall I be bold?"

Miss Garratt sent me a frightened glance, which I ignored.

"We were talking about Randal Cope," I said, as Ida joined us.

The faintest look of displeasure showed, for an instant, between her eyebrows. Then she laughed.

"No!" she exclaimed, railing at us, as if we were always doing it.

"We simply cannot make up our minds," I continued.

"Make up your minds?" It was an excellent effect of wondering indifference, and Miss Chamier sat down to the piano.

"Whether one is safe, after all, in predicating great things of him."

She struck two or three chords, into which, I fancied, thought passed. "Why predicate anything?" she said. "Why not wait?"

"That's so difficult," I sighed, "when one is dying to foretell and be gloriously vindicated. We complain, your aunt Gussie and I, that he gives us nothing to go upon but our instincts."

"I am out of temper with him," said Miss Garratt,

taking up a book.

Ida glanced from one to the other of us. "I don't see that it matters," she said. "I don't see what right you have — any of us have — to expect him to please *us*."

"That view," I said, with infinite guile, "simply shows you non-speculative, dear. Or perhaps not so deeply interested as your aunt and I are in his mother. We want to see Mrs. Cope fulfilled in her son, and he seems somehow to present a baffling front to his destiny. It's absurd, as you justly remark, to be irritated, but we both are."

"Oh, his mother!" exclaimed Miss Chamier, and fell to the brilliant execution of the "Appassionata." She paused abruptly to say, "He seems to take a good deal for granted about his mother."

"Not too much, surely."

"Well, he is always telling one what she thinks or what she does."

"How delightful of him! I wish he would tell *me*."

"Doesn't he?"

"Never a word. He tells me little stories, usually about bishops."

"He suggests having always lived among them," put in Miss Garratt, with an air of mournful detachment. "Bishops and high-thinking men. But he is the enviable inheritor of all the great traditions, isn't he? In letters and morals and politics."

"And there's something in him," I contributed, "so hoarded, so precious, so absolutely the last expression, that its inaccessibility — "

I stopped. Ida had left the piano, and waited, looking at me oddly, with her hand upon the door. She broke almost passionately upon my hesitation.

"I can't think," she said, "why you and Aunt Gussie talk about him so much! I can't think!" Then she went quickly out.

"And now," demanded Miss Garratt, in low tones of panic — "and now what have you done?"

Well, we could wait. After all, it came to that, and her aunt and I made all, I venture, that could be made out

SARA JEANNETTE DUNCAN

of the fact that this obvious course was Ida's own suggestion. Meanwhile a leading magazine published another of her Italian sketches, which she immediately locked up in a drawer. I did not hear of it till long afterwards.

Mr. Cope's commission was from the *Period*. His reticence could only be described as protective, but so much he had divulged, not being able to help it, since Miss Garratt asked him point-blank. The *Period*, we agreed, was precisely the medium through which a Randal Cope could show his essential quality to the world. You found, as your great-grandfather had found, the best thought in England in the *Period*; and one could imagine its welcome to young Randal. They had given him generous imperial range; I understood he was only beginning with Canada; and he seemed to me to be almost hampered with facilities. The name of the Lieutenant-Governor of the province came up between us.

"I know Sir George," he said. "He was kind enough to ask me to stay there."

"And you didn't?" I queried.

"Well, no. I think a fellow had better keep out of Government Houses. He's a bit too much in the middle of it there, I find."

"How are you getting on?" I asked, looking out of the window. "I believe it will rain, after all."

"Oh — thank you — there's immense material, isn't there? I — I've sent them something."

Presently he turned and looked at me with directness, a simple and sudden regard. The rain struck softly on the trees and murmured over the grass. The quiet breath of it came into the room.

"You know I ought to do something," he said, and in his eyes, with almost a pang, I saw the problem that had been perplexing us all.

"But you will. You can hardly" — I hesitated — "help it."

"That's just it." He paused appreciably, and then added, "It seems to me that I've got — more or less — to trust to that. I hope one may. One has dreams."

He gave me a look full of courage and patience and nice feeling, but he had come to the end of his confidence.

"I'll walk out to the Hunt Club, I think," he said; "it's such a jolly day."

He brought it to me himself, the August *Period*, on the veranda, while there was still light enough to read. I remember thinking, as one notes trifles at great moments, that the *Period* had never approved of undignified anticipation; when the time came you got your *Period*, and not in the third week of the previous month. Almost at the same moment the gate clicked, and Ida came quickly up the path. She went to her room without a glance at us, and she carried a book-seller's parcel.

My eye fled down the list of contents on the cover. There it was, the fourth article: "Canada and the Empire. — I. By Randal Cope."

My eye fled over the first sentence, lost itself in the middle of the next paragraph, and dashed back to take the task seriously, with powers collected. The queer premonitory shiver that sprang upon me I paused to denounce as foolish, premature; but the very rebuke revealed its apprehension. I tried to soothe a jumping pulse with the assurance that this was a matter with which, after all, my concern was remote; what was it, indeed, to me though Randal Cope spoke with the tongue of men and of angels and had not imagination? Then I set out to read the opening paragraph, deliberately, and quite in vain. It was concerned, I perceived, with facts of the first importance in the balance of political science, but their category escapes me now as then; the character of the thing, its quality, its significance beyond its meaning, leaped out from it and obscured the words. Presently I gave up the effort and looked at it, just looked, and at the next paragraph, and the next.

Then, hastily, I regarded the article by pages, from top to bottom, from beginning to end; it bulked very respectably among the contents of the *Period*. The eye could take it in that way, I realized in my dismay; its lines and proportions stood square and plain; it had formal definition; it was instantly realizable, in scope, intention, achievement. And we who thought to ponder it, to wonder and exclaim! To be confounded by directness and set at naught by exactitude was perhaps in the nature of proper chastening, but the structure proffered also the consideration of material, and there was no escape from the dejected conviction that it was all built of bricks.

Closer examination here and there showed the bricks substantial, with plenty of straw, but when one had looked for a marble palace! Irreproachable bricks, set with precision, and what would have been, in any other material, a certain dignity of sequence and design, a great subject in ground-plan, and an eminence like a railway station. And curiously colorless and withdrawn, never the flush of a prejudice, never the flash of a mistake! I dropped the thing in my lap. "*How* they have taught him!" I almost groaned aloud. At that very instant I saw Gussie Garratt from her retreat by the drawing-room window pounce upon the postman, who delivered to her the magazine in its unmistakable wrapper. As she scuttled across the end of the veranda with it I waved my copy at her. "Never — never — never!" I cried. She gave me a frightened glance and sped on. Then Randal Cope came back and dropped into a chair. His face was still bright with the pleasure and excitement of it. He had won his spurs, and there they were, for my intelligent consideration. I turned them over. There was plenty to say in honest praise; one had only to forget the signature.

We talked for a while, and presently a vagueness grew upon him.

"Would you be so good as to show the article to — to Miss Chamier?" he said elaborately at last, poor dear boy. "She has kindly expressed a wish to see it;" and I went upstairs, feigning to consent, well knowing that Miss Chamier, alone in her room, had long since considered the article in its fullest import.

I do not know what induced me to throw the publication across the room; it was quite a disproportionate display of feeling; but I did, and there it was lying, face downwards, when Ida Chamier, with barely a knock, walked in.

"I came," she said, with an odd challenge in her voice, "to show you Mr. Cope's paper in the *Period*." She put it before me and stood looking over my shoulder. "It's quite excellent, I think — wonderfully sound" — and then her eyes caught the dishevelled thing on the floor. "But you've seen it already!" She walked over and picked up the insulted magazine, smoothing out its ruffled leaves, and sending me, on a glance, a full charge of indignation. "What did you do this to it for?" she demanded; and there was nothing else for it, so I said out of my pure wonder,

"I was disappointed with it."

"Of course you were! And Aunt Gussie — no doubt she's 'disappointed' too! You both expected something different, something from his mother or his grandfather. His mother is a poet and an essayist — well and good, very charming. His grandfather was just a great Englishman, and there are lots of them. And he is himself!"

Her eyes were bright with excitement; she was really talking very impulsively.

"Just a big, strong, splendid man, his own stamp and his own pattern — "

"My *dear* Ida!" I expostulated.

"You had no *earthly* business to be disappointed," she went on, undaunted. "Can't he inherit all that — that you thought of — in his most" — she seemed to seek, in the magnificence of her concession, for words that should hold nothing back — "his most lovable and princely nature? Can't he himself be the sole person to benefit — and perhaps the particularly happy woman whom he marries? Imagine any individuality that is worth its salt condescending to take the mould that is prescribed for it! But of course there was always the danger — and I *was* so afraid he might be some sort of repetition. I don't think anybody could permanently l-like a man who was only that."

"Ida! You don't — you're not going to — "

"But I do — and I just am! He doesn't know what I waited for, but I don't mind telling you it was this. I wanted to be quite sure. And I wish you'd say," she went on, with beguilement, "that you think it's a good article."

"If I were in love with him," I retorted, "I should think it a splendid article;" at which Miss Chamier pressed her lips together with immense self-control and left me.

"You and Aunt Gussie," she put her head back in the door to say, "did put one off so dreadfully!"

The book appeared in due course, and the only thing the copious reviewers never found to say of it was that the world would clearly have no share in Randal Cope's inheritance. They missed this obvious deduction, though other volumes have proved it with increasing clearness since. The younger Copes live in Westminster near the Colonial Office, where Randal has got a "job" — his wife delights, I think maliciously, to dwell upon it under that unlovely term. He is generally acknowledged to be rather good at his job. Miss Garratt, who has a flat in their neighborhood, nurses a grievance that these things should not appear to surprise the people of England. She discovers here a subtle form of ingratitude not confined to republics. And she cannot be bullied into any recantation about the shape of his head.

~

Harper's Monthly Magazine 110 (March 1905): 625–631.

Isabel Ecclestone Mackay (1875–1928)

THE DESPAIR OF SANDY MACINTOSH (1905)

Isabel Ecclestone Mackay, poet and fiction writer, was born in Woodstock, Ontario, on 25 November 1875 to Priscilla Ecclestone and Donald McLeod Macpherson, a Scot who was one of Oxford County's early settlers. "Bell" Macpherson was educated at Woodstock Collegiate and was an early literary contributor to the Woodstock *Daily Sentinel* and to Methodist publications. In 1895, she married Peter J. Mackay, a court stenographer; they had three daughters. In 1909, the Mackays moved to Vancouver, where she was prominent in the literary life of the city until her death on 15 April 1928. Mackay was vivacious, outgoing and active in literary organizations; two of her closest literary friendships were with Marjorie Pickthall and Pauline Johnson (see pages 157 and 169). On Pickthall's return to Canada in 1920, for instance, she summered with the Mackays.

　　Isabel Ecclestone Mackay first became known as a poet: in 1907 she won the Toronto *Globe* prize for historical verse. She published several volumes of poetry — largely lyrical nature and love poetry — including *Shining Ships*, a volume of verse for children. Some poems indicate her social awareness. "Calgary Station" apostrophizes Canada and the immigrant influx in a spirit of optimism and acceptance: "a new nation clamours at our gate." Mackay was a staple contributor of stories to *Canadian Magazine* and several other well-known North American periodicals. She turned to fiction from poetry in the belief that, as she put it, "prose is good mental training, and not dependent upon a moment's exaltation." Her five romantic novels include *Blencarrow* (1926), which draws upon her interest in small-town life, also evident in "The Despair of Sandy MacIntosh." *Indian Nights* (1930), her rendition of some West Coast tales, may owe something to her friendship with Pauline Johnson. In the last two years of her life, Mackay's interest turned to short plays, some of which were performed at Hart House Theatre, Toronto.

"The Despair of Sandy MacIntosh," like Adeline Teskey's "A Common Man and His Wife" (see page 21), is in the tradition of "kailyard" fiction so popular at the time. As Elizabeth Waterston has made clear, the figure of the minister is at the heart of such stories and the dark side of life — drink, despair — is not scanted. Mackay's characters are Scots; her heritage was Scots and Scotland (through such authors as John Galt and J. M. Barrie) nurtured "kailyard" fiction. The story's conclusion questions unrelieved Calvinism and affirms the need for the mercy of the New Testament rather than the rigour of the Old. The theme of drunkenness ties in well with the prevalence of the temperance question in the Canada of the day, a subtext also present in Nellie McClung's "The Live Wire" (see page 246). Many of Mackay's stories also deal with the occult, another preoccupation of the day.

✌

Suggested Reading

Mackay, Isabel Ecclestone. "Through the Wall," *Canadian Magazine* 23 (Feb. 1909): 331–340.

——. "Ashes of Dreams," *Canadian Magazine* 50 (Dec. 1917): 95–105.

——. *Indian Nights* (Toronto: McClelland and Stewart, 1930).

Waterston, Elizabeth. "Canadian Cabbage, Canadian Rose" (1973), rpt. *Twentieth Century Essays on Confederation Literature*, ed. L. McMullen (Ottawa: Tecumseh, 1976), 93–101.

THE DESPAIR OF SANDY MACINTOSH

Isabel Ecclestone Mackay

It was a windy, blustery day of early spring. The snow still lay in the shaded hollows, but the sunny spaces were showing green. The sky, which had lost its distant winter blueness, was softer and nearer to earth. The roads were a quagmire bordered by little rivulets of icy water, but an early robin sang from somewhere near, and the clear, pure air had a tang in it which made the blood leap gladly.

The minister of the Presbyterian kirk at Embro stepped out of the manse door with a song on his lips, to the tune of which he carefully picked his way through the many puddles which lay across his garden walk. But though he sang his mind was occupied with weighty matters, and Sandy MacIntosh lay heavily upon his conscience. Speaking as a philosopher, he considered Sandy in the light of a cross which must be borne. Speaking as a man, he admitted that he liked Sandy; but speaking as a minister, there could be no doubt that Sandy was a terrible scandal in the kirk. Only in this matter he and his elders saw not eye to eye. The elders were used to Sandy. For forty years he had carried the "Book" before the minister with stately step and reverend mien. What if it was true that he took a "wee droppie"; better men than he have their little weakness, and if, as a matter of fact, he was guided home from the "Rising Sun" every Saturday night, it was never said of Sandy that he had to be carried, and Sunday morning always saw him clothed and in his right mind ready to carry the "Book" with steady step.

When it was at last decided that the session of Embro kirk should extend a call to the Rev. Robert MacPherson, B.A., there were a few who shook their heads.

"He iss a ferry fine lad," said Elder Mackay, judicially, "and herself will not pe sayin' he iss not a ferry fine preacher, but he iss not speakin' the Gælic."

"He iss speakin' the Word," rejoined a brother elder, solemnly; "it iss to our hearts he will pe speakin' it."

"Och, yes," agreed Elder Mackay, "but her heart would pe likin' the Gælic pest."

Before long, however, even Elder Mackay realised that the minister was making a grand fight of it. He had come determined to win a place for himself in the warm, sturdy Highland hearts, and winning it he was. A fine, strong, brave young man the Rev. Mr. MacPherson, grave beyond his years, as befits a minister who takes his calling seriously, full of faith and hope and good works, sure of his doctrine and his God as only a Scottish Presbyterian minister, in times now a little out of date, could be sure. Of the Gælic he knew enough to use in his prayer, but not enough to attempt a Gælic sermon until he had been minister of Embro kirk for many years. Yet, as the feeling of distrust amongst the congregation began to wear away, the minister himself began to feel less sure of his ground. As the Highlanders trusted him more and began to know him better, he found that, though a Highlander himself by birth, there was much about them that he did not understand. His education had not been among his own people, and he could not but find that in many things his view-point was very different from theirs, and realised that much adjusting must be done. So he was going slowly and feeling his way.

In the matter of the advisability of Sandy MacIntosh continuing to carry the "Book," he had been feeling his way for some time with little success. He was a man of strictest purity of life himself; he hated sin with what he was fond of describing as a "Godly hatred," and he could not reconcile it to his conscience that a "drunkard" should carry the "Book." In this he knew that he had not the support of his elders. To them the word "drunkard" could not apply to any man who came soberly to kirk on Sabbath and listened to the sermon with proper attention and discernment. To his Highland members Sandy was a man who "would pe takin' more than would pe good for herself," and by the Lowland folk he was described as apt to "taste a wee oor muckle."

As for Sandy himself, well, it was of Sandy himself that the minister was thinking as he tip-toed over the mud puddles on that blustery morning. He had decided to speak to Sandy. He was on his way now to Sandy's home. He would be mild, but firm — he would — ah, there was the subject of his thoughts now, coming from the usual direction of the "Rising Sun," jogging along beside his old blind horse, across whose saddle was lying a bag of potatoes and a small, suspicious looking keg.

"Caught in the act," thought the minister, with a feeling very much like triumph.

Sandy on his part was surprised to feel a trifle sheepish. Not that he was ashamed of the spirituous burden carried by old Nancy, but because the minister's absurd prejudice about "whuskey" was well known. So, entirely for Mr. MacPherson's sake, he sought to avoid a collision which might prove embarrassing to the minister.

"It is a fine morning, Sandy," began the minister, bringing old Nancy to a standstill by a firm hold upon the bridle.

"She would pe takin' home a few small potatoes," said Sandy in an explanatory tone, going straight to the point at issue.

"Yes, but the keg, Sandy — what is in the keg?"

To gain time, Sandy produced his snuff box and, after tapping it nervously, offered it to the minister.

"Och, the wee keggie," said he cheerfully, "Och, nossing — nossing at all — a bit whuskey whateffer."

There was an awful pause. Sandy's eye fell before the minister's and Sandy's feet began to shuffle. Guileless innocence was not going to work this time. Wildly he cast about in his mind for a reason — any reason which would satisfactorily explain the presence of the wee keggie. His eye fell upon the potato sack.

"Whuskey and small potatoes," he began slowly, then with a burst of confidence —

"Whuskey and small potatoes would pe good for the measles."

The minister sternly repressed a desire to laugh. Ordinary men might find Sandy's subterfuge delightful, but in the pursuit of his duty he was not as other men.

"This must cease, Sandy," said he firmly. "I cannot and will not countenance it any longer."

"God forbid!" said Sandy, greatly shocked. "It iss not herself that would be asking you, Maister Mac-a-ferson."

"But can't you understand that as long as I permit you to continue in your service at the kirk that I am countenancing it. You must surely see that, Sandy." There was real distress in the minister's tone.

"She would not pe understanding, but she would not pe likin' to be vexin' you, Maister Mac-a-ferson," said Sandy in conciliatory tones.

"Then will you promise to do better, Sandy — not to — not to — visit the wee keggie too often?"

"Och, yes, inteed, she'll no do that whateffer," said Sandy, earnestly; "she would not pe tastin' more nor would pe good for herself."

And with this the minister was forced to be content.

But it so happened that that very Saturday night the minister himself, returning late from a sick bed, was the disgusted spectator of Sandy's nocturnal home-bringing.

Sandy had not broken his word. His interpretation of what was "good for herself" was different from the minister's, that was all. But Mr. MacPherson did not realise that the fault lay in his own narrow notion of how much a hard Scotch head can stand and be "none the worse whateffer." And so it happened that while Sandy slept the sound sleep due to a "wee droppie" and a clear conscience, the minister sat in his study and composed a new sermon on the text "Without are drunkards."

This was a sermon talked of for many a day by those gentle-minded Lowlanders who had the privilege of hearing it, as "fut tae mak' the hair stan' on yer heid," and even the stolid Highlanders admitted that as a discourse it was "ferry powerful whateffer."

Indeed the stern young minister spoke from the depths of his heart and it was not his fault if those depths were severely Calvinistic. He felt himself filled with holy fire, a chosen vessel for the warning and rebuke of an endangered Israel. The hot words poured from his lips, he forgot that he was young and inexperienced and that he had determined to go slowly and feel his way. He only remembered that he was the minister of God and these were his people of whose spiritual welfare he must give account, and the congregation heard him gladly, rejoicing to know that the "meenister was speakin oot."

After the service Mr. MacPherson waited awhile in the session room, lingering in the hope that Sandy, a repentant sinner, might wish a word with him. And Sandy came.

Very warmly he grasped the minister by the hand, though this was a salute almost unknown among the undemonstrative Highlanders.

"Och, Maister Mac-a-ferson," said he in frankest admiration, "it wass a fine stirrin' word that you wass givin' us, och, yes. But herself was sinking that if there wass anyone that would pe given to tastin' more than wass good for herself she would not pe feelin' ferry comfortable, whateffer."

When Sandy was gone the minister sat down by his open Bible and laughed a little hysterically. Perhaps it was the reaction of the morning enthusiasm.

It was that day with the black reaction upon him that he spoke of his trouble to Alexander Morrison, one of the wildest yet most sympathetic of the younger portion of his flock.

"The elders wont see it, and Sandy can't see it," he complained, "but everybody else sees it — and it is a scandal in the kirk."

And Alick was very sympathetic, saying that surely it could not last much longer; and, as he said it, in his mischievous, hair-brained head a plan grew, for Alick was very fond of the minister and Sandy was an old enemy of his not far distant youth. This plan of his was a fine plan: it would at once relieve the minister of the reproach of Sandy's carrying the "Book," and would provide for himself amusement and revenge.

So it chanced that no one, with the exception of one conscience-stricken scamp, ever knew what made poor Sandy's one wee drap so unusually potent upon a certain Sabbath morning. None could guess the cause but the effect was patent to everyone. Elder Mackay said afterwards that he "saw somesing wass wrong when Sandy came in wis the 'Book' and was 'ferry sankful that the meenister would not pe noticin."

The sermon that morning was upon the text "His own received Him not," and the minister was at his best. His voice, always low though clear and sweet, was to-day deeper and more tender than was usual. The congregation listened with awe and reverence to what was to them indeed and in truth the Word of the Lord. They never for an instant doubted that the Lord was in His Holy Temple. I have been in many churches and listened to many services but I have never found the atmosphere of reverent worship which I remember in the old frame Presbyterian kirk where our fathers met their God.

Into the midst of this solemn quiet, through which the low voice of the minister spoke to the hearts of his hearers, broke a terrific snore, then another, then another, then a crash, for the violence of the last snore had lifted Sandy bodily from his seat and deposited him upon the floor.

The minister paused, flushed painfully, and then tried to go on mechanically with his sermon. But he had lost himself. Again and again he broke, and finally, bringing his words to a hurried conclusion, came down from the pulpit and vanished into the session room.

From the first snore everybody knew that Sandy's fate

was sealed. They had no sympathy or consideration for him now. He had disgraced himself and defiled the kirk and shamed the minister. Never again would he carry the "Book" with stately step and reverend mien. His service in the House of God was over.

The congregation dismissed that morning without the singing of the usual psalm. They went out slowly, saying little, leaving Sandy slumbering upon the floor. Presently the minister issued from the session room and walked quickly away, speaking to no one. His heart was full of Godly rage towards poor, misguided Sandy.

Of Sandy, when he awoke in the deserted kirk I may not tell. After a few minutes' thought and remembrance he came to himself and his heart knew its own bitterness. No one would have recognised in the shrunken, shamed man who crept out of the side entrance and hurried away, the fine, erect officer of Embro kirk. By many side ways he reached his home and, without a look around, went in and closed the door.

Two weeks afterwards came Elder Mackay to the minister.

"I would be speaking aboot Sandy," began the elder without preliminaries.

"I refuse to discuss the subject," said the minister coldly.

But the elder laid his big hand upon his arm.

"She iss a broken man, Meenister," he said, simply, "and it iss written 'the bruised reed will I not break.'"

The minister was troubled. He knew that his elder must have felt deeply to have said so much. For the first time in the two weeks he felt a little distrustful as to the Godliness of his rage; perhaps, after all, he might —

"Where is he?" he asked abruptly.

"She will pe at home," said Elder Mackay briefly, knowing that he had won his point.

"I will see him," said the minister, and taking their hats the two set off in the direction of Sandy's cottage. The minister alone went in.

There was a low fire in the little stove which had

replaced the oldtime fireplace and over it a man was bending, a man who was old and bowed and who did not glance up as the door opened. The last trace of the minister's Godly rage vanished before that silent despair.

"Sandy," he said kindly; "haven't you a word for me?"

"She would pe pleased to see you, Maister Mac-a-ferson," said Sandy in an expressionless tone, rising painfully to place a chair in his old reverential fashion.

"You don't look well, Sandy," said the minister sympathetically.

"She is not ferry weel," replied Sandy dully.

Then the minister took the bull by the horns.

"When are you coming back to the kirk, Sandy?" he asked, and no one in the congregation would have been more surprised than himself as he said it.

A spasm passed over Sandy's face, leaving it duller than before. And for the first time the minister noticed the whiskey jug beside him on the floor. Sandy did not answer.

"We were very sorry for what happened — " began the minister, and then he stopped, feeling uneasy, like a man who has referred to another's shame before his own face.

"When are you coming back, Sandy?" he asked again.

Then Sandy lifted his face and looked at him with the look of a man condemned.

"Let us pray," said the minister, who felt that in the face of the man's trouble he was powerless. He stood and prayed, then he sat down and spoke again kindly, encouragingly, even entreatingly, but all his efforts were as fruitless as if he had beat his hand against a rock.

It was a minister with a white, exhausted face who left Sandy's door that day and joined the elder outside. The two men walked for a while in silence. Then the elder asked nervously:

"You will haf seen Sandy, Maister Mac-a-ferson?"

"I have seen a man who has lost his self-respect," said the minister with a shudder, "and God forbid that I should ever see another."

The elder said no more, but he put his sympathy in a

Isabel Ecclestone Mackay

handclasp as they parted.

Every day the minister visited Sandy MacIntosh, until Sandy's death, which occurred some weeks later, and was hastened, as the doctor said, by immoderate drinking. If that were so, and he sought relief in drinking, it was certain that he did not find it, for not once was his brain stupefied into forgetfulness. The heartsick minister toiled as he had never toiled before to win the man back to his self-respect, to give him some hope, all without avail. Sandy spoke little, and seldom at all to the purpose.

"She will haf disgraced the kirk," was all that he would ever say. And to all the minister's pleading of extenuating circumstances, of infinite mercy and goodness, of hope for everyone, of the experience of the thief upon the cross, he had but the one answer:

"She will haf disgraced the kirk."

That was all, save once, when he was dying, and the minister hung above him with a prayer upon his lips, Sandy's haunted eyes opened and his gaunt hand pointed somewhere into the darkness —

"Without are drunkards!" he said, and fell back dead.

◦

Canadian Magazine 24 (April 1905): 551–555.

Alice Jones (1853–1933)

AT THE HARBOUR'S MOUTH (1905)

Alice Jones, novelist and short story writer, was born in
Halifax, Nova Scotia, on 26 August 1853, the daughter of
Margaret Wiseman Stairs and Alfred Gilpin Jones. The
latter, a wealthy and charismatic Halifax businessman,
had profited from the West Indies trade and served as
Lieutenant-Governor of Nova Scotia from 1900 until his
death in 1906. Alice Jones's mother died in 1865. Alice was
educated in Halifax, and travelled widely in England as well
as in France and Italy, where she studied languages. Her
brother, Guy Carleton Jones, married their cousin, Susan
Morrow, another writer (see page 57). In 1905, the year
before her father's death, Alice Jones settled in France,
where she died at Mentone on 27 February 1933.

Alice Jones published travel essays, short stories and
five novels, sometimes using the nom de plume "Alix John."
Her social situation and European experience allowed her to
develop the international theme of the innocent abroad. Art
is also a preoccupation in much of her writing. *Bubbles We
Buy* (1903) begins with a Nova Scotian family, which has
made a fortune in the age of sail in West Indies and South
American trade, then shifts to Boston, to an English country
estate, and to Florence and Paris. The protagonist, a talent-
ed painter, is one of Jones's characteristically strong women
characters.

"At the Harbour's Mouth" has two such characters,
Julia Perrier and her grandmother. For setting, Alice Jones
turned to an evocation of the maritime landscape of her
native Nova Scotia. The central character evokes the more
than 165,000 Maritime women who left Canada between
1881 and 1921 to seek employment on the eastern seaboard
of the United States. That Julia Perrier became a dressmaker
is also realistic: by the mid-nineteenth century, sewing had
replaced weaving as the major source of income for unattached
women. The fictional and romantic elements of "At the
Harbour's Mouth" present us with a female protagonist who is

an amalgam of the enterprising, responsible new woman and the traditional sweetheart who yearns for a man "to take care of one, and help one up the steep places," although she has managed to climb by herself, helping others up too. An historical counterpart to this fictional character is chronicled in *No Place Like Home: Diaries and Letters of Nova Scotia Women, 1771–1938*.

Alice Jones's use of the omniscient mode of narration allows us insight into a young woman who has experienced the bustling, more materialistic urban life, and an old woman living in comparative isolation, for whom the ship at last brings back "one of all it has taken away."

⌒

Suggested Reading

Conrad, Margaret, Toni Laidlaw and Donna Smyth, eds., *No Place Like Home: Diaries and Letters of Nova Scotia Women, 1771–1938* (Halifax: Formac, 1988).

Davies, Gwendolyn. "Alice Jones," *Oxford Companion to Canadian Literature* (1983).

Jones, Alice. *Bubbles We Buy* (Boston: Turner, 1903).

———. "The Blue Cloak," *Canadian Magazine* 21 (March and April 1904): 418–426, 538–544.

———. "A Little Immigrant," *Canadian Magazine* 28 (Dec. 1906): 147–150.

"Notes on Canadian Books," *Canadian Magazine* 21 (July 1903): 289.

At the Harbour's Mouth

Alice Jones

Editorial Note — In the Province of Nova Scotia, the great
tragedy of the period is the migration of the young people to
New England. This story gives a glimpse of the effect of this
migration and of some typical results. [*Canadian Magazine*, 1905]

> "Into the mist my guardian prows put forth,
> Behind the mists my virgin ramparts lie;
> The Warden of the Honour of the North,
> Silent and veiled am I."

Old Josephine Perrier had never heard of Rudyard
Kipling, nor of the "Seven Seas" of which he has
sung, but for seventy years and more she had
watched the "guardian prows put forth" into Chebucto
Bay, had heard the boom of salutes, loud on the north
wind, dull on the south, from the "virgin ramparts" on the
hill above the town, up the harbour.

It was a bit of world's history that she had looked out
on from her white-washed cottage on its small patch of
level land below the steep fir-clad slope — crowned by the
great new fort that the men from along the shore had
worked on for the last three winters. How good of Queen
Victoria to give them work through the bad time of year —
and what a pity she had died! How the guns had roared
that fierce January day of bitter north wind and driven
snow!

The old woman remembered, as though it were
yesterday, the years when light painted, slimly-rigged

steamers lurked inside the harbour's mouth, often being there at night and gone at daylight. The pilots had called them blockade-runners, and said that they were dodging the Yankees outside, and that there was war.

She had watched disabled craft, like wounded duck, towed in out of reach of the winter storms, had seen a cholera ship over there at the quarantine island and had helped secure and tow out to deep water the straw mattresses thrown overboard from it.

She had seen two Princes of Wales, father and son, at an interval of forty years, steam up the harbour with thunder of salutes and fluttering of flags, to visit Britain overseas. Last year she had seen shiploads of Canadian soldiers sail away to fight for the Empire, and had seen some of them return.

All these sights had woven themselves into the philosophy of her tenacious, shrewd brain. There was, however, only one passing that ever had a personal interest to her and that was the going to and fro of the Boston boat.

Friends, kinsfolk, children, grandchildren had gone in that boat, waving a handkerchief to the white cottage below the fort. Some had returned, some had prospered in that mysterious "Boston town," some had died there, or worse, had sunk into its depths. That distant city was ever in her mind as some fatal, alluring syren which had drawn away her children, which might yet draw her if she did not cling very closely to her boulder-hedged cottage.

It was with the attraction of terror now that she watched the weekly boat pass, for were not her middle-aged children writing urgently that she must come and end her days with them. They had stranger husbands and wives, and children, whom she only knew from photographs. All, except one, and that was her orphan granddaughter, whom she had brought up here by the shore.

And what a part of the shore life the girl had seemed, always about the boats and the nets, until suddenly she had taken a fancy into her head to leave the cottage and Josephine, and even Louis Minette, who, when his pilot boat was waiting behind the point, was always at her elbow,

ALICE JONES

to leave this old life and go up to the town to learn dress-making.

Her too, in time, the Boston magnet drew, and Josephine shed one or two of the scant, weary tears of old age as the steamer smoke mixed with the sea-fog on the horizon.

The girl was good though, writing every Sunday, and sending money to buy the barrel of flour, the tea and the pork, staples of longshore life. She had prospered. And when the other women came in for a gossip Josephine was never tired of showing them the letter in which Julia told of the three girls she employed, and the photograph of Julia in a beautiful big hat and with wonderful lace frills around her neck.

"Them French is always the same. They'll spend every penny on their backs, be they high or low," said a virtuous dame of Scotch descent, as she and her crony left the cottage.

Now that, even on the sea shore, the August sun was hot, Julia wrote that she was coming home. Work was slack, the heat had been terrific, "and I lie awake, and think and think of the wind blowing in from the sea, and the tide lifting the seaweed around the rocks."

"Bless the child's heart, she isn't changed after all! But it's a wonder that she never so much as asks after Louis Minette, and them such friends once," the old woman pondered wistfully.

Joyful thought! Her new rag mat with the red and grey squares was nearly finished. That would make the third that Julia had not seen. How glad she was now that she had not sold them, though it seemed extravagant at the time! She had honestly meant to sell the red and grey one before the winter, but now she must keep it to put in front of Julia's bed.

She was of too grandly simple a soul ever to think that the girl might find her old home poor and mean; but all the same, she limped about, scrubbing inside and white-washing out, to give everything its best air. A neighbour brought her from town, on market day, a roll of common brown wall paper, rudely stamped with gay bunches of poppies, and with this she papered the slanting attic that had always been Julia's. She, herself, slept in the downstairs room behind the kitchen.

There was only one thing more to be done, and that was to have a flag and some sort of a pole ready for the Sunday evening when the Boston boat should pass up the harbour. "For sure, it will bring one back of all it has taken away," she said to herself with vindictive satisfaction.

Once she had had a real flag, a beautiful printed Union Jack, that had flared out red against the sombre hillside. It had been torn to bits though in that fierce October storm after Julia went away, when she was down with the rheumatiz, and the neighbours had forgotten to take it in for her. Now she must do the best she could with some bits of red flannel which the officer's wife, who came sometimes in summer time down to the Fort, had given her for her mats.

"Well, I never saw such a crazy thing! Old Josephine would make merry with a skitter's leg," said the critical Scotch neighbour, as she saw the thing of rags and patches flaunting bravely in the wind, and thereby symbolising Josephine's seventy years of life.

At last came the Sunday when the Boston boat, poking her nose round Sambro, would bring Julia home. All through the summer her whistle sounded about four o'clock, and there would be plenty of time for David Minette, Louis' elder brother, who kept a fish-shop in town, to bring Julia down in his whaler before dark.

Everyone was so kind about this home-coming of Julia's except Louis Minette, who, when his pilot boat was lying in the cove, never came along the shore to the cottage as he used to, never asked news of her.

The sun was still high when the *Chebucto* steamed up the harbour, near enough for the flutter of a white handkerchief to be seen from the shore.

An hour or so later, amid the evening opalescence of sea and sky, a tawny-sailed whaler slid down on a last puff of wind, losing which under the shadow of the land, a few vigorous oar strokes ran her in on to the skids below the cottage.

David Minette who managed her was still, in spite of the town fish-shop, a pilot all over, from his peering eyes and tanned face to his Sunday suit of shiny black broadcloth.

"Here's the stray lamb, Josephine," he called out, but the old woman, seated on her boulder perch, because somehow her legs refused to carry her to the shore, had eyes and ears for nothing save that one figure steering in the stern, a figure curiously out of keeping with the surroundings.

By some atavistic freak, no sooner had Julia Perrier become acclimatised to city life than she had developed into the type of the little Parisian dressmaker. She may have learnt that fashion of dressing her shining black hair, of trimming that big, poppy-wreathed hat in Boston, but she had made them French, and her counterpart might have been found that August Sunday afternoon on the promenade of any provincial town of old France.

The grey, black-fringed eyes, the clear, pale skin, the trim, small figure, all were French, without any Norman or Alsatian dilution. Her voice, however, was that of her surroundings, as she called out, "Ah, Grandma, here I am, home again to bother you!"

There were tears over the smiles on Josephine's cheeks as she stretched out her hands.

"Little Julie! So big and fine!" she sobbed.

A light spring from the gunwale of the boat landed Julia on the seaweed, and she was up the bank and in the old woman's arms, being fondled, patted and crooned over like a child's recovered toy. There was a pleased, childlike admiration in Josephine's face as she held the girl off to inspect her.

"What clothes! I never knew that there were such beautiful clothes in the world!" she said, laying a timid hand on the pretty green and white dress.

Julia laughed.

"*This*, Gran'ma! Why the ladies would scarcely think

it good enough to wear shopping of a morning! You ought to see the silks and satins I make for them. But you shall see them, for I've brought you a bundle of silk scraps, enough to make a whole patch-work quilt, and I've got woollens, too, for the mats, every bit of them bright colours. Just wait till you see them."

The wrinkled old face was transfigured with joy.

"Bright colours? Greens and blues — and perhaps *pinks*?" she queried in incredulous delight.

"Greens, and blues and pinks, every one of them, and red too, bright red. They're the colours worn this year, and I saved the very best of them. You see!"

A rapturous thought struck the old woman. "If only I could finish up a mat for the show in town in October. Simon Devreau's wife over at Tuft's Cove, she got a prize last year for one that wasn't near a patch upon mine, but I never had a chanst with good scraps, real good ones that is to say."

Her granddaughter looked at her with a dawning comprehension.

"You always liked pretty things around you, didn't you, Grandma? I shouldn't wonder now but what I got my ideas about clothes — what the ladies I work for call my 'French taste' from you."

"Oh, child, why I don't know enough about anything to teach a baby — and you so smart and clever," Josephine protested.

The girl made no further effort to propound her dim theories of heredity.

"Never mind, Grandma. Come up and let's give David his tea."

"Lord sakes! And I was forgetting you would be hungry, and I've got hot cakes for you" — then, peering anxiously into Julia's face — "now that I think of it, child, you look thin and peaked, like as though you hadn't been eating overmuch of late."

"Oh, that's nothing. The heat pulls everyone down till they look like tallow candles," Julia said, though she flushed nervously.

There was a great reception that evening in the cottage kitchen and general living room, a reception that once or twice overflowed on to the steps as the indoor space proved inadequate. To one and all Julia had the same tales to tell of Boston, its streets and shops, and theatres, and even the cynical Scotch neighbour, listening, took it for granted that she was a successful and self-satisfied girl.

"Goin' to the theatre in what she calls a flowery foolard dress — old Josephine's gran'darter! Well! and there's my Jenny's girl glad to get a place as a general! Talk about the devil's own luck! Them Papists!" the neighbour sniffed on her homeward way, though all the same, she made occasion the next day to walk over the hill to her cousins, the MacNaughtons, up by the Presbyterian Church at Falkland to tell the news.

II

The next morning Josephine sat in silent happiness among shining heaps of vari-coloured silk scraps.

"And to think I never even dreamt that such things were in the world. Seems as though God must ha' made them colours like the flowers without any man's help," she murmured in her soft old voice. "Ah, child, you must be happy to live among stuffs like them, and to touch them with your hands!"

Julia had been smiling down at the old woman in her rocker, but at the word "happy" a little shadow came over her face, though she laughed carelessly.

"Happy! Oh, I suppose so, though you see, maybe one's best workgirl says she has a headache and must go home, or maybe one is tired, and has a headache one's self —— "

"A headache?" and the anxious eyes peered up tenderly at her. "But for sure, you never had headaches when you run about among the rocks, Julie."

"No, Grannie, perhaps life was easier then. But you see, if I had gone on running about among the rocks where would these scraps have come from, and my clothes —— "

"And the warm winter dress of beautiful black woollen, and the wadded quilt you brought me. Ah, my girl you've worked for me!"

"Don't talk about black woollens and wadded quilts to-day, Grannie. It's too warm. I'm going out to pick blueberries to make a pudding like we used to have, and to feel the wind coming in from the sea with the tide. The tide is nearly full now. I know by the smell of it."

And the girl standing in the cottage door, silhouetted against the blue plain of sea, threw back her head to sniff in the crisp air.

The tide was full, brimming up among the granite ledges and boulders, swaying the tawny seaweeds, and splashing against the pulled-up dories and flats on their skids with suggestions of wayfaring.

A little black tug had puffed into the military wharf, and was disgorging a string of khaki-clad men in broadbrimmed hats.

Julia, watching this operation with interest, broke out suddenly: "Gracious goodness, Gran'ma, whatever are those queer brown men that look like the mountain dwarfs in a play I saw once, called Rip Van Winkle — surely they're never soldiers — English soldiers?"

"That's just what they are, my dear. The sergeant up to the fort told me, when they went to fight last year away out there somewhere across the sea — I saw the ships go — the Englishmen in the pretty red coats that are plain to see, was all shot down, while the Canada men in that dingy colour was safe as could be. So, says the English officer to his men as wasn't shot — 'You'll wear it too,' says he. 'No more men in red for me' — and that's the way of it, but I'm sorry, for there's no one as wants to shoot them here, and the red coats were nice and cheerful to see on a dull day — that they were," she ended, regretfully.

Julia seemed to have lost interest in His Majesty's troops.

"Any pilot-boats up in the cove?" she asked in the most casually conversational tone.

"Let me see," Josephine meditated. "It was Saturday

as No. 4 went up, and she must be there still, for only this morning early did I see No. 3 beating out, and it won't be their turn outside yet awhile. Yes, there's most always two of them there."

"No. 4's the Minettes' boat, isn't it?" asked Julia, still watching the dun line of figures winding up the road to the fort.

"Yes, Simon and Louis Minette, both, and some day when Simon settles on shore Louis will be Captain."

"Well, I mustn't stay talking if I'm going to have blueberry pudding for dinner," Julia announced, swinging her basket with a fine air of energy as she set off down the pathway, a trim figure in her navy blue cotton. She had too innate a sense of the fitness of things to appear this morning in the smart green and white dress of yesterday.

It was natural that Julia should take the path leading up towards the Cove, for there the granite cliffs and stunted spruce woods gave place to the sweep of open blueberry barrens, but it was not natural that as soon as she found herself alone, the brightness should pass from her face, leaving evident marks of the toil and strain of city life.

The curve of her cheeks sank into two little hollows, and under the velvety grey eyes were dark shadows, telling of long vigils. The south wind stirred her loose hair and flapped her skirts with its message of summer gladness, the wavelets flashed up their welcome from among the boulders, the birch trees rippled their delicate tracery of leafwork, turning her blue cotton into the semblance of an elaborate brocade, but the subtle joy of these summer sights and sounds was dulled by a grim column of figures that haunted her night and day.

To the simple home folk, Julia seemed a successful and magnificent young woman, but she herself knew another side to the story, a side that spelt failure. She knew now how careless she had been when she first worked for herself; careless in the trifles spent on small pleasures; careless in giving credit and in ordering materials from the amiable young salesman who came to her with samples, and with vaguely polite statements as to the credit his house always gave to dressmakers. Never had this young salesman been anything but amiable and polite, even when he had had to ask in vain for his money.

"I'll make it all right with them, for sure I will, Miss Perrier. Don't you go and worry about it now. You just quit working for a spell and go home and have a rest down there among those Bluenoses of yours, and when you come back you make up your mind to marry me. Between us, what with your taste and my hustling, we'll soon have one of the smartest shows in Boston, and, you bet, you won't have any worrying about bills then. A cute little thing like you wants a man to take care of her anyway."

Julia knew that he was right, and that between them they could command success; but why, as the pink-faced, sleek little man beamed affectionately upon her, did a sudden vision come of a young face, weather-tanned and impassive from sea-vigils, that impassiveness belied by the pleading of grey eyes?

Miss Julia was too fond of approbation, too frightened of hurting people's feelings, ever to find it easy to say "No" outright, and so there was a certain amount of prevarication in her answer. The salesman, assured that no moneyless girl could reject so magnificent an offer, saw her on board the *Chebucto* with many amorous references to the September that was to bring her back again.

"If only the bill was paid, and I never need go back at all," Julia was saying to herself. "I ain't fit to run things for myself, that's a fact. If I was free of it all, I believe I'd just stay here up in town and go out by the day. Only, if Grannie got sick and couldn't get about, would I have enough then for us both? No, I've got to go back; I've got to go back."

As the words repeated themselves like a weary refrain, she heard the sound of a heavy step on the pathway behind her, and glancing back, saw a smart young artilleryman coming along at a pace that would surely overtake her.

No dull khaki here, but the dark blue with its touches of red and gold that had once been so familiar a sight to her, though the slouch felt hat was a change from the jaunty little cap of yore.

The girl's neat figure and well-set head almost unconsciously trimmed themselves up for masculine inspection, as the steps drew nearer.

"Beg pardon, Miss," came a hoarsely amiable voice behind her, and she paused and stood still, as the remarkably red-faced young warrior addressed her: "You didn't 'appen to ha' dropped this 'ere letter in the path as you come along, did yer?"

The paper he held out was a folded one without address, and something in the twinkle in the round blue eyes suggested that it probably belonged to the youth who produced it as a trumped-up excuse. This, however, was no great sin in the eyes of Julia, who was quite ready to take what small diversions came in her way; even though No. 4 pilot-boat might be lying in the Cove. Most likely her crew were all up in town amusing themselves. And so she smiled sweetly, with just a shade of polite reserve as she answered:

"No, I'm sure it isn't, for I haven't got a pocket in this dress, and I put away my purse and letters in my trunk this morning. Thank goodness, one doesn't need those kind of things down here!"

"Down here!" the artilleryman repeated diplomatically. "Now I didn't see any picnic parties landing to-day; but — "

Julia felt the implied compliment, that she could not be of local origin, suspecting all the time that her identity was known.

"Oh, David Minette brought me down last night in his whaler. I'm Josephine Perrier's granddaughter, and I came in the Boston boat yesterday."

"Well, I never!" ejaculated the youth. "Did you really, Miss? It seems to me that every man, woman and child in this blessed country has either gone to Boston or just come from it, or got the rest of their family there. I suppose it's like London is to us at 'ome," and he jerked his thumb eastwards, "and draws the restless ones. Now, might you say, Miss, as this 'ere Boston would be a likely place for a smart young time-expired man, who's a fair hand at electric lights and such, to make a start in the world?"

This last question was brought out with bashful earnestness, showing a forgetfulness of his neighbourhood to a pretty girl, in the revealing of an air-castle.

Julia answered with corresponding frankness:

"I think it is a good place for anyone who ain't afraid to work; but lord, one must work; no mistake. The folks round here seem half alive after the stir there."

"And you, Miss? Might I make bold to ask if you did well there yourself?"

The downright question checked Julia for a moment, then she laughed out:

"Oh, yes. I went there just as a sewing girl, and now I work at home with two girls under me. I suppose that's doing well?"

The round blue eyes stared at her in greater admiration than ever.

"I should just think it was!" came the hearty comment. "But, then, anyone can see with harf an eye as you's clever — downright clever, that's what you are, Miss."

This sincere homage was not unpleasant.

"Oh, I don't know as to that!" she disclaimed. "Well, if I'm going to pick any blueberries to-day, I guess I must be on the move."

"If I might make so bold, I'm on my way to the ferry myself — it being Bank 'Oliday at 'ome, and us 'aving a day orf in consekens," the youth suggested.

"What's Bank Holiday?" Julia asked, as they set off up the old grassy road.

"Bank Holiday? Why — it's just Bank Holiday you know. Comes four times a year, and every one as can stops working."

"Oh, something like the 4th of July, I guess, though there's only one of it."

"What's the 4th of July?" asked the English youth, perplexed in his turn.

"That's the great day in the States when people make speeches and let off fire-crackers," she explained.

"Lord! what a queer way to amuse themselves? I shan't want to do that if ever I goes to live there."

Again Julia laughed.

"Oh, well, I guess you wouldn't be a big enough man to make speeches, or a small enough boy to let off firecrackers, so you'd be safe."

"Well, but what would I do then?" he persisted, with the tenacity of a slow mind.

"Oh sakes, how do I know? Sit in the shade and eat watermelon."

"What's watermelon?"

Julia was rapidly tiring of the ingenious youth, and this last question so exasperated her that she answered recklessly. "Oh, a sort of apple!" a retort which bore inaccuracy on the face of it.

Her mind was busy with the unpleasant possibility of a certain young pilot making a reconnoitring tour on this pathway, and that the plump artilleryman would, in that case, spoil a very effective meeting. It is always the unpleasant possibility that becomes a fact. Just as she was making up her mind to desert the path and her admirer on the plea of berry-picking, a trailing blackberry vine caught her skirt so securely that the artilleryman had to go down on his knees to disentangle her, forming an idyllic group for the benefit of a youth who came strolling around a turn in the path in the leisurely fashion of sailors ashore. At the sight, the grave, bronzed face darkened, and the loosely hanging hands clenched, but Julia made a brave effort to control the situation, crying with somewhat forced gaiety:

"Well, I never, if it ain't Louis Minette! Come along and say 'welcome home' to me, like the blackberries do."

"Seems to me as you look pretty much at home already," came the grim retort, with a scowl at the artilleryman, red-faced from his struggle with the bramble.

"Well, and did you think as I'd be sitting on the shore waiting for you to give me leave to come home?" she answered shrilly with a note of rising anger.

"I knew you too well for that."

Just as she caught the bitter words, the bramble condescended to disentangle itself, and the soldier picked himself up and stood first on one leg and then on the other to relieve his embarrassment. Julia's face was very pale, and her voice came in a little breathless way as she said:

"Thank you most kindly for the trouble you've took." She hesitated, wondering what his name was, but it did not occur to the youth to supply it.

"So she goes walking the very first day with a sodjer as she don't even know the name of," commented a jealous heart.

"Well, and I guess you'll be getting on to the ferry now," she said amiably to the stranger, "and as I'm going up this path to the blueberry patches, I'll say goodbye"; then, with a sudden chill in her manner, "If you're going towards the Fort, Louis, and happen to see Gran'ma at the door tell her I'll be back in plenty of time to peel the potaters."

And with a flounce of blue skirts the young woman turned to climb the hillside, while the soldier and the sailor went on in different directions.

Not for anything would Louis Minette have turned back to the Cove with the intruder, though the object of his walk was gone.

III

A week of hot August days passed without any startling development.

The artilleryman prowled about between the Fort and the Cove, cropping up in all sorts of unexpected places when the blue cotton appeared, sometimes receiving a few careless words and smiles, sometimes being urged on his way with the briefest of excuses. If Louis Minette were on board his boat in the Cove, he stayed there and attempted no more expeditions into the enemy's country. As for Julia she had always a stream of gay talk ready to amuse old Josephine, sitting on the doorstep in the soft evening dusk, telling long tales of the splendours of town life; devoting a whole stormy day to cutting out and fitting the new winter dress of black woollen; attempting wonderful feats of cookery at the little cooking stove, and even persuading her grandmother to eat some mushrooms which she had brought home and served up as a savoury dish.

"They're pison, rank pison, and my mother always told me as it was only witches as could ate them," Josephine protested, but she ate them as she would have done anything that Julia wanted her to do.

For all her bustling and cheerful ways, the girl stayed as thin as ever, and though her face tanned to a healthy brown, the hollows were still in her cheeks.

It was a week after her arrival and a letter having come from her commercial traveller, she carried it off to the hillside for further meditation.

She had found herself a mossy nook among the spruce trees, open enough to give her a lookout down on the stretch of water below, shut in enough for there to be little chance of her amorous artilleryman hunting her out.

"I simply couldn't stand his bank 'olidays and his watermelons to-day. I'd scream right out," she said to herself with an ungrateful remembrance of their first meeting.

A pearly haze of fog hung over the sea, and although there was no wind a southerly swell was booming among the granite ledges below.

A military launch had landed some passengers at the wharf, and, looking down from her perch on to the winding road to the Fort, she saw a lady in dainty white walking up beside an officer in uniform. They were both young and good-looking, and from the cosy way in which she put her hand through his arm and smiled up into his face, they were evidently husband and wife. How happy they looked! she thought to herself, and how nice it must be to have someone to take care of one, and help one up the steep places. She, Julia, had always had to climb by herself, sometimes helping up others too.

And then she put her hand in her pocket and pulled out her letter and re-read it, wrinkling up her face a good deal in the process.

The letter was dreadfully affectionate, expressing a strong sense of proprietorship. "When the days have been extra hot, and business extra aggravating, I just camp down evenings in any cool, dark place, a beer-garden, a ferry-boat or such, and think about a certain honeymoon trip to Niagara, and a certain pretty little bride getting her picture taken beside her husband, wearing one of those shiny blue silks, and a pearl brooch that I have a look at every now and then in Solomon's window, and after that I feel like another man. I don't want my little girl to hurry back to work, but I want her to come back in time for that honeymoon —— "

Goodness gracious! How certain he seemed about it all! She had never intended anything like that when she had promised just for the sake of keeping him quiet, to think it over.

And this was the man who when he came for his money she would have to tell that she could not pay it!

For all his smiling pinkness, she had marked his underlying tenacity, and knowing her own weakness, she felt certain that if she went back it would end in his marrying her.

"And oh, I don't want to, I don't want to!" she sobbed in a sudden outburst of despair. "I want to stay here by the sea, among my own folks — but I can't, I can't!"

It was almost a luxury to give way to that passion of weeping that seized her as she hid her face in the cool, green moss, letting her hair fall thick about her face, and her sobs break from her burdened chest. She had been brave and had laughed back at the world for so long. Now she would have her hour of tears to herself.

A sailor walks with a certain loose restraint that makes his footfall much lighter than that of landsmen. Perhaps that was the reason that Louis Minette, returning from a night's fishing with the Falkland men, came across the hill-side and down the meadow slope behind the spruce trees without her hearing his approach.

A flicker of light on the blue cotton caught the pilot's eye, and he paused to look down in silent dismay at the dishevelled, sob-shaken heap.

"Julie! Why Julie!" he said, with a dawning tenderness of voice and eyes, and stooping laid a big brown hand on the girl's heaving shoulder. The effect of words and touch was magical. In a moment Julia was on her feet, shaking back her loose hair, and facing him with stormy eyes.

"And so you speak a civil word to me at last do you, Louis Minette?" she panted out. "What is it to you if I have a toothache, or a headache, or — oh well, anything that makes me cry — and what do you mean by coming spying round —— "

But Louis was not to be tempted into a quarrel to-day.

"There, there," he said with a soothing hand on her arm. "I know well enough as you wouldn't have the heart to say that to me, Julie, if you weren't, so to say, upset and put out by something. And if you'll just tell me what it is, and if that fool of an artilleryman — at least, he mayn't be a fool though he looks one for sure —— "

A mollified laugh broke from Julia. Why do women so enjoy masculine jealousy?

"That artilleryman! As if I'd go all the way to Boston and back to cry about him! Why, he's twice the fool he looks, if that's possible."

"Well then, if it ain't that it's something else!" Louis persisted. "And I want to know what it is, and to see if I can't help you, Julie."

The girl's lips quivered, and a little sob rose as after swell of the past storm.

"It's nothing, Louis. I was only just foolish, and thinking how soon it'd be when I'd have to go back to work and worries —— "

She paused, and he took her up promptly, though with a visible effort.

"There's no need to go back at all, Julie. You know how hard I took it for you to be working away off there by yourself. You were set on going; but now, when I'm getting enough to keep you comfortable, and you'd live in town or in the Cove just whichever you liked best —— "

His voice had grown hoarse and now choked with the force of his pleading.

Julia looked bravely into the dark face bent towards her and shook her head with a wistful smile. Then, all at once, she let herself go in an impulsiveness which some-times proves the truest wisdom.

Flinging her arms up to his neck, she clung to him, her tear-stained face against the oilskins he carried on his arm.

"Oh, I wish I could! I only wish I could!" she cried. "But whatever happens I must go back next month. It wouldn't be honest if I didn't, Louis."

His face was haggard with mingled passion and disap-pointment as he clasped her close.

"But you'll come back to me for sure?" he muttered.

"For sure," and the commercial traveller's letter crackled in the front of her dress as though protesting.

This was all very fine as far as it went, but if Louis were not as conversationally nimble as Julia, he held tena-ciously to his purpose, the purpose of knowing the reason of her tears and her insistence on returning to her work. The temptation was strong to tell the tale of her troubles with her head on his shoulder, but all the strength of will that had driven her out to fight her own battle in the world revolted against an acknowledgment of failure. No, rather than that she would go back, and giving up her little estab-lishment would go out again to work by the day.

It was a come down, but she felt pretty sure that by working hard and stinting herself of all her little pleasures, she could by the early summer have saved enough to pay her debt without letting Louis know of it or of the com-mercial traveller. He would want to pay the debt she felt certain, and that would be too humiliating an end to all her grand schemes.

And so, rubbing her cheek against his shoulder like a meditative kitten, she cooed:

"Don't let us bother about anything now. I've a month more holidays, so let us get all the good of them, anyway. Take me out cod-fishing this afternoon, won't you? I haven't been once yet."

And what could Louis do but capitulate to this programme.

IV

All dwellers upon these Nova Scotian shores know the signs of the "August storm," outer edge of the West Indian hurricane circle, that sweep up hot and dark and fierce, working havoc on their way. As a child, Julia had enjoyed seeing the coasting schooners running in for shelter, and the fishermen hauling up their boats and making everything fast before the coming peril.

To-day though, when the overcast sky was of such a steely hardness, and a shrill whistle sounded in the rising south-westerly wind, her restlessness was not of so pleasurable a kind. No. 4 was out, and she had climbed the hillside more than once before she saw the pilot-boat running in before the wind, past the cottage up to the cove, where sheltered between the island and the mainland, no southerly storm could reach her.

The rain had not yet come, and presently Julia was strolling up the shore path where she had once met the artilleryman. But the poor artilleryman had been sent with his blighted hopes over to one of the forts at McNab's, greatly to Julia's relief, and it was somewhere near the same spot as she had met him before that Louis now appeared. There was the freshness and life of the sea in his face, as he hailed her cheerily:

"I saw you on the lookout as we passed. Did you think we'd be drowned inside Sambro? A fine sailor's wife you'll make."

"I wasn't looking for you," she asserted. "I was just watching the soldiers landing."

"Looking for the artilleryman?" he asked.

Then they strolled leisurely homewards, though the first warm drops of rain struck their faces. But as they turned to the bare seaward slope the force of the storm met them, and it was with Louis' arm round her waist, and with their heads bent that they faced it.

Down the rocky hillside they scuttled, making for the shelter of the cottage. As they came within sight of the open door Julia clutched his arm sharply.

"What's that, Louis?" she gasped, and then ran forward towards something black that was huddled on the wet stones by the well.

"Grannie!" she cried pitifully, and a feeble wail answered her.

"Yes, I've done it this time. There's something cracked up in top of my leg, and I thought as I'd have to lie here for ever. I wanted water for tea —— "

"Oh, never mind that now. Let Louis and me try to lift you —— "

It was a heart-rending business when she quailed and groaned at their touch, and fainted outright as they raised her. Even Louis was haggard-faced by the time that they got her on her bed, and the tears were streaming unheeded down Julia's face as she tried to force brandy between the old lady's teeth.

"Look here," Louis said desperately; "when John Marlin over to Falkland broke his leg they just laid him out flat in a whaler and took him up to town to the hospital. Now, it's clear as she's broke *something*, and if you like, I'll get the Pettipaw's boat and 'range a mattress and tarpaulins all right, and start off."

"But the storm?" Julia protested in dismay.

"There ain't no sea yet to harm us running before it," he persisted.

A pressure of the poor bony hand Julia held made her bend lower. "What's he say?" came a hoarse whisper.

"Grannie dear, will you let Louis take you to town to the hospital? We'll cover you up warm and I'll be close beside you."

"You're good children, the both of you, but I ain't going to no hospital. Here I am in my own bed, and here I'm going to stay till I go up over the hill to the graveyard."

They knew her too well to attempt argument.

"Then I've got to get a doctor somehow. Guess I'll walk up to the ferry. Don't be downhearted, if we're not here before morning, though I'll do my best. Dare say I'll get Dr. Haskell to drive down. I'll send one of the neighbours to you, Julie."

And so Louis went out into the night, and Julia with a neighbour's help did her best for Grannie through the long hours that intervened between his return with a youthful doctor of sporting proclivities who, finding these shore folk a change from the monotony of town patients, had become a sort of physician in ordinary to them. He got her hip set, but shook his head when asked as to her recovery.

"At her time of life — and I can see she's worked hard — there's not much chance of her ever getting about again," he said to Louis. Though the latter kept this to himself, it was not long before Julia had realised the fact for herself. Grannie was growing weaker every day. It was impossible that in a few weeks' time she could be left alone, and yet, if Julia stayed with her where was the money for their daily needs to come from unless she married Louis? That she felt she could not do until her debt was paid.

True, for Grannie's keep she might appeal to her married children, who if never over-generous, could hardly leave her to die neglected. She herself might get sewing to do in town. Mrs. Demoine who kept the boarding house would recommend her, and she could easily send the work back and forth.

It was with such schemes that she tried to keep up her courage as she went about her simple household duties.

They had moved Josephine's bed into the front room where the cooking-stove was, and where through the open door she could see the ocean steamers and the white-winged sailing craft pass up and down the harbour.

"All my life long, they've been company to me," she murmured, half apologising for her interest in a great, white American man-of-war that had come in.

Grannie had always taken much pains to hide her frivolous delight in the wonderful outside world at which she had had so few peeps.

"A Yankee cruiser!" she said over to herself at intervals; then beckoning to Julia, "There ain't no war, nor no blockade-runners now, is there?"

"No, Grannie, of course not," Julia answered, not quite understanding what she meant. She had heard the old folks talk of the American war, without realising that it could ever have affected the lives of those around her.

She had finished her tidying up, and now took her sewing and sat near the door where her grandmother could see her. She knew how persistently the wistful eyes followed her about. She was uneasy too, for to-day the pale face seemed as though pinched by invisible fingers, it looked so strangely small, and the worn hands wandered restlessly on the red and white patchwork quilt.

"The priest says as we'll meet fathers and mothers and husbands in heaven, don't he, Julie?" the thin voice questioned.

"Yes, Grannie."

"But I wonder how it'll be with folks as ain't relations, folks as p'raps we've only seen once or twice — long ago, long ago, and yet we've remembered all our lives. What do you think, Julie?" and the words had a strange intensity in them.

"I don't know, Grannie," Julia answered with an anxious glance down the pathway. She wished some of the neighbours would come along, though she could not have told why she was frightened.

V

A restless sigh had followed Julia's words, then raising her head for a furtive glance around, Josephine beckoned.

"Shut the door, Julie, and come here close by the bed. There's a thing as I've got to tell you before it's too late."

Something in the compelling eyes made Julia obey in silence, though she shivered as she shut out the September sunshine.

"You lift the mat over there by the dresser and you'll see a loose board. Yes, that's it. Take a knife and lift it up — there — now you see a little box, don't you?"

Julia stood up, holding a small pasteboard matchbox in her hand.

"Bring it here," and the wrinkled hands grasped it like a recovered treasure. Slowly the box was pushed out —

ALICE JONES

"Look at that!" Josephine whispered, like a devotee before an uncovered shrine.

Julia was by now in such a state of bewilderment that she thought nothing would have surprised her, but she gave a gasp of amazement at sight of a man's heavy ring in which shone a large diamond. She had a friend in Boston whose father was working jeweller in a big firm, and who had amused himself showing the girl enough of their treasures for her to make a guess at the value of this stone if it were real.

"Why Grandma, where'd you get that?" she asked in all the sharpness of surprise.

"Pull up the rocking-chair close, and I'll tell you" — and then feebly at times, now and then strong with excitement, the old woman went on to tell the tale of her life's romance.

"It was when I was a girl — before your father came from Chezzetcook and married me" — of late she had more than once confused Julia with the daughters married and gone from her — "those was the days when the Yankees in Boston was fighting the people who lived south of their country, English I think they really was, though there was another name they called them by —— "

"Rebels," suggested Julia, but the old woman frowned and shook her head.

"No, no, that wasn't it. Anyway, they used to come here in steamers to get things to take home to their families, as the Yankees wouldn't let them have — blockade-runners they called them. They were painted such pretty colours, pale blues and pinks and greys, so as the Yankees shouldn't see them at night. I used to watch 'em over there by the Eastern Passage. The Yankee cruisers would dodge about outside to catch them, but often they'd come down here and wait till after dark to slip out in a fog.

"There was one — she was pink — and more than once when she was loaded she came and lay hidden away in the Cove, where she could only be seen from the land side, and there she would wait for the best time to go out.

"There was a man — father said he was the captain —

as used to come strolling about, and sometimes he passed our door and talked to me — he was big and splendid, with a yellow beard, and such a kind, gentle voice. He used to call me a queer name, Evangeline — I don't know what it meant —— "

Julia knew, and tears were in her eyes as she realised Grandma's youth, and the stranger with the kind and gentle voice. She guessed that Grandpa's ways had been anything but kind or gentle.

"One hot summer day I hadn't seen him, but I knew that he had crossed to go to the town, and that his ship had her steam up.

"Our men were getting their nets ready, and I heard them say as they must be careful to-night, for there was a Yankee cruiser going up and down near the shore as might run them down.

"'Then that blockade-runner had better stay safe where she is,' says father.

"'She's been waiting three days, and she'll try it for sure to-night if there's a wisp of fog,' says Louis Minette's grandfather.

"Well the men went out towards sunset and it was quiet, deadly quiet along the shore. There wasn't a breath of wind, not a bit of lop to break on the beach.

"I was sitting out there on one of the rocks, as it seemed less lonely like than inside, when I saw two men coming up the path. Sailors they were for sure, though different from any I'd ever known. They asked to fill a jar at the well, and then they talked a bit about how quiet it seemed with the men out, and were any men from the blockade-runner up above ever about? They thought they'd seen one of them being landed over by the point this morning.

"Then somehow I guessed as they were enemies to my captain, and I just wouldn't tell them one word, though I made pretence to answer them fair enough.

"'Oh, she's a fool! Come along,' one of them mutters, and as they go off I heard him say, 'Steam's up, and she goes out to-night as soon as he's aboard.'

"'Yes, as soon as he's aboard; but what if we catch him first,' the other says with a laugh.

"I made a show of sitting down on the rocks with my back to them, but presently I just stands round a bit, and I sees them join two others as was waiting, and go along the shore, and somehow I felt sure as they were hiding behind that big rock up above the path. They meant to catch my captain as he came back, and I, a poor stupid girl, was the only one to do a thing to stop them.

"If he had his own boat to meet him on the other side, he'd be safe enough, but if he crossed in the ferry and walked along the shore they'd have him for sure.

"It was getting dark, not real dark, but just enough to be dusky against the hill, while out on the water it was clear enough.

"I wondered if I could get along the shore up to the blockade-runner and call out to them to go to meet their captain. I walked a little way when presently I sees a head bob out behind the big rock up on the hill, and I guessed if I tried to go further they'd stop me. So I just sat down and looked around idle like. I looked at the shore and I looked at the water, and didn't I see a boat coming over from the ferry, right to where I was. If only I could have called to them to go higher up, for I knew the captain was there going to land just below those men on the hill.

"I'll chance it, thinks I, and I sets off to run down as light as I could between the bushes, but by the time I reached him the boat was gone and he was walking along the path, brisk, and humming to himself.

"'Hullo, Evangeline! Did you fall from the sky?' says he, as I come down through the bushes. I was panting so as I could scarce speak, but I caught him by the arm. 'There are four men hiding up there behind that rock,' I says, pointing, 'as mean to stop your getting on board to-night.'

"'Do they?' says he, cheerful-like. 'That's kind in them. Four to one is big odds too, but we'll see what we can do.'

"He puts a whistle to his mouth and blows twice, sharp and loud. 'That should bring the boat, but I must lose no time. You're a good girl — see here,' and he pulled this ring off his finger. 'If they get me, they shan't get this. You keep it for me until I come back, and if I never come back, keep it for yourself. Good-bye, child,' and he just kissed me, and was off up the path at a run.

"There I stayed, but it was duskier now, and though I heard heavy feet among the loose stones on the hill I could see nothing, only presently there was scuffling and sounds as though shouts were being choked and I was half mad when I thought they'd got him. Then there were sounds of oars as sometimes I thought went towards the sea, and sometimes towards the Cove. I was so bewildered, I couldn't even make that out.

"By'n-bye, there was nothing more anywhere, and I crawled home, but I listened for hours on the doorstep, and still never heard a thing.

"It was morning when father gets home, and by then I had been up to the Cove and seen as there was no block-ade-runner there.

"I told father about it — all save the ring; I kept that to myself for fear he might want to sell it — and he said as it wasn't the first queer thing of the kind as had happened along the shore this last year or so. Whether the captain had got off or hadn't was none of our business, and we'd best hold our tongues about it all," — she drew a deep breath as for remembered sorrow — "and we did, and that was the end of it, for though I waited and waited, and even when Elias was ill I wouldn't show the ring or sell it, for the chance as he might come back for it. But now, I'm pretty well done for, and perhaps when I'm gone you might use it to buy a nice white cross to put over me. It would seem like being friendly with him still. I guess it might be worth that?" she asked anxiously.

"It'll buy nicer things than that," was the resolutely cheerful answer, though there were tears on Julia's cheeks. "A soft, easy chair for when you sit up —— "

"There'll be no need of that. But I'd be glad if it gave something for you. It's yours now, Julie."

"I'll take care of it for you, Grannie," and Julia hung

the ring by a ribbon round her neck, and tucked it inside her dress.

This matter of her one worldly care settled, Josephine rapidly let slip her hold on life. Her little craft, moored so long, was drifting out with the tide into unknown seas.

"It's a comfort there won't be no more winter storms," she whispered, one still Sunday afternoon when Julia sat close to her, watching the breaths that came slower and slower with a lengthening pause between each.

On the stillness came the deep whistle of a steamer, and the heavy eyelids lifted while that wonderful smile of the dying lit the wrinkled face.

"The Boston boat!" the old woman said out clear and strong. "It's a bringing back all them it took away."

The head fell back in a final fashion, and listen as she might, Julia could hear no breathing. Josephine was dead.

Far up on the rocky hillside she was laid, the hillside where it seemed as though these seafaring folk still watched the passing of the ships.

Then, in spite of Louis' protests, Julia locked up the poor little cottage and went back to Boston.

"Only for a month, Louis. I'll be back in a month. It's just to get things fixed up."

She kept her word, and before the red of the blueberry barrens had faded they were married and settled in a nice little cottage in the Cove, where the wooded point sheltered them from the battering sea storms.

∾

Canadian Magazine 26 (Nov. and Dec. 1905): 59–65; 162–168.

Jean Blewett (1862–1934)

THE EXPERIENCES OF A WOMAN BACHELOR (1905)

Jean McKishnie Blewett was born on 4 November 1862 at Scotia, Kent County, Ontario, to Janet McIntyre and John McKishnie, Scottish immigrants. An interest in writing was a family trait: Blewett's brother, Archie McKishnie, achieved some success as a novelist. After attending St. Thomas Collegiate, Jean Blewett published a novel, *Out of the Depths*, in 1879, the same year she married Cornishman Bassett Blewett. She became a regular contributor to the Toronto *Globe* and served as editor of its Homemakers' Department from about 1898 until ill-health compelled her retirement in 1925. In the interim, Blewett became well known for her poetry, her journalism and her readings across Canada. In 1919, with the support of the Imperial Order of the Daughters of the Empire (IODE), she published a booklet, *Heart Stories*, to benefit war charities; these are local-colour stories and dream-come-true tales of Great War casualties miraculously restored. Such stories were a staple of writing by women on the Home Front. After Blewett's retirement in 1925, she lived with a daughter in Lethbridge, Alberta, until her return to Toronto in 1927. She died in Chatham.

Jean Blewett was well known as a poet. For the most part sentimental and didactic, her poems range from simple narratives of farm life to nature poetry and lyrical love poetry. Blewett was interested in suffrage and social reform from a conservative perspective. In this respect, some of her fiction is more intellectually complex than her poetry. The poetry tends to unreservedly endorse conventional notions of wedded domestic bliss. In a typical poem, a male narrator exalts his wife:

> And ah! her mission seems to me
>   The highest and the best;
> And so I say with pride untold,
>   And love beyond degree,

> This woman with the heart of gold
>   She just keeps house for me.

By contrast, Blewett wrote one story, "Dr. Dorothy Treherne," in which both love and quest are valorized, although the protagonist's decisive romantic attractiveness lies in her womanly tears. Other stories by Blewett, for example "The Emancipation of Dorothea," make suffragism an object of hilarity: the heroine is rescued from an oafish vagabond by her suitor, irrefutably proving to her that "We [women] can talk, and hold meetings, and theorise, but when the big, unforeseen, elemental things turn up, where would any of us be, if you [men] didn't 'just happen along'?"

In "The Experiences of a Woman Bachelor," Eunice Complin enthusiastically embraces independence and the single life, but her ideas about intellectual, platonic relationships with men are shown to be naive, amusing and untenable. The story relies heavily for humorous effect on gender stereotypes (hypochondriacal husbands, possessive wives, puritanical maiden aunts). The domestic bliss of the "woman bachelor"'s friend Kate Deming is triumphant. There is an ironic tension in the narrative, however, created by Deming's injunction to her friend to realize new womanhood with its intellectuality and self-assertion, so unlike the fate of wives, who are destined to "hug their chains." With deft use of the epistolary form, Blewett creates a story with a documentary style and an ironic subtext.

∽

Suggested Reading

Blewett, Jean. "Dr. Dorothy Treherne: An Easter Love Story," *Canadian Magazine* 20 (April 1903): 558–564.
——. "The Emancipation of Dorothea," *Canadian Magazine* 35 (June 1910): 139–144.
——. *Heart Stories* (Toronto: Warwick and Rutter, 1919).
Middleton, J. E. "Writing-Lady," *Educational Record* (*Quebec*) 62 (April–June 1946): 98–100.

The Experiences of a Woman Bachelor

Jean Blewett

Being the confidential letters which passed between Eunice C. Complin, B.A., and her bosom friend, Kate Deming, on the subject of platonic love and kindred theories.

KENTOWN, ONT., March 15th, 1904.

MY DEAR EUNICE, — I hope the fact of a Montreal periodical calling you a genius will not puff you up with vanity. Geniuses, my dear, differ from fools in only one respect; fools are quite destitute of wisdom, while geniuses are wise, subtly wise, in streaks. You'll be looking for this letter; it should have reached you days ago, had I not been too busy defending you to the Kentownites, and explaining that there is nothing culpable in the fact of your getting to be a bachelor.

Poor Aunt Lydia hasn't held up her head since the news first reached her. I went in yesterday morning to talk the affair over. She was in bed — I believe in my heart she climbed in when she heard me coming, for she was flustered and her cheeks were quite pink.

"What's the matter?" I asked suspiciously.

"Nothing, nothing," she answered, and began to

smooth her hair back by way of drawing my attention to a wonderful thing, the very newest thing in the way of a nightcap. It was of lace, and shaped a good deal like a baby's bonnet. In the crown was a lining of puffed cream satin, and there was a full ruffle of lace falling about her face. There was also a smell of violet sachet powder. Two silver safety pins fastened this bit of millinery to Aunt Lydia's scant tresses. 'Tis a pity she can't wear it in the daytime, for it's the most becoming thing in the line of headgear I ever saw on her. But, bless me! I start out to say all sorts of grave and clever things to you, and waste my time and paper in describing a nightcap! Such are common, everyday women, Eunice. You, of course, are different. You have had advantages. You are a bachelor.

I expect great things from you. What are you going to make of yourself? You surely won't fall in love and marry. Leave all this sweet foolishness to us who know nothing of the delights of brand new womanhood; who can't write books, speak on platforms, box, fence, run, row or analyse our emotions; who hang to our embroidery frames, our smelling salts, our whims — created from the beginning to be in bondage to the sterner sex, and to hug our chains. This last sounds a trifle, er — well, indelicate; but you know what I mean. There's Cousin Augustus, a ridiculous name for a prosaic fellow; but he's not to blame; the sin rests on his mother. He was in love with you last year. He may be in love with you this; but man, being born to inconstancy, as the sparks to fly upward, I'll not venture to assert that he is. You were never nice to him. There has been a jolly little girl visiting his sister for the last six weeks, and he has hung about the house a lot. He displayed no emotion when speaking of you to me, so I imagine the flame which was wont to burn in his bosom has simmered down to a comfortable little pile of embers. You might kindle it up again. Somebody says that a love revived is the tenderest love of all, but I've no experience. If I were you, though, I would be a bachelor girl for a long time. I would live and work and enjoy. You are a genius; I wish you weren't, for though I'm proud of the fact of your being one, I know you'll be just as apt to do the wrong thing as any other genius. Geniuses are happier before they marry than after, as a general thing — so also are those they marry, for the matter of that. What a Job's comforter I am! And all because I am jealous away down in a corner of my mind of those awe-inspiring letters tacked to your name. Aunt Lydia says you had better come home and behave yourself. Maybe you had, Eunice Complin, B.A. I'm lonesome for a look at your pretty face. Yours, with heaps of love,

KATE DEMING.

P.S. — Dick sends you kind regards. By the way I am going to celebrate my wooden wedding next month. Tell me how to go about it. What's the good of being a B.A. if you don't know everything?

K.D.

∽

ELMDALE AVENUE, MONTREAL,
April 10th, 1904.

MY DEAR KATE, — Here is your six weeks' old epistle confronting me with a bold air of fault-finding on this glorious April day. Conscience urges me to write; inclination urges me to get out and watch the grass growing, and the crocus flaunting herself. Every time I look out of my window two big dandelions stare back at me. If, presently, I cease writing, the fault will be theirs; two more inviting, cajoling things you can't imagine. They make me want to get down and cuddle them, and pat the yellow heads for being so brave and so bonny. As big a fool as ever, I can hear you saying, and 'tis true. The green and gold, the sap and bud, the stir of growing things make me so glad that I cannot help crying at times. I love the season.

"Spring with the hyacinths filling her lap,
And the violet seeds in her hair,
With the crocus hiding its satin head
In her bosom warm and fair."

So the Kentownites do not approve of me! I don't
know why I should wish to go on living, or — but never
mind the Kentownites. They are like mosquitoes, always
buzzing and singing. I can't bear mosquitoes, prefer snakes
— they bite harder, but they don't bite so often, and they
aren't forever droning an evil lay. So much for the
Kentownites. You and Dick are among them, but not of
them. Then, there is your cousin Augustus — he couldn't
be anything but good if he were to try. Not that he is
always good to me; he says I have impulse enough to spoil
my calculations, and calculations enough to spoil my
impulses. I'm a bright personage according to this. As
to falling in love and marrying, I am not contemplating
anything so rash. What am I going to do with myself?
Why, what any sensible young woman with good health,
a fair share of good looks, and a modest but sufficient
income ought to do with herself. I'm going to keep my
independence, have a good time, and grow better and
wiser every day.

I'm not a marrying person; Aunt Lydia often deplores
the fact. I don't believe in affinities and one woman losing
her heart to one man; in fact, a woman very much in love is
rather a nuisance to herself and everybody else. I always
avoid her if possible. It's as bad with the other sex. The
man who at a party stands moodily watching the door till
the woman of his choice enters — we meet him often —
ought to be sent home until such time as he can appear in
public without making a ninny of himself. There is no
excuse for him. I'll tell you something, Kate. You may
think me joking, but I'm not; I'm in earnest, cross my
heart, as we used to say. Listen, then. The only kind of
love I am going to give or receive is platonic love. There
are splendid men in the world, and men, my dear, make
better friends than women. There are people narrow
enough to deny that a close friendship can exist for any
length of time between a man and a woman — perhaps I

should say, rather, between a young man and a young woman. It is to refute to my own satisfaction this libel on human nature that I have chosen for my device "calm, passionless, platonic love."

Already I am happy in the possession of a man friend of whom any woman might feel proud. Not that he is handsome — I've never admired handsome men, as you know — or witty, or even exceptionally clever. He's just an earnest, good fellow, and so broad-minded for a preacher — a Presbyterian at that. He makes an ideal friend; I give him advice, and sympathy, and quite a lot of my time. Now don't smile and look knowing, for there's no more question of love between us than on the first day of our meeting some six months ago. I'm going to be perfectly frank with you always; you may believe every line of my epistles. If I find that this platonic love is, as some one declares, "hard to find, and harder to hold," I'll tell you about it. At present my faith is strong. The parson is tall and slim — too slim — and has near-sighted blue eyes, but he has a heart of gold. We both enjoy our friendship immensely in spite of the ill-natured remarks of those envious of us. There is a girl here, Nadine Ghant, big-eyed and good looking. She asked me yesterday if I had ever been in love, and when I answered that I had not, she laughed.

"Then why encourage the attentions of the Rev. John Hobson?" she asked.

I explained to her just how matters were, but she only made fun of me. She's very plain spoken, this Nadine.

"The parson's a big fool, and you're a little one," she said. "Platonic friendship, indeed! It's the platonic friendships that make so many old maids. A man gets into a position to take to himself a wife, but instead of going among the marriageable young ladies of his acquaintance, choosing a wife, and starting a happy home life, what does he do? He strikes up a platonic friendship with some pretty matron, or some silly girl who thinks because she has studied a host of theories that she knows more than her great-grandmother about men and women. Humph!"

Oh, the scorn expressed in that "Humph!" I didn't get vexed. Nadine is fond of John Hobson; she is clever and bright, and will make him a good wife. Think I shall try to do a little matchmaking. Marriage will not interfere with our delightful companionship. Your cousin Augustus is another of my friends. He's under bonds never to mention the word love in my hearing, so no building of air castles, you wily schemer. There's a professor, McDill — but no more about my "affairs" this time.

My love to Dick. Tell him he chose the only woman in Kentown worth marrying. And about your wooden wedding, dear! Are you really a five-year-old bride? I can't believe it.

Have your room look as rustic as possible, with rustic furniture and little wooden buckets to hold the flowers. Send your invitations out on birch bark, and when the evening arrives don the pretty silver poplin you were married in and look your old sweet self. This is all I can tell you. When I'm five years married you won't find me asking advice of a girl bachelor.

I wish you would have a baby, Kate. I'll go down and pet it most to death. If 'twas a girl you could name her Eunice, and I'd be her godmother. Think it over. If I were to mention twins I suppose you'd gasp, but twins, Mrs. Dick Deming, are the loveliest things on earth. Yours lovingly,

EUNICE COMPLIN.

❧

KENTOWN, ONT., May 7th, 1904.

MY DEAR EUNICE, — You don't seem at all anxious for my advice, but you shall have it nevertheless. I'm not one to see you running on the rocks and not try to direct your stubborn course. I use the word stubborn advisedly. At five you were a pigheaded mite, who followed your own sweet will, whether it got you into difficulties or not, and at twenty-five you are just as bad. Faithful are the wounds of a friend, my dear. I want you to give less of your sympathy, your smiles, and your time to the near-sighted preacher.

Platonic love does exist in this weary old world, and a sweet and true thing it is. Some of the most beautiful friendships I know of are between men and women. For myself I like a man friend best, and if I were wrecked on a desert island would rather any day find a Friday than a Mrs. Friday. This is between ourselves; am telling it you to prove that I'm no mean prude, with a born distrust of human nature, but a sensible, large-minded woman.

You are too young and pretty to do well at the platonic business. I do not care how many maternal airs you give yourself, or how goody-goody he is, you are going to get into trouble. He may be as harmless as a dove, and you as wise as a serpent, but all the same you will find he will get to think too much of you, or you will get to think too much of him, or, worse still, both of you will get sentimental.

Let the parson go to the appreciative Nadine for smiles and sympathy. Remember friendship belongs to the old; love to the young. If a girl desires to be the near and dear friend of some man not related to her, she had best pick on one twenty years her senior. I know men and women, you dear big baby, and I tell you in confidence, that the average woman has no business writing her letters till she's fifty, and the average man has no business trying to establish platonic relations between a pretty girl and himself till he's too old to notice whether her eyes are brown or blue — and dear only knows how old that is.

Of course, you'll gang your ain gait; you've a wonderful opinion of your powers of discretion, but don't forget there are a few things one can't learn in a university.

Augustus is still attentive to the girl who visited his sister; it is just possible that he may be in earnest. Do you know that you are a careless and perverse person? Your dearest Kate writes you that she intends celebrating her wooden wedding early in April, and asks your counsel, and on the very last day of April you answer. If this is to be a genius, I thank heaven I'm not one.

And such counsel! Rustic furniture — as though such things could be gotten for love or money in this old-fashioned town. Don the gown I wore on my wedding day, five years ago — don it, forsooth! Easier said than done. I tried my best to get into it, but couldn't, and Dick had to come and help me out of it. He laughed so hard I lost my temper and bundled it and its ribbons and ruffles back into the closet in a hurry. This is only a scrap of a letter; we are in the throes of housecleaning. But do not pay heed to what it contains, Eunice, and be as sensible as you conveniently can. Yours, with lots of love,

KATE DEMING.

P.S. — Who and what is Prof. McDill? He had almost slipped my mind. By the way, did you get the little book, "Ministering Marthas," which Aunt Lydia sent you? She is anxious to know.

K.D.

〜

ELMDALE AVENUE, June 6th.

MY DEAR, — It's good to be alive in June, isn't it? The lilacs are rioting in the garden, the two big apple trees at the back of the house are pink and white, the jessamine at my window is full of tiny flowers, the tall chestnut beside the gate tosses up its white plumes proudly, and the breeze smells like something escaped from the hug of a sweetbriar. I believe God never looks on the world in June without being glad that he created it.

But you'll be telling me again that I write a poor letter. There is nothing of interest to some people but personalities. Why doesn't she begin and tell everything about the Rev. John Hobson, you are saying? I don't care to tell about him. The truth is, he wasn't the sort of man I should have chosen for a friend. He got foolish notions in his head, and — and, well he behaved badly. It was some weeks ago. We had been reading Browning's "By the Fireside," together in the back parlour. I thought I would talk to him of Nadine, and, as a beginning, remarked that a preacher held a responsible position.

"Yes, oh yes, there isn't a doubt of it," he admitted.

"You know how heartily I sympathise with you." He looked pleased.

"Don't you think," I said insinuatingly, "that if a minister marries he widens his influence?"

"I'm certain of it," he said; "it is his bounden duty to take a wife." ·

"Then, John Hobson," said I, soberly enough, "why don't you do your duty?"

"Because," bashfully, "you've always seemed so against it."

"Indeed, you are much mistaken," I began, and was going to tell him that I knew of a dear girl who would make him an excellent helpmate, but he got hold of my hand, and — if you laugh, Kate Deming I'll never forgive you, never — proposed to me. I never was more disappointed in a person in my life.

Of course our delightful friendship is at an end. I don't mind owning to you that I missed him dreadfully, but I've gotten over it. A woman has to love a man or hate him to give him a prominent place in her thoughts. He seemed lonely for a time, but Nadine took him in hand. He will do his duty.

Am I convinced that platonic affection is a snare and a delusion? Certainly not. One swallow does not make a summer, nor one failure the end of an undertaking. My slim, near-sighted preacher is not of the stuff of which platonic friends are made — he is susceptible — and romantic. Then his imagination is big — he fancied himself in love with me, nothing more.

Prof. McDill will not fail me. He makes a delightful friend. Who and what is he? He is a big, homely fellow who knows all about the stars, and several things — wise and good. He is also the happy husband of a very clever woman who writes and lectures on heredity, and physical culture, etc., the kind that Augustus admires. I thought many times of your steadfast old cousin when the preacher upset my plans so rudely. Old friends are best after all, dear. What comfort-loving king used to call for his old shoes because they were easiest on his feet? There is something rather pathetic about it. Poke fun at me if you choose, I am still your candid

EUNICE.

KENTOWN, July 10th.

POOR OLD GIRL, — You must be in a bad way when you find something pathetic in the fact of gouty King James calling for his old footwear. Pack your trunk and shake the dust off your shoes at that broken reed (a happy comparison), John Hobson; the professor with the wonderful wife, and all the rest of it, and come home on a visit. You think that bit of a garden on Elmdale Avenue something to brag of on a June day, but you should see the wheat fields, and corn fields and meadows about Kentown, now that midsummer is at hand — to say nothing of the orchards where the early peaches are getting a blush on them, and the early apples a perfume so inviting that 'tis no wonder the small boy succumbs to the temptation of plucking. Come on. Leave all your ponderous tomes behind you and revel in such delicate mental fare as we get at the public library.

I haven't said "I told you so" once; all the same I warned you how things would turn out. You haven't had lesson enough, eh? You must needs begin all over again. And this time it is worse — a man with a wife. She will be giving some private lectures before long, I am thinking, this woman who knows all about heredity and physical culture. Of course she has a lot to attend to, and leaves the wise, good professor to get along the best way he can; but she won't relish your interest in him for all that. It is the woman who treats her husband like a dog who resents it most when some other woman takes any notice of him. If I could only teach you a little worldly wisdom! The idea of a nice girl like you turning up her nose at marriage — flouting all love that is not platonic, and making herself ridiculous generally. But I must stop lecturing or you will be exclaiming "Save, save, oh! save me from the candid friend."

Dick has the toothache. He had typhoid fever a year ago, and didn't make half the fuss. I want him to get it out, but he has a dozen excuses. The truth is he is afraid — nearly all big men are cowards — the bigger the man the bigger the coward. Aunt Lydia desires to be remembered to you. She talks continually these days of my worthy uncle's political career. Don't ask me what he has done, for beyond the fact that he spends quite a lot of money having a good time in Ottawa, I know of nothing. Your faithful

KATE.

P.S. — Aunt Lydia and I went for a walk yesterday, and came on Augustus and Jenny Dole — the girl I told you of — leaning over the bridge spanning our river (call it creek if you dare) listening to the frogs, as happy as you please.

"How gallant he has grown!" whispered Aunt Lydia; "he is in earnest, I doubt not."

But I told her one never could tell, seeing that conscience has no more to do with such philandering than it has with politics. Whereat Aunt Lydia, thinking I was quoting my own sentiments instead of some philosopher's, remarked that "I ought to be ashamed of myself," and my uncle a member.

K.D.

✺

ELMDALE, October 22nd, 1904.

MY DEAR KATE, — I promised you the whole truth, and nothing but the truth, so at whatever cost to my pride — but let me begin at the beginning. I came back from my long visit with you feeling that I had been having an idle, pleasant time of it long enough, that I should get to work and do something. I would write a book. Prof. McDill was much interested, and it ended in our forming a partnership.

He knew so many things that I did not that he was invaluable. He was at the house every day, and mother hinted a disapproval, while I paid no heed to it. We progressed at a great rate. I think it was Chapter X we were at when he began to act unlike himself, to be nervous and ill at ease. Now, don't look mortified and begin imagining the professor a gay Lothario. He had no thought of making love, I can assure you. And I believed in him so — he is one of the big, kind-looking men who inspire you with confidence. I used to think what a tower of strength he would be in a time of trouble, and feel so glad because of our friendship. Kate, he proved himself a fraud out and out. I believe what you told me, the bigger the man, the bigger the coward, for when the time came for him to assert himself he daren't say his life was his own.

It was Mrs. McDill. It seems that she made up her mind to put an end to the professor's visits, and set about it so vigorously that he nearly died of fright. He didn't stand up for his rights at all; he simply wilted. He made one last hurried call. The blandness and kindness were gone, he was dreadfully sheepish-looking and uncomfortable.

"But our book," I urged. "Why didn't you reason with her?"

"You don't know her," was all he answered.

I wanted to shake him. "She surely has confidence in you, and —— "

"She hasn't a particle," he interrupted; "and when she forbade me to continue friends with you, what could I do but promise her that it should be as she wished?"

I thought of my book and my big ambition, and grew angry. "You could have been a man; you could have said that our friendship was a pure and wholesome thing and that you would not treat one who had shown you only kindness, discourteously," I answered proudly.

"I'm sorry," he said, without lifting his eyes; "but she's got the notion into her head that you were too — too — well, rather fond of me. Now, Miss Complin" — it had been Eunice for weeks — "I know better, but I can't convince her. She never believes what I say."

And do you know, right there I felt sorry for him,

angry as I was.

"Nonsense," I said impatiently, "she knows very well that I don't care for you in that way. You're hardly the man to capture a girl's fancy. Mrs. McDill ought to remember this. Too fond of you! I think your wife is a horrid woman."

"You are angry; I don't blame you," he said, and got himself away without loss of time.

This is a thousand times worse than the John Hobson affair. I'm almost ready to let somebody else prove the safe and sure delights of love platonic. There still remains Augustus, dear steadfast fellow! His sweethearting — as Aunt Lydia terms it — with Jennie does not take all his time. I get a letter every week. Write, my dear girl, rail at me, say anything you want to. It will be meekly borne by your disheartened

EUNICE.

P.S. — I'll wager Prof. McDill's mother was too big a coward to go to bed in the dark. Heredity, Kate!

⤳

ELMDALE AVE., Dec. 23rd.

MY DEAR KATE, — Am busy, but must send you a Christmas letter. We have been very gay here of late. What with parties and private theatricals and literary gatherings, I've had hardly time to think. The book is still unfinished — have a notion to send it as a Christmas box to the professor. Poor old fellow, still looks frightened when we chance to meet, and hurries along as though he thought the eagle eye of his better half might pierce the distance and detect him bowing. By the way, I was honoured with a call from her a few weeks ago. She came in as friendly as you please, nearly shook my hand off.

"You're looking well, real well. Did you feel vexed when I put an end to the professor's foolish flirtation? Now, don't look cross, it was a flirtation, I don't care what name it went under. I did it for the best. If we sensible people didn't have a care of you foolish ones the world would be upside down in no time. I like you, but I can't allow you to puff the dear old professor up with vanity and foolishness."

She said all this with the greatest air of goodfellowship. I suppose you think I improved the occasion and told her some unpleasant truths. Not a bit of it; I just sat and stared. "I want you," she went on, "to come and hear Doctor Agnes Farr — a power in the social purity movement, my dear — speak on 'Woman as Wife and Mother.' The meeting is for ladies only, and you'll hear something worth remembering. I never like to waste my time; inherited my father's practical disposition; I am like my father."

"Then your father was big, and coarse, and a bully," I said — but I didn't say it until she was gone. Beast!

So Augustus is having the homestead rejuvenated with paint and paper, is he? I think it a dear old place. What happy times we've all had playing hide-and-seek among the hollyhocks and building play-houses under the maples! It is lovely of you to want me to go down for Christmas, but I can't do it; will go in time for your wedding anniversary in April. I mustn't forget to tell you that we have an invitation to attend the nuptials of the preacher and Nadine Ghant. What do you mean, Kate Deming, by asserting that I have failed in my quest, and had better abandon it? Have I not Augustus still? There is no danger that he will want to wed me any more than he will turn coward and forsake me. I like a man who is always the same, don't you? Aunt Lydia, of course, will be pleased at the idea of his marrying Jennie. She used to be mortally afraid he would marry me. With oceans of love, and wishes for a Merry Xmas. Yours lovingly,

EUNICE.

KENTOWN, Jan. 1st, 1905.

MY DEAR EUNICE, — Am I not beginning the year in a right and proper manner? All sorts of good wishes, darling — happiness, peace and prosperity be yours during the next twelve months. We had a quiet Christmas at home, Dick and I, and kept regretting your absence. Come down in April, by all means, but there will be no wedding party this year. The very next festal occasion will be a — oh, Eunice! You think no one can keep a secret but yourself — christening! Think of it! How I laughed at your account of Mrs. McDill's visit! The professor's punishment is heavy enough; he has to live with her. If I were you, Eunice Complin, B.A., I would resolve on this New Year to throw away some very silly, nonsensical ideas and get sensible ones in their place. The common, old-fashioned love is good enough for you or any other woman. It's discouraging to think that at twenty-six you are such a fool. You wouldn't have Augustus for a lover, and so his feelings simmered down to friendships. You two will never marry now, for I've noticed one thing; you can, if you manage rightly, turn your lover into a friend; but when you have accomplished it, nothing short of a miracle will turn him back into a lover again. Heigho! I was right about the preacher, and about McDill. You'll find I'm right about Augustus. Thanks, dear, for the Christmas box, centre-pieces and doylies are beautiful. All my acquaintances are envious — what more could a mortal desire? Your wise and loving ·

KATE.

P.S. — Forgot to tell you that Augustus is away spending New Year's with the Doles. He will come back engaged to Jennie it is more than likely.

ELMDALE AVE., Jan. — .

DEAR KATE, — I don't like people who know everything and never make mistakes; they are so important and
aggravating. This doesn't mean you for you don't know
everything, and you do make mistakes. For once you can't
say, "I told you so." Oh, wise little woman! Augustus is
engaged but not to Jennie Dole. The wedding will be in
June. He left for Kentown this morning, and I would miss
him dreadfully if I weren't so busy wondering how Aunt
Lydia will bear up under the new trial. So glad about the
secret, dear one.

EUNICE.

KENTOWN, Jan. 8th, 1905.

EUNICE, — If I weren't so fond of you I would lecture
you well for the worry your platonic love affairs have
caused me. I might have known you would not come to
grief; as I remarked some months ago, geniuses are wise —
in streaks. There are a lot of clever and sarcastic things I
could put in this letter, but the truth is I'm so tickled I
haven't the heart. Dick and I send our united blessing.
Your happy

KATE.

Canadian Magazine 26 (Dec. 1905): 154–161.

Marjorie Pickthall (1883–1922)

ON ILE DE PARADIS (1906)

In the first two decades of the century, Marjorie Pickthall was hailed by Canadian critics as a writer of great promise in the romantic vein. She was born in Gunnersby, Middlesex, England, the only child of Helen Mallard and Arthur C. Pickthall, an engineer. An intelligent, frail and rather solitary child, she emigrated to Toronto with her parents in 1889, where she was educated at Bishop Strachan School. Her literary, musical and artistic affinities were evident from childhood: she won a Toronto *Mail and Empire* literary contest in December 1899 for a short story and a poem. The award helped to bring her the support of such influential critics and academics as Professor Pelham Edgar of Victoria College, University of Toronto, and Sir Andrew Macphail of *University Magazine*, men who saw themselves as her mentors and protectors. She appreciated their help, but kept a wry and ironic perspective on their image of her as a delicate, unworldly "poetess."

Pickthall's poems and stories were well received, and her scores of stories appeared in such prestigious periodicals as *Atlantic Monthly* and *Scribner's*. After the death of her beloved mother in 1910, she suffered a nervous collapse and was unable to write for a time. She worked as a library assistant at Victoria College between 1910 and 1912. She then sailed for England in search of health and financial self-sufficiency as a writer. She spent the next seven years in England, summering at Bowerchalke Cottage near Salisbury with a cousin, writing and enjoying the closeness to nature, always important to her. At the onset of the war, she undertook war work, first training as an ambulance driver, then labouring as an agricultural worker and as an office clerk, but her health was unequal to such tasks. In 1920, she returned to Canada. She spent the first summer with her friend, the writer Isabel Ecclestone Mackay, in British Columbia. She lived at various locations in and around Victoria and Vancouver until her death of an embolism after surgery on 19 April 1922.

As Lorne Pierce has pointed out, Pickthall's stories are frequently narratives of adventure set in exotic locales which deal with quest or pursuit, and are coloured by her reading of Conrad and Kipling. "On Ile de Paradis," with its Conradian atmosphere, is no exception. Pickthall often created male protagonists, possibly in reaction to her own musings on femininity, crystallized in a 1919 letter to a friend:

> To me the trying part is being a woman at all. I've come to the ultimate conclusion that I'm a misfit of the worst kind, in spite of a superficial femininity — emotion with a foreknowledge of impermanence, a daring mind with only the tongue as an outlet, a greed for experience plus a slavery to convention — what the deuce are you to make of that? — as a woman? As a man, you could go ahead and stir things up *fine*.

As a short fiction writer, Pickthall delighted in the depiction of states of mind and in the evocation of the subtle, delicate or dramatic details of nature for atmosphere. "On Ile de Paradis" is a good example of her predilection for symbolic action, here the struggles of the soul in a wilderness setting. The male tenderfoot is vulnerable and doomed, one "to whom the woods played step-mother." Feminist critics have remarked on the affinity of women writers for a physically or mentally afflicted male protagonist, perhaps as a mirror of the afflictions and restrictions of female gender.

෴

Suggested Reading
Pickthall, Marjorie. "The Rock and the Pool," *Atlantic Monthly* 3 (March 1913): 430–431.
——. *Angels' Shoes and Other Stories* (London: Hodder, 1923).
Pierce, Lorne. *Marjorie Pickthall: A Book of Remembrance* (Toronto: Ryerson, 1925).

On Ile de Paradis

Marjorie Pickthall

"The wilderness," says Antoine with a shrug, "is a sister to those who seek her in comradeship, a mother to those who seek her in sorrow, but a step-mother to those who seek her in ignorance."

That is the Reverend Antoine MacMurray's way of putting things. He had it from his mother, a Frenchwoman, together with his Christian name, his soft heart, and his skill in cookery. From his father he got an uncompromising conscience and an iron will. The result of these two conflicting strains in one nature is sometimes peculiar. He gives peppermint balls to the children to keep them quiet during the sermon, and is much distressed because all the Henris and Picauds and Pierres of his scattered flock call him Père Antoine. He is strong on the sins of the Laodiceans, and tells fairy tales to the little Jeannes and Douglases o' Sundays.

"The wilderness is a step-mother to the ignorant," says Père Antoine. "I learned that on Ile de Paradis many years ago."

Ile de Paradis is not unknown to fame in its own land. It is a big rock set among brawling rapids in Rivière de Paradis, producing balsams, berry-bushes and bears in season.

"It is also full of caves," says the Reverend Antoine MacMurray, "and there is a daft tale about a loup-garou that runs whining through interminable wet caverns. Ouh! it is a queer place, not quite canny. I was near believing in that loup-garou — once." It befell some ten or twelve years ago. Antoine was preaching one Sunday at New Edinborough, a score of little shanties, redolent of balsam, dropped down among the hills near Rivière de Paradis. To be precise, it was a mile from the river and some twelve miles above Ile de Paradis. On the other side of the river was Allansville, seven miles away, hidden in the lumber country. To Antoine, smoking at ease with Factor Macgillicuddy of the H.B.C. post at New Edinborough, came a wet and incoherent messenger from Allansville. Picaud Le Soldat had been crushed by a falling branch — no, no carelessness, all in the day's work — and now lay sick to death, craving for Père Antoine.

"Cosh me!" cried the Reverend Antoine fiercely, "has the man none of his own faith to send to? D'ye think I'll put my finger in everyone's pie? Careless, idle, reckless — Give me some more brandy in the flask, Factor. Eh! poor lad, poor lad! Only a year married, they tell me. Yes, I'm ready. How's the river?"

The messenger, a tall, wild lad, three-parts Indian, flung out his hands in an expressive gesture. It was April. What might be expected of the river? "The snow melts in the hills," said he, "and the river runs flood-full. It is thick with old trees and logs and mud from the hills."

"Well," quoth the Reverend Antoine, "if you can get across, so can I."

It was one of those riotous April evenings of which there are many up north. The sky was dark with the threat of rain, the wind sang across the woods as if driven by an excess of life. And the river, when the two men reached it, was a sullen flood, brown, foam-flecked, full of dead branches and all the rubbish of a winter, having strong sucking eddies where the banks were caving in.

But they embarked. O yes, they embarked in a little leaky birchbark canoe! Each took a paddle. And then the roaring river whirled them away.

They intended to strike a landing place somewhere within a mile or so, working over on a long slant. But instead, a careering log struck them amidships. The messenger from Allansville fell into the water, and after a little buffeting, the flood tossed him ashore with a broken arm. But the Reverend Antoine was sucked down and drawn under and driven on. Strange pains and fires flashed through his head. "It's all up wi' me," he thought; "now I may as well say a Psalm for the good o' my soul." But he could think of none but the forty-second, "which," he explained, "in that situation, was irony."[1] Then he thought of a pair of boots left out to heel in Prescott, the last place of his sojourning. Then he thought of a hole in his grey stockings which the Factor's niece had darned for him with pink wool. And then for a space he thought of nothing.

He came to himself, "struggling with impediments," as he puts it. The impediments were the wet branches of a tree, and to these he clung like a limpet. "Praise the Lord, O my soul," whispered the minister. And after a few long breaths, he managed to lift himself astride the floating tree, and so rode clear above the brown flood.

He felt very weak and dizzy, and he laid himself almost flat on the trunk, gripping it with arms and knees. The brown river roared around him, clots of cold foam were flung in his face, the tree danced and quivered like a match-stick. It was growing quite dark. Every now and then the flying rain-clouds parted to let a glint of stormy moonlight through. "I'll be needing a mackintosh before the morning," thought Antoine vaguely. Then his senses must have gone from him again.

He was shaken back to life by the jar of the tree trunk grounding on rocks. He was tipped off into brawling shoal water, all foam and cutting stones, and here he struggled and clawed for some moments, his mouth and his hands full of sand. Then he felt a firm rock under one foot, clutched desperately at low black branches above his head, and scrambled forward into blessed young grass and briars, where he lay gasping, his head in a muskrat's doorway.

---

[1] Psalm 42 refers to water: "Like as the hart desireth the water brooks."

By-and-by, when breath and life had in some measure returned to him, he picked himself up and looked about. It was quite dark now. He could hear the tree upon which he had ridden grinding in the shoal water. The roaring of the wind and the roaring of the river seemed to make the very rocks quiver. "I wonder where I am?" said the Reverend Antoine.

Behind him, a black bulk of rock and pine stood against the driving gloom of the sky. The roar of rapids came from either side. Truth flashed upon Antoine. "Cosh me!" he exclaimed, "I'm on Ile de Paradis!"

He stood, wet and cold and shivering, considering his position. "Now, it's a matter of four years since I was here," he said, "but it seems as if there ought to be the mouth of a cave somewhere at hand. Now, if I can get a light — "

He felt in his pocket, and pulled out a small and sodden Bible, a copy of the Westminster Confession of Faith, three fish-hooks, a tiny surgical case, and finally, a water-tight box containing matches. He found a resinous pine branch, and succeeded in kindling a torch after infinite trouble. Then he went in search of the cave.

Twice the wet wind descended and blew out the valiant flame. Twice Antoine patiently rekindled it in a sheltered cranny of the rocks. At length he saw the mouth of the cave, a still black void in the tumult. Stepping within, it was like entering a warm haven of rest.

The cave was some seven feet high at the entrance, floored with dry sand, airy but warm. Antoine cast a cautious glance about for signs of bears, but found none. This was satisfactory. He stuck the steadily burning torch in a little cleft, and sat down upon the dry sand to gather his wits.

"I may have to stay here four, even five days," he said ruefully. "I wonder what happened to Picaud's messenger? I don't expect he was drowned, for a half-breed has as many lives as a cat. Poor Picaud! Well, I did my best. We're all in the hands o' the Lord. Five days on Ile de Paradis! 'Tis no picnic. How's the commissariat?"

He felt in another pocket, and pulled out a little

Marjorie Pickthall

parcel containing half-a-dozen sandwiches wrapped in oiled paper, which the Factor's niece had put there. "Good lass," he said, "they may be the saving of me." The flask of brandy had dropped to the bottom of the river. "However, there's a-plenty of water," sighed the Reverend Antoine.

Upon a flat stone he laid out his property to dry — the sandwiches, the Bible, the Westminster Confession, the fish-hooks, and the surgical case. "They'll come to look for my body when the river goes down a bit," he thought contentedly, and leaned back against the side of the cave, up which the sand had drifted in a grateful incline. The tumult without sounded softened to his ears.

He declares he only closed his eyes for a moment. Anyhow, whatever space of time had passed, he opened them again very suddenly. The long torch was still burning, flaring with resin like a gas jet. And for the flash of a second, it shone upon a pair of eyes, watching the Reverend Antoine from where the cave narrowed down into the darkness of unexplored passages. Then the flare sank down smokily, and the eyes vanished.

"Cosh me!" exclaimed the Reverend Antoine, as well as he could for a sudden unreasonable tightening of the throat. He sat upright and stared at the dark shadows. The Scotch side of him thought wistfully of a rifle and bear-steaks. The French side, perhaps shaken uppermost by the stress of the night, recollected, with lavish detail, the story of the loup-garou. There was a conflict in his soul, and he departed suddenly in quest of more wood.

The brown river still roared down in spate from the hills, and the rapids sang with innumerable voices. The great wind had blown the sky clear, and the April moon shone brightly in the west. The Reverend Antoine succeeded in finding an armful of burnable wood, and with this he returned to the cave.

When a good fire was crackling between himself and the shadowed passage, the cave had a very prosaic appearance. Antoine's Scottish side began to assert itself. A bullet was the best thing to send between eyes which gleamed at people from unknown caverns. Supposing now —

He glanced at the darkness which still hung heavily beyond the little fire. And there were the eyes again, the eyes belonging to some vague shape whose outlines the fire did more to hide than show.

"Lord preserve 's from all evil!" cried the minister in the strongest voice he could command. He said afterwards that he was almost too frightened to breathe. There was something so weird in the silent appearance of those eyes, shining with a little greenish flicker in the firelight, and then disappearing. Nevertheless, he snatched a flaming pine root and hurled it at the shadow that crouched among the shadows at the end of the cave. The brand whirled and fell, hissing. The thing, whatever it was, whined and fled. There was a scrambling and clattering of loose pebbles in the darkness, and then silence, save for the many-voiced thunder of the rapids.

"It's a bear," murmured Antoine the Scot; "what could it be *but* a bear? If I had a gun and a bullet or so — "

"Maybe a silver bullet," thought Antoine the habitant, with a chilly sensation at the roots of the hair. The minister spent the hour or so before the dawn in sitting bolt upright behind the fire, imagining inexplicable eyes at every point of the compass. But with the dawn his shaken nerves steadied, and he ate a ham sandwich.

Day came in a translucent flood of infinitely tender green and gold and blue, outpoured behind the ramparts of the hills. Light flashed into the cave, light, blessed daughter of Life, victorious, recreating. And with the light, the Thing came again.

Antoine heard it in the passage, heard it shuffling upon the rocks, heard the tchink-tink of disturbed quartz-pebbles. Then it came into view, slinking furtively in the shadows, dumb, infinitely pitiful. Antoine raised his hands as if to ward it off, shaken for the moment from all semblance of courage.

For the Thing had been a man . . .

"Unclothed, scarred, worn to an incredible leanness, there was nothing human about this Thing from the caves of the rocks, except that unappeasable loneliness of the

MARJORIE PICKTHALL

eyes. Understand me, they were human eyes only in so far as they were more wretched, more vacant, than the eyes of any beast. This who had been a man, had lost everything. He was not mad in any popular sense of the term, but he had lost everything. . . . I never learnt the whole story. But he had been ignorant. And that step-mother, the wilderness, had brought him to this pass." Thus the Reverend Antoine in after days.

"At the time, I remember I felt more afraid of him, poor creature, than if he had been the veriest loup-garou that ever scared a voyageur. It is so terrible to see the empty house of the spirit which the Lord breathed into man. It is worse than a wrecked church. But pity will conquer horror. And I held out my hand to — to that which had been a man, and spoke to him evenly and kindly, as one might speak to a stray pup. And he came to me — came to me, away from the loneliness that had encompassed him and destroyed. He came, and crouched at my feet, and clawed at my hands with some hideous travesty of shaking them. My wits had come home to roost by then, like a string o' frightened fowls. And I wrapped him in my coat, and gave him a ham sandwich." . . .

"For two days I was there on Ile de Paradis with that shadow of humanity. There was less to him, less character, less nature, than there is to a beast. He felt neither love nor hate, neither joy nor sorrow, nothing but terror if he lost sight of me, and hunger. When he was hungry, he grubbed for roots and 'guddled' for fish in the pools. I suppose he had done this before he — lost everything. He gave me all I liked to take of his roots and fish, and he preferred those I cooked for him to the raw. Beyond that, he felt nothing, was concerned with nothing. He would sit awake all night, staring into the darkness, and shuddering. By day he would sleep sometimes in the sunshine, jerking all over. He had no speech, no thoughts, nothing but two or three dim memories or inclinations, and this overmastering fear of being alone. The wilds had taken from him everything else.

"For two days I was there alone with him. Then I

saw a canoe coming down stream, with Buck Terry and Lucien Le Soldat in it. They saw the signal smoke I had kept burning, and made for the island, shouting. The flood had gone down a little, but it was a risk.

"When they leapt ashore, and Terry caught my hands, and Lucien held me in his arms, I think I must have cried . . . My — my companion was not frightened as I feared he would be. He only looked at them, with a dim expression of pleasure that there were two more between him and the loneliness. Nor did Buck and Lucien feel much of the horror that I had felt. Buck swore, and Lucien crossed himself — for which I forgot to rebuke them. And then they laid him in the bottom of the big canoe, where presently he went to sleep, twitching like a dog. Then they helped me in, for I was weaker than I had thought, and we began our journey back.

"It was slow work. We only made seven miles up stream before night. So we camped on the bank. *He* sat at the foot of a tree, staring and shivering till morning. And I told Terry and Lucien everything I knew or could guess. But, first they told me that there was hope for Picaud, after all.

"'Without doubt,' said Lucien, when I had finished my story, 'without doubt, he was a tenderfoot. And the woods have not been kind to him, mon Dieu!' 'I mind something,' said Buck Terry, 'of a tenderfoot that started from Fort St. Henri in February, early February. And he was heard of no more. He would take no guide. P'raps this is him.' Perhaps it was, but there was nothing by which we might identify him. Nothing. It was all lost.

"But we suppose that he started off in some such fashion, and got lost, and then his brain went. Brains fail so easily, so easily, in the wilds. It is all perfectly simple, perfectly explicable, perfectly horrible. To Terry and Lucien, it was almost commonplace.

"'Some of 'em gets over it, and some of 'em don't,' said Terry to me; 'this 'un won't.'

"He did not. He never recovered feeling, speech, or thought. We went to Allansville, and there they cossetted me up for a few days, and then I came round, and helped nurse Picaud back to life. But he to whom the woods had played step-mother, he sat and shivered at the darkness, or slept in the sun, or ate what was given him. I had the fancy that his soul must be somewhere wandering in the woods, looking for its lost house. Men came to see him, hoping or fearing to identify him with lost relations or friends of their own, but they never did. He remained, unclaimed flotsam of the wilderness, and at the end of the summer he died."

～

Canadian Magazine 26 (March 1906): 417–421.

E. Pauline Johnson (Tekahionwake) (1861–1913)

THE HAUNTING THAW (1907)

Emily Pauline Johnson was born in 1861 on the Six Nations Reserve, near Brantford, Ontario. A status Indian, the younger daughter of George Henry Martin Johnson, a Mohawk chief of distinguished lineage, and of Emily Howells, an Englishwoman and sister-in-law of an Anglican minister on the reserve, her heritage shaped her life and her art. Pauline Johnson was educated at home, the imposing "Chiefswood" built by her father for his bride. She later attended a native day school and Brantford Collegiate (1877–79). After the death in 1884 of her father, an activist in Indian social issues of the day, the twenty-two-year-old Pauline, her mother and her older sister were compelled to move to cheaper lodgings in Brantford.

In 1885, Pauline, whose literary interests had been fostered in her parents' extensive library, published her first poem in *Gems of Poetry* (New York). She became a frequent contributor of lyrics to the *Week*. She also wrote sketches for the London *Express* at this time. In 1892, she participated in a poetry reading in Toronto, the point of departure for a successful — but gruelling and financially uncertain — life as "The Mohawk Princess" on recital tours between 1892 and 1909. During performances in Canada, London and the United States, she was a striking and dramatic figure in ceremonial dress; her Indian poetry won the praise of English critic Theodore Watts-Dunton. In 1895, *White Wampum*, her first book of poetry, appeared as the result of an introduction by Canadian novelist Sir Gilbert Parker to the London publisher John Lane during her first visit to England. When ill-health prompted her to give up touring in 1909, she moved to Vancouver. There, through a friendship with the Squamish chief Joe Capilano, she absorbed and transcribed versions of traditional Indian legends, an expression of her concern that even the aboriginal peoples themselves were losing touch with traditional lore. The result was *Legends of Vancouver* (1911). Pauline usually added the signature "Tekahionwake" ("Double Wampum") to her name on literary works, in order to emphasize her aboriginal heritage: the name had been that of her famous ancestor, Chief Smoke Johnson, a hero of the War of 1812. She saw herself as a spokesperson for her people and told the writer Ernest Thompson Seton: "There are those who think they pay me a compliment in saying I am just like a white woman. My aim, my joy, my pride is to sing the glories of my own people." She died in Vancouver of cancer in 1913, and her ashes are buried in Stanley Park.

Pauline Johnson was known primarily as a poet and recitalist, but her stories were also well received. Betty Keller, her biographer, described the genesis of "The Haunting Thaw" in 1904 during one of Pauline Johnson's arduous national tours with her collaborator Walter McRaye:

> In Edmonton on 23 May the last patches of snow still littered the streets when Pauline and McRaye watched an exhausted dog train struggling into town, its sled runners grinding on bare ground more often than on snow. Later that day Pauline showed McRaye the rough version of a new poem which would be called "Train Dogs." A few days later, the same incident became the basis of her short story "The Haunting Thaw."

Like many of her stories — for example, "A Red Girl's Reasoning" (1893), in which a Metis girl rejects her husband when he questions the validity of her parents' native marriage ceremony — "The Haunting Thaw" asserts the dignity and equality of native peoples. The valorization of a native partner in the fur trade is echoed in recent historical scholarship, which has focused on the competency and drive of native involvement in the fur trade. The depiction of nature as a psychic force in "The Haunting Thaw" finds echoes in Pickthall's "On Ile de Paradis" and Susan Jones's "The Frenchwoman's Son."

Suggested Reading

Johnson, E. Pauline. *Legends of Vancouver* (Toronto: McClelland and Stewart, 1911).

Keller, Betty. *Pauline* (Vancouver: Douglas and McIntyre, 1981).

The Haunting Thaw

E. Pauline Johnson (Tekahionwake)

For three minutes the trader had been peering keenly at the sky. Then his eyes lowered, sweeping the horizon with a sharp discernment that would not admit of self-deception.

"Peter!" he called.

Peter Blackhawk came to the door, though he only came to that insistent voice when it suited him.

"Peter," repeated the trader crisply, yet with something of deference in his tone, "we can't wait another hour for Louis. He should have been here with that pack of stone-marten a week ago. There is a thaw threatening and we can't wait." Then almost pleadingly: "Can we, Peter?"

"No, Mr. McKenzie. I am afraid it will be hard to make Edmonton as it is," answered the Indian.

"You have *got to* make Edmonton, or you and I will lose two thousand dollars apiece. Do you know that, Peter?"

The words *got to* lacked the tone of authority. The trader could never bully this Indian.

"Then I'll make it," acquiesced Peter, with the pleasantness born of independence. "The dogs are fit, and I have got the mink and beaver ready, and a few ——"

"How many mink skins?" demanded the trader.

"Sixteen hundred."

"Not bad, not bad. They're the primest skins that ever went out of the north, and the price gone up sky-high. Not a bad pack, Peter."

The strain on the trader's face relaxed. "But we must get them to the market, or they're fur, just plain fur, not money."

The Indian scanned the horizon. "I'll start in an hour, if you say don't wait for Louis and the stone-marten."

"Then don't wait for Louis and his d —— d stone-marten," jerked the trader, and turned on his heel with a curse at the threatening thaw.

Within the hour Mr. McKenzie was shaking hands with the Indian.

"Got everything, Peter?" he asked genially, now that the dog-train was really off. "Everything? Plenty of Muck-a-muck, tobac, dog-fish, matches, everything?"

"Everything," said Peter Blackhawk, knotting his scarlet sash about the waist of his buffalo coat. "Plenty of everything but time." He shook his head gravely. "I'm starting too late in the season, I will have to work them too hard," he added, turning towards the dogs, which were plaintively yapping to be away, their noses raised snuffing into the wind, the chime of their saddle bells responding to every impatient twist of their wolfish bodies. Another hitch to the scarlet sash, an alert, quick glance at huskies and pack-sled, then — "Good-bye, Mr. McKenzie."

"Good-bye, Peter, my boy."

The red and the white palms met and the dog-train hit the trail.

An hour later the trader came to the door and looked out. Far against the southern horizon a black speck blurred the monotonous sweep of snows and sky. "He'll make it all right," he assured himself. "He'll beat the thaw if any one can. But, d — m him, he wouldn't have gone if he didn't want to. You can't boss those Iroquois."

Swinging into the southward trail towards the rim of civilisation, Peter Blackhawk was saying to himself, "I'll beat the thaw if any one can; but I wouldn't have come if I didn't want to. Those d——d traders can't boss an Iroquois," which only goes to show that absolute harmony existed between those two men, trader and train-dog driver though they were.

Blackhawk had come from the far east with three score of his tribesmen on the first Red River Expedition. Voyageurs they were of a rare and desirable type, hardy, energetic, lithe, indomitable, as distinct from the western tribes as the poles from the tropics. Few of them had returned with Wolseley. The lure of the buffalo chase proved stronger than the call of their cradle lands. In the northern foothills they made their great camps, mixing with no other people, the exclusive, conservative habits of their forefathers still strong upon them. And young Blackhawk had grown into manhood, learned in the wisdom of the great Six Nations Indians of the east, and in the acquired craft and cult of the native-born plainsman of the west. McKenzie considered him the most valuable man, white or red, in all the Northwest Territories.

～

The third night out something disturbed Blackhawk in his sleep, and his head burrowed up from his sleeping bag. It was the heavy hour before dawn. The dogs lay sleeping, exhausted by their over-mileage of the previous day. The gray-white night lay around, soundless, motionless. What had awakened Blackhawk? His tense ears seemed to acquire sight as well as hearing. Then across his senses came the nearing doom — the honk, honk of wild geese V-ing their way along the shadow trail of the night sky. He heard the rush of their wings above, then again their heralding honk as they waned into the north. They were the death-knell of winter. Blackhawk whistled to his dogs.

"Soft snow after sunrise, boys," he said aloud, after the manner of men who face the trail without human companionship. "We must travel at night after this, when sundown means hard surfaces."

The dogs stretched sulkily. They devoured their fish, while the man brewed coffee of cognac strength to fortify himself against limited sleep and increased action.

When the sun looked up above the rim of the white

E. PAULINE JOHNSON

north, its gold was warm as well as dazzling. The snow ceased to drift under the keen night wind. The hummocks grew packed and sodden. The dogs slipped in their even trot, their feet wet and their flanks sweating. Peter put up his whip and prepared to stay until nightfall. He could not deceive himself. The snow was going and Edmonton dozens of leagues away! But with sunset the biting frost returned. The south outstretched before him, smooth, glassy, frozen hard; it was the hour of action for man and beast. Again the north became draped with an inverted crescent of silvery fringes that trembled into delicate pink, deep rose, inflammable crimson, and finally shifting into a poisonous purple, with high lights of cold, freezing cold, blue.

"God's lanterns," whispered Peter. "He must mean me to make Edmonton. I cannot miss the trail with those northern lights ablaze."

And night after night it was so, until one morning came a soft, feathery Chinook wind, the first real proclamation that spring was at his heels. That day gray geese in numberless flocks fishtailed the sky. As Blackhawk passed each succeeding slough, scores of brown muskrats crouched in the sunshine on the thin ice at the doors of their humped-up houses.

That night for the first time the Indian lashed the dogs, feeling in his heart the lash of his partner's tongue. Again hanging in the north were "God's lanterns," but the invisible spirit of the coming thaw urged him on like a whip. At night he could feel its fingers clutching at the sled, balking its speed. He could see its shadowy presence ahead in the trail obstructing the course of the dogs, weighting their feet with its leaden warmth. It began to trail beside him, to mock and jeer at him, to speed neck and neck with him hour after hour. In the day-time it outstripped him, throwing up uncovered tufts of grass and black earth in the trail, so that the sled could not carry and the dogs almost bleated like sheep in their exhaustion. At night he distanced it flying across the newly-frozen crusty snow and sloughs.

But the haunting thaw was on his track, coming nearer and nearer now even in the night time. It was tracing lines on his forehead, painting worry in his eyes. It was thinning the limbs and emptying the bellies of his dogs. It was whispering, then speaking, then shouting the word "Failure" at him. And that night a thin sickle of moon was born with its frequent change of weather. Snow fell, spongy, wet stuff. Once more the dog-train made time, and late the next afternoon, up the slush and mud of the main street in Edmonton trudged a weary-footed Indian, the sole alert thing about him being the shrewd bright eyes that snapped something of triumph to the casual greetings of acquaintances. At his heels lagged a train of four huskie dogs, cadaverous, inert, spent, their red tongues dripping, their sides palpitating, dragging the fur pack as if it were a load of lead.

But when the great fur-buyer greeted Blackhawk with a thousand questions, Peter had but four words to say, and he said them fifty times that night: "I beat the thaw."

And when the sickle moon arose, round and ripened, Peter turned his back on the southern trail, facing once more God's lanterns of the north. This time the dogs trotted free of burden, and Peter took his ease astride a cayuse which had already begun to shed the long ragged coat it had grown for self-protection against the winter cold, leaving but the rich dark fuzz beneath, soon to be bleached buckskin colour by the hot Alberta sunshine. The little people of the prairies were thinking of spring garments; the rabbit and weasel were discarding their snowy coats for jackets of russet; the white owl was abandoning his ermine robe, calling through the night for darker, obscuring feathers; the wary lynx, which had grown huge, mat-like snowshoes of fur about his feet last November, was replacing these articles, useful only for winter prowling, with his usual summer footwear of soft, silent padding.

E. Pauline Johnson

~

For the third time that day Trader McKenzie came to the door and looked out. Then once more far against the southern horizon, a black speck blurred the monotonous sweep of prairie grass and sky.

"Peter," he yelled, and taking a key from his leathern fob, unlocked a door that swung clear of the wall. From behind it he took a black bottle, ripped off the capsule, pulled the cork and set it on the table with two large horn cups.

They did not say much as they met and clasped hands, palm to palm, red and white. But McKenzie spoke: "Did you beat the thaw?"

"Beat it by driving like hell. Sold every pelt at the top-notch price — here's the credit."

For an instant the two men eyed the paper with a gratification utterly devoid of greed. Then the Scot's hand reached for the bottle.

The horn cups were spilling full as each man raised one to his lips.

Then McKenzie said with some emotion: "Bully for you, Peter. Here's ho!"

"Ho," said Peter.

~

Canadian Magazine 29 (May 1907): 20–22.

Mabel Burkholder (1881–1973)

THE HEART OF KERRY (1907)

The work of Mabel Burkholder, writer, journalist and local
historian, shows her deep engagement with Hamilton, the
city where she spent her life. She was born on Hamilton
Mountain on 15 March 1881, the third of four daughters of
Peter Burkholder, Jr. and Dinah Anne Street, his second
wife. Her father, a grandson of one of the area's original settlers, was wont to praise his overwhelmingly female brood
(six daughters, one son) with the comment: "There isn't
much *my* girls can't do." Mabel Burkholder's self-reliance
was spurred when the women had to run the farm after her
father's death in 1886. She attended Central Collegiate
School in Hamilton from 1895 to 1899, and subsequently
taught school for two years. She preferred writing, however,
an ambition she began to realize while spending a year in
Denver as companion to an invalid sister. Burkholder remi-
nisced near the end of her long life that she could never picture herself "as a homebody mending pants and washing and
ironing." She contributed fiction to *Onward*, a leading
Toronto Methodist Sunday School publication, and also
wrote plays on biblical themes for church performance. In
1913, she joined the Canadian Women's Press Club, and
later wrote a biographical sketch of journalist Kit Coleman
(see page 43), her friend and its first president. By the 1920s,
Mabel Burkholder had begun a long association with the
Hamilton *Spectator*, ultimately contributing a regular column
about local history. She published the successful *The Story of
Hamilton* (1938) and *Out of the Storied Past* (1969).

    "The Heart of Kerry," like Sime's "Munitions!,"
deals with women during the growth of industrialization.
Burkholder wrote her story at a time (1900–1913) when
Hamilton was undergoing an unprecedented surge of immigration and industrialization. Given the activities of such
unions as the Knights of Labor and the American Federation
of Labor, the city was becoming Canada's best example of
a labour-activist, heavy-industry town. As historian, old

settler, and Methodist with something of a social gospel orientation, Burkholder responded in her fiction to the changing urban environment. She published *The Course of Impatience Carningham*, a novel with an industrial milieu, in 1912. Other women writers like J. G. Sime, Nellie McClung and Agnes Maule Machar (who published the novel *Roland Graeme, Knight* in 1892) also dealt with social and labour themes. It was uncommon, however, for the middle-class magazines of the period to address such topics in their fiction. For example, "The Heart of Kerry" appeared in *Canadian Magazine* in 1907; the magazine published only one other story on labour unrest at this time — "The Food Ship" (1915) by Ethel Hamilton Hunter, an anti-strike story set outside Canada.

"The Heart of Kerry" opens "in medias res," plunging us into the plot. The story blends romantic fictional norms (boy miraculously escapes death and gets girl) with some social awareness. As critics like Ellen Moers and Elaine Showalter have pointed out, the fiction of this period often presents the heroine's moral choice (in this case a choice between social responsibility and self-absorbed materialism) in terms of a love choice between two men: here "a champion of the working man" versus a "rich rogue." The hero is ultimately the heroine's moral "master" — her ethical mentor as well as her elocution teacher.

The story employs another motif popular in fiction of the time, that of the performing heroine. A female artist articulates moral choice. In "The Heart of Kerry," the heroine's rendition of a poem to striking workers, rather than to a wealthy gathering, indicates her decision to repudiate the role of social butterfly. This repudiation is central to a type of social feminism also found in the work of Nellie McClung (see page 243) and others. Historian Wayne Roberts has written of such fiction:

> The conversion of all these heroines demonstrates the magnetism of the new standards being set for women during the turn-of-the-century period. Women were renouncing the frivolity, passivity, subordination, and privatized familial role prescribed for them.

Lady Aberdeen, feminist wife of a governor-general, might have been echoing Burkholder's thinking when she declared in 1893: "[In the upper classes] lies the hope for the country, if they will come forward as a duty, mixing with the working man, fighting their battles, leading them in the right way."

∽

Suggested Reading

Burkholder, Mabel. "His New Chance," *Canadian Magazine* 28 (Jan. 1907): 241–245.

———. *The Course of Impatience Carningham* (Toronto: Musson, 1912).

Hunter, Ethel Hamilton. "The Food Ship," *Canadian Magazine* 45 (Oct. 1915): 526–528.

Morley, William F. E. "Farewell to Clio: A Tribute to Mabel Burkholder the local historian . . .," *Douglas Library [Queen's] Notes* 20 (Feb. 1971): 1–2.

Roberts, Wayne. "'Rocking the Cradle for the World': The New Woman and Maternal Feminism, Toronto, 1877–1914," *Canadian Historical Review* 63, 2 (1982): 15–45.

The Heart of Kerry

Mabel Burkholder

So she dared.

Again he held before his unbelieving eyes the great, green bill whereon her name was flaunted in tall, black letters. Then, while he still struggled with his incredulity, the girl who had dared came in. There was a slightly defiant arch to her proud, black brows, as if she knew that he knew she had dared. Ostentatiously she flung off her gloves, rustled over to the window, and gazed down into the foggy street.

"I thought I should never get here, Mr. Phillips!"

He folded the green bill leisurely. "I was not expecting you," he replied.

"King and Main streets are blocked with an idle, yelling horde. Ugh! They are loathsome, though they are your dear, dear workingmen, Mr. Phillips. How this strike must rejoice your democratic soul!"

He accepted the thrust without a quiver, for a half-turn of her face was revealing a malicious gleam of ivory between the scarlet threads of her lips. She was wilfully misunderstanding him, so he would not take the trouble to explain that he had been holding the street railway men in leash for a month, while he proclaimed from every available platform the advisability of enduring their grievances a little longer, before trying the last, desperate expedient of a strike.

In lieu of explanations, he unfolded the green paper, and opened fire abruptly on the subject that claimed both their thoughts. "Under the patronage of the Mesdames Chesterfield and Conway-Moore, your charity concert should be a decided success." His large, homely features were screwed into innumerable sarcastic curves and wrinkles, as he mentioned the names of the society leaders under whose wings his favourite pupil was about to make her *début*.

His favourite pupil nodded.

"I see your programme includes *The Heart of Kerry*." He was wont to say of *The Heart of Kerry*, that it was his masterpiece; that if he lived to be a hundred and strove to earn fame every day, he would still be remembered solely as the author of *The Heart of Kerry*. It was only a simple poem, depicting the struggles of a workingman and his family against poverty, sickness, and abuse. Perhaps because Phillips was himself poor, struggling and abused, was the reason it played so wonderfully on the feelings of the public.

"I see your programme includes *The Heart of Kerry*," he repeated, giving her a compelling look, under which she flushed rosily.

"Confess, Professor, that you were flattered to have your favourite poem so ably handled, before a critical audience, by your favourite pupil."

He made a bitter gesture. "Is it from the generous notion that you can make them subscribe a large charity fund?"

"Partly. A thousand dollars is a donation the Kerrys of this city will not despise."

"Donation! Charity! Rank words! Let them pay Kerry his wages. Good Heavens, he asks for a chance, not charity."

She hummed a frivolous air.

"I had hoped," he continued, more calmly, "that you would recite *The Heart of Kerry* for me sometime — at one of our great mass meetings, before men and women who would understand. Will you cast my pearl before swine?"

"In behalf of the Chesterfields and the Conway-Moores, I thank you."

"You will never read *The Heart of Kerry* until I give you permission. I will prevent it."

"But how?" she laughed.

"Gracious, girl, the poem is mine!"

"It is also mine. You have poured it red-hot from your soul into mine."

Clearly, compulsion did not answer his turn. As a master-strategist, he allowed a mellow tone to creep into his voice. "Lally, truly now, why do you want to tell the story of Kerry to those people who can never understand Kerry's heart?"

Evading his eye and hand, she sprang up like a queen of tragedy. "Why? Oh, because of its room for fine shades of inflection, because of its pathos." She began a semblance of shivering, and her voice iced the room as she recited:

Ever the storm-wolf howled and raved abroad,
Nosing the battered door for toothsome prey.
Within, a little, dolorous, human shape,
Upon his bed the sick child lay; and all
Above lay heaps of rags, this coat, that shawl,
To coax the heat within the wasted frame.

Then raising her arms tragically:

He died! Hear me, O smiling, plenteous earth!
For one so young has little need to die
He died for breath withheld —

"Stop! Do not tell us how he died. That requires soul."

She stopped, bit her lip in chagrin, while her black eyes flashed menace on the thousand hapless Kerrys thronging in the street below. Then, when her voice was steady, she said irrelevantly: "I see your *protégé*, Patsey Quin, looking up at me with his ridiculously solemn eyes. I say, what makes him look like that?"

"Hunger," said Phillips promptly.

"Nonsense! He doesn't like me, and therefore my best smile is frozen in his icy frown of disapproval. Oh, look! Quick! That horse! Mercy, will the boy be killed?"

MABEL BURKHOLDER

When Phillips reached the window, he merely saw Patsey riding on the bridle of a restive and powerful horse, whose owner was pushing into his left hand a coin. The man had a thick face and muddy eyes. He was on the stairs. He stood in the door in their very midst, like a ponderous cat, crouching with claws concealed. From mere revulsion Phillips went pale as paper.

"Is Miss Van Allan here?" A pipe being the constant adornment of the left side of his mouth, he had learned to talk out of the right side, which conveyed the expression of an habitual sneer. "Ah, Lally, is your lesson over? The streets are no longer safe for pedestrians. A pretty turmoil you have stirred up, Mr. Phillips, with the devil knows how much bloodshed before it receives its quietus."

Again Austin Phillips smilingly laid bare his bosom to the stab, but he turned appealing eyes on Miss Van Allan with the unspoken entreaty in them that she should send this man about his business.

"Lesson!" exclaimed Lally, coming out of the shadows; "I have had no lesson to-day — except one in deportment. Mr. Phillips has been so horrid; at least, I mean we have both been quarrelling. My gloves! There, dear Dick, I believe I am quite ready." Moreover, because the stairs were dark, she took "dear Dick's" arm to the street.

Phillips strode to the window. The violent bay was making nasty plunges, with Patsey Quin still riding on his bit. They laughed and chattered an unconscionable time while tucking in the robes, and when they were ready, the audacious girl looked up and waved her hand. "There, I'll leave him on the rack for a while," she murmured. Unluckily, she knew Austin Phillips to be a very fit subject for torture.

How long had she been calling Richard Haliday "dear Dick?" Phillips wondered. "Dear Dick" was the man who had spoken of her before a crowd of men as "the charming little Van Allan, by George!" He was the man who opposed his heart interests at every turn, whether in the complex game of love, or as a leader of capital against a leader of labour, or as a rich rogue against an honest man.

Stop, he must consider it was pure jealousy swishing the lash across his feelings, and blinding him to Haliday's better qualities. "Lally!" "Dear Dick!" It was unbearable. It must be stopped. Then he braced up, laughed shortly, and called Patsey Quin. There was still left to him — his work.

Austin Phillips had turned his genius for rhetoric into two channels. As a teacher of elocution, he had directed the voices of youth to sweeter speech, purer accent, nobler thought; also he used his own silvery logic from the public rostrum to swing men around to broader views on public questions. Gradually becoming identified with the great labour movements, he stood in the city for personal liberty, the champion of the workingman everywhere.

"Can you get over to Camden Crescent?" he asked of Patsey Quin.

Patsey bent on him great caressing eyes. "Yes, sir," he replied, promptly.

"I believe you can. You will avoid King street."

"Yes, sir."

"Find out whether the Haliday, Toone and Tompkins bunch have made any concessions to the men or whether the strike is to continue."

Patsey grunted at the mere mention of concessions coming from the company. He was a well-informed unionist for one of only ten years.

"Say to Merriman I will speak to the men in the armoury to-morrow night."

"Yes, sir." Patsey was off with a bound, Phillips watching him skilfully thread his way around the corner until he was lost in the side street.

Ever through the street rolled the angry surges of humanity. Crash! A plate-glass window went shivering in, and a wooden-headed policeman was belabouring a couple of innocent boys who had ventured too near. Down the street came the tramp, tramp of the soldiery, who held the city under martial law. On the very sidewalk they rode their horses, driving men, women, and children before their merciless steel. The crowd took refuge, momentarily, in alley and lane, but surged in again behind the troops with hisses and groans. It was to these people Phillips must speak, to these frenzied workingmen, these Kerrys, who demanded for their families the decent comforts of life, and demanded it from the adamantine Haliday, Toone and Tompkins combine. What should he say? Should he tell them to be calm, to wait? He clenched his hand. No. Just God! The day of patience was past. He would tell them to fight tooth and nail.

But ever over his ponderous and weighty plans fluttered the remembrance of a green concert bill, like a bee teasing a bull. He knew that Lally's act meant more than appeared on the surface. It meant that she had gone over to the opposition, body and soul. She was tired of his hopes, his promises, his wonderful plans that only soared to fall. He was an idealist, a visionary, he had so little money, and possessed so few of the luxuries that women regard as essential. Conscious of the fact that he was being burned at the stake of public opinion, he had risen manfully above the ordeal to a height where he could look down on his tormentors, but this last wound bled beyond the power of staunching, because he had been coddling himself with the belief that she was different, that she understood.

↶

When Austin Phillips emerged into the street on the night of his engagement at the armoury, he realized that the reading of the *riot act*, and the subsequent wounding of several citizens, had had no effect in quelling the mobs. A brick, clumsily aimed at his head, stirred in him the lust of battle. He pushed forth like a war-horse scenting smoke. An unusual uproar raged about him, for which he searched the cause. He was not long in finding it. A battered street car, run by two sullen strike-breakers, pushed its way up King street; while Tompkins, the most intrepid of the company, strove to look at ease as he rode.

"He will be killed!" screamed women's voices, as a very shower of stones descended on the hapless car. Phillips ducked his head, sprang from under the feet of a rearing horse, and turned to encounter — Lally Van Allan! She sat in Richard Haliday's buggy, whose owner had left his seat for one precarious moment. He noticed that she was richly dressed, and the thought flashed through his mind that she was on her way to the charity concert, there to amuse the Chesterfields and the Conway-Moores with tales of poverty which held all the charm of novelty for their dainty ears. Was she gathering inspiration from the real story hissed into her ears, prefaced with curses and punctuated with stones. In a moment he had realised her danger and was fighting toward her.

Her danger lay chiefly in her proximity to Haliday. The hated manager had been greeted with hisses as soon as he appeared in the street. He, too, was fighting toward the buggy, and the girl, frightened at last, cowered in the corner and raised appealing arms to the mob.

Phillips reached the wheel and sprang upon the hub, intent on one purpose — to get between the girl and those mad stones. His loosely-knit figure, and homely, well-beloved face might have had the effect of subduing the rioters had he been seen in better light. In the darkness, however, someone mistook him for Haliday, and a cruel stone, surely aimed, crunched against the side of his head. He dropped between the wheels without a groan; while Haliday, seizing the moment of dire consternation, leaped into the rig from the opposite side, urged the horse over the prostrate figure, and cleared the curbing at a bound.

Meanwhile, through the doors of the armoury surged a motley throng of wild-eyed, dishevelled workingmen, relieved here and there by capitalists of wealth and influence; for all men questioned in their minds what *he* would say in the face of the crisis. Little knowing that a tragedy had been enacted without, they waited patiently, with expectant faces turned toward the platform. Eight o'clock came and half-past eight. Some went out, but more came in. Eyes riveted on the side-door became strained, breathing became tense and audible. Presently the lights were turned on brilliantly, a door clicked sharply, and profound expectancy reigned in the vast hall.

MABEL BURKHOLDER

The crimson curtain quivered and was thrust aside, disclosing, not the stalwart figure of Austin Phillips, but that of a rarely graceful woman. Her sparkling face was surmounted by a coronal of hair, braided in subtle, serpentine curves around her head, and void of all ornament save its own mystic, blue-black gloss. There was a dash of wine-red in her dress, which harmonised with the vivid curves of her lips. Her dark beauty almost suggested the warmth of an Oriental sun.

It was plain that she had a message for them. Her lips parted for speech, but rich and poor, bending together, caught only the strange words, "The Heart of Kerry."

Then it seemed that she held up a great mirror, and invited every man to look in and see himself. It was not Kerry who struggled, raved, prayed, and waited; it was each one of them, portrayed with marvellous faithfulness. They wept for his hunger, shivered for his cold, wondered at his patience, recalling each his own like experience. Perhaps it was Lally Van Allan's finest triumph that they forgot her. She was only a vibrant, all-pervading voice. Even her master could, now, hardly have accused her of soullessness. In truth, she, too, had forgotten Lally Van Allan. In those intense moments, her soul fled to theirs, and she loved them, as he had vainly tried to teach her to love.

When she stopped speaking, the silence was oppressive, until, like a great sob, the audience took its breath. Then arose groans, and shouts, and stamping of feet, while the girl stood helpless before the *furore* she had created. What had she done but raised the tiger in them? It was as if there had been communicated to her soul the decision reached by Austin Phillips when he said: "The day of patience is passed! I will tell them to fight tooth and nail."

"Now, what are you going to do about it?" muttered a deep voice behind her, and, turning quickly, she saw that Richard Haliday stood at her elbow. She had not known that he followed and protected her steps from the house of mirth, when she ran away into darkness and danger; her eyes looked her thanks. But he was going forward, lifting his hand to enjoin silence. The crowd halted sullenly, for wrath and murder were stirring in their hearts, and he was the object of their deepest malevolence. But Haliday was no coward. His bold, full eye, which had cowed many a slinking delinquent into submission, compelled them to his mood; and when from mere curiosity he had them hanging on his words, he said:

"I beseech you, men, for God's sake, do not go out and do useless murder. Some of you (he waved his hand toward the door) know that Tompkins, the intrepid leader of capital, lies dead at this moment from the madness of the mob. Some know, too, that Phillips, the equally brave leader of labour, is also dead." Lally sank into a chair, and a deep groan rose from the stricken audience. "Kerry, who has trumpeted his message into your ears, has also brought his message for mine. It means that this present illicit condition of affairs must cease. And as there has been wrong on both sides (for the first time they saw it), so both must unite to bring about a more satisfactory state of affairs. Let each right-thinking man go quietly home. Send your leaders to us, at our office in Camden Crescent, at twelve o'clock to-night. I promise you, if Kerry behaves as wisely and patiently as we have reason to expect, we will see that he gets his rights."

Then Haliday noticed and pitied the abject misery of Lally. "Come home," he said gently.

"To him! Oh, to him!" she panted, catching his arm. Haliday turned away, and, in the one brief moment allowed him, swallowed his bitter cup. Then he took her hand and led her away, while she, torn as she was with grief for her master, wondered why his arm trembled.

Bravely he led her to the man she loved, away, ever away from himself. When she knew for a certainty that he was dead, she might, sometime, in the dim future, think of him, though Lally was one to live her life on a memory. Had he not in life ridden over Phillips? Was it not meet that, in his death, his antagonist should crush him to the ground?

Silently they turned the corner of King street. A strange, funereal silence held the block. The hoarsethroated cries at the armoury sounded faint and far. In a moment Lally knew what they had done. Ropes were stretched around the house, and straw laid down; while a hundred of his chosen devotees stood guard to ward off noise and disturbance. Now, she knew why he loved them. They were turned into very angels at his inspiration, ministering angels, tireless in endurance, undaunted in danger. She took them all to her heart by leaps and bounds.

By permission of the guards, the two passed noiselessly over the straw-strewn pavement, guided by the feeble light that shone from his window. At the stair, entrance was barred by Patsey Quin.

"Let me pass!" cried the woman, flinging him to one side. The child threw his wrathful eyes on her from the darkness.

"You can't go in!" he whimpered in petty fury.

"Why not? Speak, boy! What do you mean? What does all this mean, anyway? This deadening of sound? These guards? Do men so guard the deaf ears of a corpse? O merciful heaven, maybe he isn't — tell me, is he — is he — "

"Naw," said Patsey Quin.

"Oh, great mercy of God!" breathed the woman, rushing up the stairs, while the man turned and retraced his footsteps into the city.

ᔋ

Canadian Magazine 29 (Sept. 1907): 465–469.

L. M. Montgomery (1874–1942)

THE QUARANTINE AT ALEXANDER ABRAHAM'S (1907)

Lucy Maud Montgomery, famous as the creator of Anne of Green Gables, was born in Clifton, Prince Edward Island, in 1874 to Clara Woolner MacNeill and Hugh John Montgomery. At twenty-one months, after her mother's death, Maud Montgomery was taken to Cavendish, P.E.I., to live with her maternal grandparents, who provided material security but little emotional warmth. She was educated at public schools, and lived one year at Prince Albert, Saskatchewan, with her father and his second family. She returned to Cavendish, and in 1893 took the one-year teaching course at Prince of Wales College, Charlottetown. She taught briefly, attended Dalhousie University in Halifax in 1895, and returned to teaching on the Island from 1896 to 1898. On her grandfather's death in 1898, Montgomery went to Cavendish to keep house for her grandmother and pursued her writing, a demanding and difficult existence. For a short period in 1901–1902, she worked as a journalist for the Halifax *Daily Echo*. In 1911, after her grandmother's death, she was able to conclude a long engagement with marriage to Ewan Macdonald, a Presbyterian minister. She moved with him to Leaskdale, Ontario, and in 1926 to Norval, Ontario. There she juggled the taxing roles of minister's wife, mother of two sons, and writer, her situation the more stressful because of her husband's intermittent bouts of severe depression. In 1935, on her husband's retirement, the family moved to Toronto, where she died in 1942.

Lucy Maud Montgomery began writing as a child, and had her first poems published in the Charlottetown *Patriot* at fifteen. She continued to write and had an increasing number of stories accepted in Canadian and American periodicals. After *Anne of Green Gables* (1908), an instant success, Montgomery continued to write long fiction, directed primarily at a young female audience. Her works included several sequels to *Anne*, for which publisher and public clamoured, and the *Emily* series. Montgomery mythologized Prince Edward Island — and childhood and adolescence — by means of idyllic settings and bright young heroines. Recent publication of the first two volumes of the journals she kept between 1889 and 1942, with more volumes in prospect, has stimulated increased interest in the woman and her work.

"The Quarantine at Alexander Abraham's" was a milestone for Montgomery. In December 1906, her fame still in the future, she recorded in her journal:

> I've been jogging along of late in a rather uninteresting rut. But a nice thing happened last Tuesday. *Everybody's* accepted a short story of mine — "The Quarantine at Alexander Abraham's" — and sent me a hundred dollars for it. *Everybody's* is one of the big magazines and to appear in it is a sign you are getting somewhere.

Montgomery journal editors Mary Rubio and Elizabeth Waterston have hypothesized that something of Montgomery's own domestic prowess and her musing over the transition from older single woman to wife — a transition impending at this time in her own life — went into the making of this amusing story. Certainly she liked the story enough to revise it to an Avonlea setting, insert a mention of Anne of Green Gables and include it in her 1912 story collection *Chronicles of Avonlea*.

The story opposes a "man-hating old woman" and a misogynistic man in "quarantine": their isolation incubates mutual toleration and then affection. His dog and her cat function as correlatives for the changing relationship of the two characters. The feisty and independent Miss Peter MacNicol of "Spinster's Glory" eventually agrees, after her opponent makes the first conciliatory gestures, to become his wife, the "Angelina" of his house. The story is comic and optimistic, perhaps because at the time of writing Montgomery herself looked forward to marriage, despite her concerns about such a transition in her life. She was, moreover, determined to be positive in life and art. As she confided to her journal about the reviews of *Anne of Green Gables* in October 1908: "Thank God, I can keep the shadows of my life out of my work. I would not wish to darken any other life — I want instead to be a messenger of optimism and sunshine."

∽

Suggested Reading

Montgomery, L. M. *Chronicles of Avonlea* (1912), Afterword by Mary Rubio and Elizabeth Waterston (New York: Signet, 1988).

——. *The Selected Journals of L. M. Montgomery*, ed. Rubio and Waterston, Volumes I (1889–1910) and II (1910–1921) (Toronto: Oxford, 1985 and 1987).

Sorfleet, J. R., ed. *L. M. Montgomery: An Assessment* (Guelph: Canadian Children's Press, 1976).

The Quarantine at Alexander Abraham's

L. M. Montgomery

I refused to take that Sunday-school class the first time I was asked. Not that I objected to teaching in the Sunday-school. On the contrary, I rather liked the idea; but it was the Rev. Aaron Crickett who asked me and it had always been a matter of principle with me never to do anything a man asked me to do if I could help it. It saves so much trouble and simplifies everything so beautifully. I had always disliked men. It must have been born in me, because, as far back as I can remember, an antipathy to men and dogs was one of my strongest characteristics. My experiences through life only served to deepen it. The more I saw of men, the more I cared for cats.

So of course when the Rev. Aaron asked me to take a Sunday-school class I said no in a fashion calculated to chasten him wholesomely. If he had sent his wife the first time, as he did the second, it would have been wiser.

Mrs. Crickett talked smoothly for half an hour before she mentioned Sunday-school, and paid me several compliments. Mrs. Crickett is noted for her tact. Tact is a faculty for meandering around to a given point by the longest way instead of making a bee-line. I have no tact. As soon as Mrs. Crickett's conversation came in sight of the Sunday-school I said straight out, "What class do you want me to teach?"

Mrs. Crickett was so surprised that she forgot to be

tactful and answered plainly for once in her life:

"There are two classes — one of boys and one of girls. You may have your choice, Miss MacNicol."

"Then I'll take the boys," I said decidedly. "Since they have to grow up to be men it's as well to train them properly. Nuisances they are bound to become in any circumstances; but if they are taken in hand young enough they may not grow up to be such nuisances as they otherwise would, and that will be some unfortunate woman's gain."

Mrs. Crickett looked dubious.

"They are a very wild set of boys," she said.

"I never knew boys who weren't," I retorted.

"I — I — think perhaps you would like the girls best," said Mrs. Crickett hesitatingly.

"It is not what *I* like best that must be considered, Mrs. Crickett," I said rebukingly. "It is what is best for those boys. I feel that *I* shall be best for *them*."

"Oh, I've no doubt of that, Miss MacNicol," said Mrs. Crickett. It was a fib for her, minister's wife though she was. She *had* doubt. She thought I would be a dismal failure as teacher of a boys' class.

But I wasn't. I am not often a dismal failure when I make up my mind to do a thing.

"It is wonderful what a reformation you have worked in that class, Miss MacNicol — wonderful," said the Rev. Mr. Crickett some weeks later. He didn't mean to show how amazing a thing he thought it that an old maid noted for being a man-hater should have managed it, but his face betrayed him.

"Where does Jimmy Fraser live?" I asked him crisply. "He came one Sunday three weeks ago and hasn't been back since. I mean to find out why."

Mr. Crickett coughed.

"I believe he is hired as handy boy with Alexander Abraham Bennett, out on the Oriental road," he said.

"Then I am going out to Alexander Abraham Bennett's on the Oriental road to see why Jimmy Fraser doesn't come to Sunday-school," I said firmly.

Mr. Crickett's eye twinkled ever so slightly.

"Possibly Mr. Bennett won't appreciate your kind interest. He has — ah! — a singular aversion to your sex, I understand. No woman has ever been known to get inside of Mr. Bennett's house since his sister died twenty years ago."

"Oh, he's the one, is he?" I said, remembering. "He is the woman-hater who threatens that if a woman comes into his yard he'll chase her out with a pitchfork. Well, he won't chase me out!"

Mr. Crickett gave a chuckle — a ministerial chuckle, but still a chuckle. It irritated me slightly because it seemed to imply that he thought Alexander Abraham Bennett would be too much for me. But I did not show Mr. Crickett that it annoyed me. It is always a big mistake to let a man see that he can vex you.

The next afternoon I harnessed my sorrel pony to the buggy and drove out to Alexander Abraham Bennett's. As usual, I took William Adolphus with me for company. He sat up on the seat beside me and looked far more like a Christian than many a man I've seen in a similar position.

Alexander Abraham's place was about three miles out from the village. I knew the house as soon as I came to it by its neglected appearance. Plainly there was no woman about *that* place. Still, it was a nice house and the barns were splendid.

"Alexander Abraham may be a woman-hater, but he evidently knows how to run a farm," I remarked to William Adolphus as I got out and tied the pony to the railing. I had driven up to the house from behind, and now I was opposite a side door opening on the veranda. I thought I might as well go to it, so I tucked William Adolphus under my arm and marched up the path. Just as I was half-way up a dog swooped around the front corner and made straight for me. He was the ugliest dog I had ever seen, and he didn't even bark — just came silently and speedily on, with a businesslike eye. I never stop to argue matters with a dog that doesn't bark. I know when discretion is the better part of valor. Firmly clasping William Adolphus I ran — not to

L. M. Montgomery

the door, for the dog was between me and it, but to a big, low-branching cherry-tree at the back corner of the house. I reached it in time and no more. First thrusting William Adolphus on to a limb above my head, I scrambled up into that blessed tree without stopping to think how it might look to Alexander Abraham if he happened to be watching.

My time for reflection came when I found myself perched half-way up the tree with William Adolphus, quite calm and unruffled, beside me. The dog was sitting on the ground below, watching us, and it was quite plain from his leisurely manner that it was not his busy day. He bared his teeth and growled when he caught my eye. "You *look* like a woman-hater's dog," I told him.

Then I set myself to solving the question, "How am I to get out of this predicament?" I decided not to scream. There was probably no one to hear me except perhaps Alexander Abraham, and I had my painful doubts about his tender mercies. It was impossible to go down. Was it, then, possible to go up?

I looked up. Just above my head was an open window with a tolerably stout branch right across it. Without hesitation I picked up William Adolphus and began to climb, while the dog ran in circles about the tree and looked things not lawful to be uttered. It probably would have been a relief to him to bark if it hadn't been so against his principles.

I got in by a window easily enough, and found myself in a bedroom the like of which for disorder and dust and general awfulness I had never seen in my life. But I did not pause to gather details. With William Adolphus under my arm I marched downstairs, fervently hoping I should meet no one on the way.

I did not. The hall below was empty and dusty. I opened the first door I came to and walked boldly in. A man was sitting by the window looking out moodily. I should have known him for Alexander Abraham anywhere. He had just the same uncared-for, ragged appearance that the house had; and yet, like the house, it seemed that he would not be bad-looking if he were trimmed up a little.

His hair didn't seem ever to have been combed and his whiskers were wild in the extreme. He looked at me with blank amazement in his countenance.

"Where is Jimmy?" I demanded. "I've come to see him."

"How did that dog ever let you in?" asked the man, staring at me.

"He didn't let me in," I retorted. "He chased me all over the lawn and I only saved myself from being torn to pieces by scrambling up a tree. Then I climbed in by the window and came down-stairs. You ought to be prosecuted for keeping such a dog. Where is Jimmy?"

Instead of answering, Alexander Abraham began to laugh — not much externally, but internally, as I could see.

"Trust a woman for getting into a man's house if she's made up her mind to," he said disagreeably.

Seeing that it was his intention to vex me, I remained cool and collected.

"Oh, I wasn't particular about getting into your house, Mr. Bennett," I said calmly. "I hadn't much choice in the matter — it was get in lest a worse fate befall me. It was not you or your house I wanted to see — although I admit it's worth seeing if a person is anxious to find out how dirty a place *can* be. It was Jimmy. For the third and last time — where is Jimmy?"

"Jimmy is not here," said Mr. Bennett. "He left last week and hired with a man down at Prestonville."

"In that case," I said, picking up William Adolphus, who was exploring the room, "I won't disturb you any longer. I will go."

"Yes, I think it would be the wisest thing," said Alexander Abraham — not disagreeably this time, but reflectively, as if there were some doubt about the matter. "I'll let you out by the back door. Then the — ahem! — the dog will not interfere with you. Please go away quietly and quickly."

I said nothing, thinking this the most dignified course of conduct, and followed Alexander Abraham out to the kitchen. That kitchen! Even William Adolphus gave a

L. M. MONTGOMERY

meow of protest as we passed through. Cat though he was, he understood that there was something uncanny about such a place. Alexander Abraham opened the door, which was locked, just as a buggy containing two men drove into the yard.

"Too late!" he exclaimed in a tragic tone. I understood that something dreadful had happened, but I did not care, since, as I fondly supposed, it did not concern me. I pushed out past Alexander Abraham — who was looking strangely guilty — and came face to face with the man who had sprung from the buggy. It was old Dr. Nicholson, and he was looking at me as if he had caught me shoplifting.

"My dear Peter," he said gravely, "I am very sorry to see you here — very sorry, indeed."

I admit that exasperated me. Besides, no man on earth, not even my old family doctor, has any right to "My dear Peter" me.

"There is no loud call for sorrow, doctor," I said loftily. "If a woman forty-five years of age, a member of the Presbyterian Church in good and regular standing, can't call upon one of her Sunday-school scholars without wrecking all the proprieties, how old must she be before she can?"

The doctor did not answer my question. Instead, he looked reproachfully at Alexander Abraham.

"Is this how you keep your word, Mr. Bennett?" he said. "I thought that you promised me that you would not let any one into the house."

"I didn't let her in," growled Mr. Bennett. "Good heavens, man, she climbed in at an up-stairs window despite the presence on my grounds of a policeman and a dog! What's to be done with a woman like that?"

"My dear Peter," said the doctor impressively, turning to me, "this house is under quarantine for smallpox. You will have to stay here."

Smallpox! For the first and last time in my life I openly lost my temper with a man. I wheeled furiously upon Alexander Abraham.

"Why didn't you tell me?" I cried.

"Tell you!" he said, glaring at me. "When I first saw you it was too late to tell you. I thought the kindest thing I could do was to hold my tongue and let you get away in happy ignorance. This will teach you to take a man's house by storm, madam."

"Now, now, don't quarrel, my good people," interposed the doctor seriously — but I am sure I saw a grin in his eye — "you'll have to spend some time together under the same roof and you won't improve the situation by disagreeing. You see, Peter, it was this way. Mr. Bennett was in town yesterday — where, as you are aware, there is a bad outbreak of smallpox — and took dinner in a boarding-house where one of the maids was ill. Last night she developed unmistakable symptoms of smallpox. The Board of Health at once got after all the people who were in the house yesterday, so far as they could locate them and put them under quarantine. I came out here this morning and explained the matter to Mr. Bennett and vaccinated him. I brought Jeremiah Jeffries to guard the front of the house, and Mr. Bennett gave me his word of honor he would not let any one in by the back way while I went to get another policeman and make all the necessary arrangements. I have brought Thomas Wright and have secured the services of another man to attend to Mr. Bennett's barn work and bring provisions to the house. Jacob Green and Cleophas Lee will watch at night. I don't think that there is much danger of Mr. Bennett's taking the smallpox, but until we are sure you must remain here, Peter. Have you been vaccinated?"

While listening to the doctor I had been thinking. It was the most distressing predicament that I had ever got into in my life but there was no use making it worse.

"Very well, doctor," I said calmly. "Yes, I was vaccinated a month ago when the news of the smallpox first came. When you go back to the village kindly go to Sarah Blenkhorn and ask her to live in my house during my absence and look after things, especially the cats. Tell her to give them new milk twice a day and a square inch of butter apiece once a week. Get her to put my two dark cotton wrappers, some aprons, and a change of underclothing in my third best valise and have it sent out to me. My pony is tied out there to the fence. Please take him home. That is all, I think."

"No, it isn't all," said Alexander Abraham grumpily. "Send that cat home too. I won't have a cat round the place — I'd rather have the smallpox."

I looked Alexander Abraham over gradually, beginning at his feet and traveling up to his head. Then I said gently:

"You may have both. Anyway, you'll have to have William Adolphus. He is under quarantine as well as you and I. Do you suppose I am going to have my cat ranging at large through Amberly, scattering smallpox germs among innocent people? I'll have to put up with that dog of yours. You will have to endure William Adolphus."

Alexander Abraham groaned, but I could see that the way I had looked him over had had its due effect. The doctor drove away and I went into the house, not choosing to be grinned at by Thomas Wright. I hung my coat up in the hall and laid my bonnet carefully on the sitting-room table, having first dusted a clean place for it with my handkerchief. I longed to fall upon that house at once and clean it up, but I had to wait until the doctor should come back with my wrappers. I could not clean house in my new suit and a silk shirt-waist.

Alexander Abraham was sitting on a chair looking at me. Presently he said, "I am not curious — but will you tell me why the doctor called you Peter?"

"Because that is my name, I suppose," I answered, shaking up a cushion for William Adolphus to lie on and thereby disturbing the dust of years.

Alexander Abraham coughed gently. "Isn't that a — ahem! — a rather peculiar name for a woman?"

"It is," I said, wondering how much soap, if any, there was in the house.

"I am *not* curious," said Alexander Abraham, "but would you mind telling me how you came to be called Peter?"

"If I had been a boy my parents intended to call me Peter in honor of a rich uncle. When I — fortunately — turned out to be a girl, my mother insisted that I should be called Angelina. They gave me both names and called me Angelina, but as soon as I grew old enough I determined to be called Peter. It was bad enough, but not as bad as Angelina."

"I should say it was more appropriate," said Alexander Abraham, intending, as I perceived, to be disagreeable.

"Precisely," I agreed calmly. "My last name is MacNicol and I live at Spinster's Glory in Amberly. As you are not curious, that will be all the information you will need about me."

"Ah!" Alexander Abraham looked as if light had broken in on him. "I've heard of you. You — ah — pretend to dislike men."

Pretend! Goodness only knows what would have happened to Alexander Abraham just then if a diversion had not taken place. But the door was pushed open and a dog came in — *the* dog. I suppose he had got tired of waiting under the cherry-tree. He was even uglier indoors than out.

"Ah, Mr. Riley, Mr. Riley, see what you have let me in for," said Alexander Abraham reproachfully.

But Mr. Riley — since that was the brute's name — paid no attention to Alexander Abraham. He had caught sight of William Adolphus curled up on the cushion and he started across the room to investigate him. William Adolphus sat up and began to take notice.

"Call off that dog," I said warningly to Alexander Abraham. "Call him off yourself," he retorted. "Since you've brought that cat here you can protect him."

"Oh, it wasn't for the cat's sake I spoke," I said ominously. "William Adolphus can protect himself."

William Adolphus could and did. He humped his back, flattened his ears, swore once, and then made a flying leap for Mr. Riley, who by that time was quite close. William Adolphus landed squarely on Mr. Riley's brindled back and promptly took fast hold, spitting and clawing and caterwauling.

You never saw a more astonished dog than Mr. Riley. With a yell of terror he bolted out to the kitchen, out of the kitchen into the hall, through the hall into the room, and so into the kitchen and round again. With each circuit he went faster and faster till he looked like a brindled streak with a dash of black and white on top. Such a racket and commotion I never heard and I laughed until the tears came into my eyes. Mr. Riley flew around and around and William Adolphus held on grimly and clawed. Alexander Abraham turned purple with rage.

"Woman, call off that infernal cat before he kills my dog," he shouted above the din of yelps and yowls.

"Oh, he won't kill him," I called reassuringly, "and he's going too fast to hear me if I did call him. If you can stop the dog, Mr. Bennett, I'll guarantee to make William Adolphus listen to reason, but there's no use trying to argue with a lightning flash."

Alexander Abraham made a frantic lunge at the brindled streak as it whirled past him, with the result that he overbalanced himself and went sprawling on the floor with a crash. When he picked himself up, he said viciously, "I wish you and your fiend of a cat were in — in —— "

"Amberly," I finished quickly. "So do I, Mr. Bennett, but since we are not, let us make the best of it like sensible people."

With this the end came and I was thankful, for the noise those two animals made was so terrific that I expected the policemen would be rushing in, smallpox or no small-pox, to see if Alexander Abraham and I were trying to murder each other. Mr. Riley suddenly veered in his mad course and bolted into a dark corner between the stove and the wood-box. William Adolphus let go just in time.

There was never any more trouble with Mr. Riley after that. A meeker, more thoroughly chastened dog you could not find. William Adolphus had the best of it and he kept it.

Seeing that things had calmed down and that it was five o'clock I decided to get tea. I told Alexander Abraham that I would prepare it if he would show me where the eatables were.

"You needn't mind," said Alexander Abraham viciously. "I've been in the habit of getting my own tea for twenty years."

"I dare say; but you haven't been in the habit of getting mine," I said firmly. "I wouldn't eat anything you cooked if I starved to death. If you want some occupation you'd better get some salve and anoint the scratches on that dog's back."

Alexander Abraham said something that I prudently did not hear. Seeing that he had no information to hand out I went on an exploring expedition into the pantry. The place was awful beyond description, and for the first time a vague sentiment of pity for Alexander Abraham glimmered in my breast. When a man had to live in such surroundings the wonder was, not that he hated women, but that he didn't hate the whole human race.

But I got a supper up somehow. I made good tea and excellent toast and I found a can of peaches in the pantry, which, being bought, I wasn't afraid to eat. As for the bread, it looked decent and I took it on faith.

That tea and toast mellowed Alexander Abraham in spite of himself. He ate the last crust and didn't growl when I gave William Adolphus all the cream that was left. By this time the doctor's boy had arrived with my valise. Alexander Abraham gave me to understand that there was a spare room across the hall and that I might take possession of it, since I had to be put somewhere. I went to it and put on one of my wrappers.

"Now," I said briskly, returning to the kitchen, "I'm going to clean up and I'm going to begin with this kitchen. You'd better betake yourself to the sitting-room, Mr. Bennett, so's to be out of the way."

Alexander Abraham glared at me.

"I'm not going to have my house meddled with," he snapped. "It suits me. If you don't like it, you can leave it."

"No, I can't. That is just the trouble," I said pleasantly. "If I could leave it I shouldn't be here a minute. Since I can't it simply has to be cleaned. Go into the sitting-room."

L. M. MONTGOMERY

Alexander Abraham went. As he closed the door I heard him say, "What an awful woman!"

I cleaned that kitchen and the pantry adjoining. It was ten o'clock when I finished, and Alexander Abraham had gone to bed without deigning further speech. I locked Mr. Riley in one room and William Adolphus in another and went to bed too. I never felt so dead tired in my life.

But I was up bright and early the next morning and got a tip-top breakfast, which Alexander Abraham condescended to eat. When the provision man came into the yard I called to him from the window to bring me a box of soap in the afternoon, and then I tackled the sitting-room. It took me the best part of a week to get that house in order, but I did it thoroughly, and at the end of the time it was clean from garret to cellar. Alexander Abraham made no comments on my operations, though he groaned loud and often and said caustic things to poor Mr. Riley, who hadn't the spirit to answer back after his drubbing by William Adolphus. I made allowances for Alexander Abraham because his vaccination had taken and his arm was real sore; and I cooked elegant meals, not having much else to do once I got things scoured up. The house was full of provisions — Alexander Abraham wasn't mean about such things, I will say that for him. Altogether, I was more comfortable than I had expected to be. When Alexander Abraham wouldn't talk I let him alone; and when he would, I said just as sarcastic things as he did, only I said them smiling and pleasant. I could see he had a wholesome awe of me.

One day Alexander Abraham astonished me by appearing at the dinner-table with his hair brushed and a white collar on. We had a tip-top dinner that day and I had made a pudding that was positively wasted on a woman-hater. When Alexander Abraham had disposed of two platefuls of it he sighed and said: "You can certainly cook. It's a pity you are such a detestable crank in other respects."

"It's kind of convenient being a crank," I said. "People are careful how they meddle with you. Haven't you found that out in your own experience?"

"I am *not* a crank," growled Alexander Abraham resentfully. "All I ask is to be let alone."

"That's the very crankiest kind of a crank," I said. "A person who wants to be let alone flies in the face of Providence, who decreed that folks for their own good were not to be let alone. But cheer up, Mr. Bennett. The quarantine will be up on Tuesday and then you'll certainly be let alone for the rest of your natural life so far as William Adolphus and I are concerned. You may then return to your wallowing in the mire and be as dirty and comfortable as of yore."

Alexander Abraham growled again. The prospect didn't seem to cheer him up as much as I'd expected. Then he did an amazing thing. He poured some cream into a saucer and set it down before William Adolphus.

Neither Alexander Abraham nor I had worried much about the smallpox. We didn't believe he would take it for he hadn't even seen the girl who was sick. But the very next morning I heard him calling me from the up-stairs landing.

"Miss MacNicol," he said in a voice so uncommonly mild and polite that it gave me a jump, "what are the symptoms of smallpox?"

"Chills and flushes, pain in the limbs and back, nausea and vomiting," I answered promptly, for I had been reading them up in a patent-medicine almanac.

"I've got them all," said Alexander Abraham solemnly.

I didn't feel as much scared as I should have expected. After enduring a woman-hater and a brindled dog and the early disorder of that house, smallpox seemed rather insignificant. I went to the window and called to Thomas Wright to send for the doctor.

The doctor came down from Alexander Abraham's room looking grave.

"It is impossible to pronounce on his disease yet," he said. "There is no certainty until the eruption appears. But of course there is every likelihood that it is the smallpox. It is very unfortunate. I am afraid that it will be very difficult to get a nurse. All the nurses in town who will take small-pox cases are overbusy now, for the epidemic is still raging there. However, I'll go into town to-night and do my best. Meanwhile, as Mr. Bennett does not require any attendance at present, you must not go near him, Peter."

I wasn't going to take orders from any man and as soon as the doctor had gone I marched straight up to Alexander Abraham's room with some dinner for him on a tray. There was a lemon cream that I thought he could eat even if he had the smallpox.

"You shouldn't come near me," he growled. "You are risking your life."

"I'm not going to see a fellow creature starve to death, even if he is a man," I retorted.

"The worst of it all," groaned Alexander Abraham between mouthfuls of lemon cream, "is that the doctor says I've got to have a nurse. I've got so kind of used to you being in the house that I don't mind you, but the thought of another woman coming here is too much. Did you give my poor dog anything to eat?"

"He has had a better dinner than many a Christian," I said severely.

Alexander Abraham need not have worried about another woman coming in. The doctor came back that night with care on his brow.

"I don't know what is to be done," he said. "I can't get a soul to come here."

"*I* will nurse Mr. Bennett," I said with dignity. "It is my duty and, thank Heaven, I never shirk my duty. He is a man and he has smallpox and he keeps a vile dog, but I'm not going to see him die for want of attendance for all that."

"Well, if you're not afraid to take the risk," said the doctor, looking relieved, manlike, as soon as he found a woman to shoulder the responsibility.

I nursed Alexander Abraham through the smallpox and I didn't mind it much. He was much more amiable sick than well and he had the disease in a very mild form. Below stairs I reigned supreme, and Mr. Riley and William Adolphus lay down together like the lion and the lamb. I fed Mr. Riley regularly and once, seeing him looking lonesome, I patted him gingerly. It was nicer than I'd thought it would be.

When Alexander Abraham got able to sit up he began to make up for the time he'd lost being pleasant. Anything more sarcastic than that man during his convalescence you couldn't imagine. I just laughed at him, having found out that that could be depended on to irritate him. To irritate him still further I cleaned the house all over again. But what vexed him most of all was that Mr. Riley took to following me about and wagging what he had of a tail at me.

"It wasn't enough that you should come into my peaceful home and turn it upside down, but you have to alienate the affection of my dog," complained Alexander Abraham.

"He'll get fond of you again when I go home," I said comfortingly. "Dogs aren't very particular that way. What they want is bones. Cats now, they love disinterestedly. William Adolphus has never swerved in his allegiance to me although you do give him cream on the sly."

Alexander Abraham looked foolish. He hadn't thought I knew that.

I didn't take the smallpox, and in another week the doctor came out and sent the policeman home. I was disinfected and William Adolphus was fumigated and then we were free to go.

"Good-by, Mr. Bennett," I said, offering to shake hands in a forgiving spirit. "I've no doubt that you're glad to be rid of me, but you're no gladder than I am to go. I suppose this house will be dirtier than ever in a month's time and Mr. Riley will have discarded the little polish his manners have taken on. Reformation with men and dogs never goes very deep."

With this Parthian shaft I walked out of that house, supposing that I had seen the last of it and of Alexander Abraham.

I was glad to get back home, of course; but it did seem queer and lonesome. The cats hardly knew me and William Adolphus roamed around forlornly and appeared to feel like an exile. I didn't take as much pleasure in cooking as usual, for it seemed kind of foolish to be fussing over oneself. The neighbors avoided me pointedly, for they couldn't get rid of the fear that I might erupt into smallpox at any moment; my Sunday-school class had been given to another woman, and altogether I felt as if I didn't belong anywhere.

I had existed like this for a week when Alexander Abraham suddenly appeared. He walked in one evening at dusk, but at first sight I didn't know him, he was so spruced and barbered up. But William Adolphus knew him. Will you believe it, William Adolphus, my own William Adolphus, rubbed up against that man's trouser leg with an undisguised purr of satisfaction?

"I had to come, Angelina," said Alexander Abraham. "I couldn't stand it any longer."

"My name is Peter," I said coldly, although I was feeling ridiculously glad about something.

"It isn't," said Alexander Abraham stubbornly. "It is Angelina for me and always will be. I will never call you Peter. Angelina just suits you exactly. And Angelina Bennett would suit you still better. You've got to come back, Angelina. Mr. Riley is moping for you and I can't get along without somebody to appreciate my sarcasms, now that you've accustomed me to the luxury."

"What about the other five cats?" I demanded.

Alexander Abraham sighed.

"I suppose they'll have to come too," he said. "It's awful to think of living with six cats, but it's worse to think of living without you. How soon can you be ready to marry me?"

"I haven't said that I am going to marry you at all, have I?" I said tartly, just to be consistent. For I wasn't feeling tart.

"No, but you will, won't you?" said Alexander Abraham anxiously. "Because if you won't I wish you'd let me die of the smallpox. Do, dear Angelina."

To think that a man should dare to call me his "dear Angelina"! And to think that I shouldn't mind!

∽

Everybody's 16 (April 1907): 495–503; revised and included in *Chronicles of Avonlea* (Boston: Page, 1912).

Madge Macbeth (1880–1965)

"Frieda's Engagement" and "Gifts" (1908)

Madge Macbeth, widowed early, successfully turned to creative writing to support herself and her two young sons — a formidable feat for a woman in a profession precarious at best. Born Madge Hamilton Lyons in Philadelphia to Bessie Maffit and Hymen Hart Lyons, she lost her father early to tuberculosis. She spent time in Baltimore and elsewhere before being sent as a boarder by her mother to Hellmuth Ladies' College in London, Ontario. In 1901, after her graduation, she married Charles Macbeth, a University of Toronto graduate in engineering and a fraternity brother of William Lyon Mackenzie King. After two years in Detroit, the couple settled in Ottawa, where Madge Macbeth's wit, vivacity and determination soon made her well known in Ottawa society. After her husband's death from tuberculosis, she struggled to establish herself as a freelance writer, one of the few socially acceptable options early in the century for middle-class women in her situation. She turned out short fiction as well as interviews, travel pieces and novels. In one memoir, *Over My Shoulder*, she recalled:

> Writing had advantages for it required no financial outlay other than pen and ink and I could dash off material at home between cooking up baby food, changing wet clothes and performing the other jobs contingent upon a nurse.

Madge Macbeth lived in Ottawa until her death in 1965. Under the pseudonym "Gilbert Knox" she wrote two well-known books of political and social satire about the capital, *The Land of Afternoon* (1925) and *The Kinder Bees* (1935). Macbeth wrote scores of short stories attractive to American and Canadian magazine editors — society stories, love stories, comic stories, sentimental moral tales, all the popular genres flowed from her febrile pen. One of her most heartfelt themes, however, is woman's place in marriage, a theme she treated both satirically and realistically in stories and novels. In "Frieda's Engagement" and "Gifts," linked stories published in 1908, Macbeth ruthlessly and cleverly satirizes social types she knew and loathed: the vapid, narcissistic, materialistic young woman of fashion and her male counterpart. The distancing effect of Macbeth's use of the satiric mode is typical of women's fiction at this period, as women questioned traditional female roles and expectations. In her colourful way, Madge Macbeth wrote herself into the plot in this story. In a third monologue in this vein, "The Pseudo-Theosophist" (1909), she mocks Frieda's gullibility and the craze for spiritualism and "Eastern" mysticism so in vogue at the time.

Of Macbeth's novels, the most interesting to feminists is *Shackles* (1926), which deals frankly with a woman writer's marital and career conflicts. The author declared in her foreword that "Woman is passing through a cultural transition. Instinctively, she is bound to the old order of things; intellectually, she clamours for the new. And vacillating, she stands between them."

∽

Suggested Reading
Gerson, Carole. "Madge Macbeth," *Dictionary of Literary Biography*, Vol. 92, ed. W. H. New, pp. 213–215.
Macbeth, Madge. "The Pseudo-Theosophist," *Canadian Magazine* 34 (Dec. 1909): 164–168.
——. *Shackles* (Ottawa: Graphic, 1926).
——. *Over My Shoulder* (Toronto: Ryerson, 1953).
——. *Boulevard Career* (Toronto: Kingswood, 1957).

Frieda's Engagement: A Monologue

Madge Macbeth

May I come in, Frieda? It's Kathleen. Don't look so surprised, my dear, though I suppose you *are* due an apology for my bursting in so suddenly; and I told your man down stairs a bit of a fib, too. I told him you were expecting me, because I was so *crazy* to see you, you darling!

Glad of it? Well, of course, Frieda, although I don't see you very often, I always think of you as my *best* friend. And that's why I came this morning — to tell you of my engagement and show you my ring. Isn't it a beauty? It was *very* expensive; I know, for I chose it myself; and, you see, the canary diamonds are very large and deep. I hate cheap rings, and said so quite frankly. This will never combine with any but the best, and I saw another one which I am going to have —— . The man? Ha, ha, isn't that funny? I forgot all about him! Why, Tom Cartwright.

No, I don't suppose you do, he doesn't care for girls, and is all for business, which is most commendable in a man — husband — isn't it? He has plenty of money, and I am going to have every thing I want, and be able to travel around just like Ethel.

However, the advantages are not all on my side; no, indeed! I am going to be a great help and inspiration to Tom. He is a little — what word shall I use? — er — sordid — earthly — you know what I mean — thinks so lightly of the higher life; and, I assure you, Frieda, his keen enjoyment of a low order of wit is most painful to me. He even enjoys puns!

You know I am so different — high-minded and spiritual — and I am always credited with being clever, you can't deny that, Frieda. Why, when I was only a little girl I wrote a splendid story. No, it was never published, but I had a personal communication from the Editor, which was very flattering; and at school my essays were considered remarkably deep for one so young.

My goodness! What queer questions you ask, Frieda! Of course, that has nothing to do with my marriage. I was just letting you see Tom is getting a woman vastly superior to him mentally. That is strictly between ourselves, as I wish the news of my engagement to be — for I am not going to tell any body for *ages*.

Oh, yes, a *few* people know. I met Jessie Hayes and Margie Walters on the way here and told them, and Fred Paxton was in Martin's where we were looking at rings, and — why that's so, his sister is a reporter — how killing! But I have only told a *few* people.

My, how unbecoming that kimono is to you, if I may say so, my dear. A person with sandy hair should *never* wear yellow. I know what I am saying, for I gave a great deal of time to the study of art.

A present? Well that makes no difference: you might easily exchange it at one of the stores for another kind. I'm sure Ethel sends me lots of things that I don't like at all, and I always manage to get rid of them.

How heavenly it will be, not to have to take many more from her! I am often bothered to death trying to remember to thank her for the right thing. Suppose she sent me a pair of gloves when I would rather have silk stockings. I change the gloves *for* the stockings. Then with my intense straightforwardness I am most apt to say in my note of acknowledgment, "thank you, dearest Ethel, for the lovely stockings," when I should say gloves, and Ethel gets cranky. She hasn't a very nice disposition, I must say.

And that reminds me of an incident which will give

MADGE MACBETH

you an idea of Tom's unpleasant failing. He asked me to go shopping with him last Tuesday, and although it was *most* inconvenient, being Lord Fitzhugh's bath day (I have to be so particular about him in summer, or he gets fleas), I sacrificed myself and said I would go. Well, I met him at Fisher's and went to buy some socks. He wanted me to choose them. I went to the counter and said, with the dignified air I always use towards salespeople:

"Kindly show me some black men's socks."

Now, Frieda, I leave it to you — is there any foundation there for a lengthy argument? Don't trouble to answer for, of course, there isn't. Nevertheless, Tom made a scene. He laid his hand on my arm and said:

"No, Kitty, they are for *me*."

"Well," I said.

"But you've made a mistake," he insisted, and the impudent sales-person tittered.

"I think not," I answered coldly; "I have not mentioned the size."

Well, the outcome of it all was this engraved bracelet, for he saw that I was very much annoyed, and any way —

Why, my *dear*, isn't that a new ring? An engagement ring? Oh, you precious darling! Why didn't you tell me before? And me your best friend! I adore being the first to know about engagements!

Why, it's huge! Do you believe it's real? Now, *don't* be cross, Frieda; I know plenty of men who give girls paste until they are really married. You see, there are loads of girls who hate giving back handsome rings; and if you were a man, and engaged to a couple of girls each summer, you can see for yourself how expensive it would be.

Engaged to be *married*? Why, why of course, you are — Oh, ha, ha, you *are* queer, Frieda! Fancy making a distinction between being engaged and engaged to be married!

Why didn't you get a marquise? With a stubby hand like yours — what? Oh, who is he? *Allen McDonald*! Why I used to be engaged to him myself!

But don't worry, Frieda, for though *I* did not care for

him, I don't doubt that he will make you very happy! Of course, you must hate being second choice, and I don't suppose I should have told you; but I would never have felt comfortable — being your best friend — with that between us. I can't see, though, how he fancied you, you are so — forgive me for speaking frankly, dear; it's because I am so fond of you — unattractive to men.

Oh, did he tell you? Well, I must say, Frieda, that you showed very little spirit — *consenting* to be second choice! You might have another chance. One can never tell!

Oh, he told you that, too, eh? No doubt he made me out a perfect dunce. It would be just like him.

I was young, and every other girl at the Island was engaged, so I went to Allen one evening (you see, I knew that he admired me immensely; I could tell by the way he listened when I talked) and simply told him I *had* to be engaged. Why, it was awful not having a letter every day; and waiting on Saturdays for the boat, when I expected no one in particular, was spoiling the whole summer for me.

So I said: "I have decided to accept you as my suitor, Allen" (I had never called him by his first name before), "and you may kiss my hand."

I assure you, Frieda, he was overcome, for he sat stock still a full minute, then laughed to cover his embarrassment, and said: "So I'm to be the goat." Do you see the point? A very neat compliment: implying that I was a lamb.

What are you laughing at? Yes, I broke it: I couldn't stand his relations. Oh, poor girl, I'm sorry for you!

When we all came back to town I went to a dinner — my first, I remember — at Donald McDonald's, and intended to announce my engagement that evening, though I said nothing of it to Allen (he was always so bashful and never would speak of it before people). Well, when I got there (a little late, and expecting to make a sensation in one of Ethel's evening gowns) everyone was making a tremendous fuss over some Mrs. Macbeth — the prodigal daughter of some one. I took an immediate dislike to her, she monopolized everything and everybody, which was exceedingly bad taste, you must acknowledge. Whenever she spoke the whole company roared, in fact, they did nothing but roar, for she never stopped talking, and no one could call her conversation clever. It was the kind that Tom would enjoy.

One of the Hoare girls asked: "Where *do* you live now, Mrs. Macbeth?" Billy Hoare answered at once: "She lives in Alaska, you stupid." "I don't, at all, Billy. You surely haven't found me as frosty as that, have you?" she said. Then everyone laughed and began to guess where she did live.

Finally I grew tired of such nonsense, and with Shakespeare in my mind said: "Why you all should know that Mrs. Macbeth lives in Denmark."

That night was enough for me. I saw at once that the McDonald family could not hold that woman and me, so I broke our engagement.

Allen was terribly distressed, and vowed that, having known *me*, he could not bear to think of ever knowing any one else like me. Poor fellow!

Are you crying, Frieda? Oh, I thought you were; and that just reminds me: I have forgotten my handkerchief — do lend me one. Thanks. I'll try to remember to return it.

Now I must hurry off. I want to see Phoebe King and ask her to be one of my bridesmaids. I've got all the rest promised.

You mustn't be offended at not being asked, dear. Truly, you were my *first* thought; then I decided that I would ask only pretty girls, and show, in that way, how able I was to hold my own without fear or jealousy. There are no mean or petty sentiments in *me*.

But if any one backs out at the last minute I will surely ask you.

Oh, don't thank me. I do this out of pure affection for you, dearie. Now, good-bye. I am sorry I must hurry off, but I am obliged to catch Phoebe. I will come again, when I have time to talk about *my* engagement.

Don't be disheartened when you meet Allen's relatives. To a less sensitive nature than mine they probably would not be so antagonistic; and you are quite phlegmatic, I think.

Good-bye! Don't tell anyone about my engagement, and I'll keep yours a secret. Good-bye. Oh, Frieda — may I tell Tom? Thanks, and Phoebe too? Good-bye again. And Frieda? Don't forget: if anyone backs out, you are to be a bridesmaid — you dear thing! Good-bye!

∽

Canadian Magazine 31 (May 1908): 21–23.

Gifts

Madge Macbeth

ate? Am I? Well, Agnes, I am sorry; but; really, if you
were as busy as I — just squeeze me in, on some one
else's hour, there's a good girl! I simply *must* have my
hair done this morning, for I haven't another minute to-day
in which I can ever stop to fix my *barette*.

Who's in there? *Who*? Well, I don't care if she *does*
hear me! Oh, it's *you*, Frieda; I couldn't understand what
Agnes said.

Oh, my dear, if you love me, let her do my hair first.
It won't take long, and I am obliged to go to Morgan's to
buy Tom's present before lunch, or else he will think I have
forgotten it.

Thanks, awfully, dear! I'll do something for you
some day.

Now, hurry, Agnes, Mr. Trevellyan said he would be
there at half-past twelve, to help me select something.

As a matter of fact, I *had* forgotten all about the
twelfth (this *is* the twelfth, isn't it?), and was going to lunch
down town, but while I was dressing I was confronted, as
usual, by that horrid bare spot on the wall (you know,
Frieda, just above where the Japanese panel hangs), and
made up my mind that I simply *had* to get a picture to fill
up that gap. Well, I actually gasped with relief when this
turned out to be Tom's birthday, and now I'll buy a picture
and give it to him.

Agnes, that particular wisp belongs on my head.
Don't tear at it, as though you could take it off.

Aren't men tiresome to give presents to? Don't you think so? Well, I do. After I had gone through the usual list of military brushes, soap-boxes, ash-trays, pipes, and an occasional scarf-pin, I settled down to the sensible and economical plan of giving Tom things for the house.

Eh? No, he gives me personal gifts, but then women require so many more luxuries than men, don't you think so?

Last Christmas I had the back hall papered old rose for Tom's present, having often noticed that even servants are affected by an appeal to their artistic natures, and my morning gowns are usually pink, so we blended very nicely. (I always give my orders for the day in the back hall, you know).

Oh, he gave me this gold bag. I hinted that Arthur Trevellyan had offered me one, also that I trembled on the brink of accepting it, being crazy for one. Well, ha! ha! it was *too* funny; Tom could not get down town fast enough to buy this, he has such queer ideas about — Agnes, *do* be careful; that soapy water is making a terrible buzzing in my ears!

One really needs a little tact in managing a man; don't you agree with me, Frieda?

Just the same, presents are always bothersome, and I simply *hate* Christmas. There always comes a raft of things that no one wants, especially from the girls (not you, of course, dear; I meant the other crowd; you know the sort) — "Wishing dear Kathleen a Merry, Merry Christmas" — some Christ Church veil case, with impossible burnt umber flowers, wretchedly painted on a saffron satin ground, generously sprinkled with Indian beads and tied with dark-brown satin ribbon. Horrors!

And the people who always say: "You have so many things, I never know what to give you; there's nothing I can buy, so I embroidered you this little pin-cushion cover, knowing you will appreciate my work, and a loving thought is sewn into every stitch!" Oh, dear!

Do let me raise my head, Agnes; I feel that I am already in for curvature of the spine. Thank goodness, I

Madge Macbeth

haven't a great deal of hair; it would take so much longer to dry, and anyway there would be so much more to turn gray.

What was I saying? Oh, yes; about the pin-cushion. One of the girls sent me a heart-shaped one, embroidered atrociously. I could see plainly what it was; the piece you cut out of the under arm seam of a shirt waist — don't you know, how, as the line slopes down to the waist, there is always a big piece to cut out? It was just that and nothing else. A few moments after it came, a boy left a box which looked so interesting, and addressed in a man's writing. I opened it in feverish haste, and found one of those horrible bon-bon dishes — thirty-nine cents at the Japanese store. You know the kind — from Hilda. Oh, I was *wild* with disappointment!

However, an inspiration seized me, and I carefully put the pin-cushion and dish back into their respective boxes, intending to send the girls' presents to each other. Of course, you know what happened: I got mixed and sent them to *the senders*!

Raging? Of course, they were, and such notes as I got from them! Though I didn't see why they should mind so much, because everyone knows that the sincerest way to give a present is to give something that one wants oneself. So they should have been glad to get those things. Eh? I always follow out that rule in giving Tom presents.

Agnes, *surely* you don't need to have that dryer at such a temperature. Of course, I'm in a hurry, but really I don't want my brains fricasseed, especially as I am going to meet Mr. Trevellyan.

Do you know, Frieda, he is the cleverest man I have ever known. We are totally and wholly congenial, as he agrees with me in every particular, and it is a great pleasure to meet a man with such lofty ideals and ambitions.

So often, when we are together, one makes a remark, and the other involuntarily exclaims: "Why, I was just going to say that myself!" Isn't that peculiar?

How much are those "transformations," Agnes? I know I have a lot of "store" hair, but only Tom sees it, and, anyway, I think I need a little more width to my head.

No, that is not as large as my new hat, which measures thirty-two inches from brim to brim. But then I can wear those exaggerated creations, where a person like you, Frieda, couldn't.

What, nine dollars? Why that's ridiculous! Does it match my hair? Um-hum, it looks very well. All right, I'll take it. Yes, I will wear the rat, too. There, that's the effect — higher and broader. Now I will get Tom to give me another pair of amber combs; or, better still, I will eat a philopena with Arthur Trevellyan and get them at once.

Nonsense, Frieda; I don't wonder you have never been a success, when you anchor yourself to such antediluvian notions as to propriety. Forgive me for saying so, but you really make yourself ridiculous!

There, Agnes, you have burnt my hair! Oh, yes, you *have*, I smell it. Tom says I remind him of baseball as it is — three and out, whatever he means by that. But I suppose I won't have the three, if you are going to be so careless. Moved my head? Goodness, do you expect me to sit like a statue?

Eh? Oh, yes, I'm going to Hattie's wedding. I have a Paris gown I'm crazy to wear. Give her? I don't know. One of my duplicates — whatever I have the most of. Just think; I haven't had to buy a wedding present since I was married.

Everyone gets so many bon-bon spoons, olive spoons, cream ladles, jelly spoons and sugar spoons. When people are stumped to know what to give, which doesn't cost much, they are always sure to select some kind of a spoon. Yes, but the marking can be taken off.

By the way, you must let me know what you want, Frieda, for, of course, I am going to give you something awfully nice.

Not only that I am fond of you, and always consider you my best friend, but I want Allen to see there is no feeling of ill-will on my part toward him. Doesn't he? Well you never can tell, he might not mention it to you. After being in love with a girl, a man always has a sore spot in his heart which does not heal. Poor Allen!

Did you ever notice in the giving of presents, how far removed from the apparent reason the sub-motive really is? It has often struck me, only most people are not honest enough to acknowledge it.

Well, dear, I'd *love* to stay and chat with you, while you are being done, I have hardly had time to get in a word, and I never saw you look as fagged as you do to-day, although the light in here may have something to do with the effect. Do you sleep well? But there, don't keep me talking. I have already given you five minutes of Arthur's time. Come to see me some time week after next. I can always spare you a moment; good-bye, dear, good-bye.

Canadian Magazine 32 (Dec. 1908): 157–159.

Edith Eaton (Sui Sin Far) (1867–1914)

MRS. SPRING FRAGRANCE (1910)

Eldest of fourteen children of a British father, Edward Eaton, and Chinese mother, Grace Trefusis, Edith Eaton lived briefly in England, Japan and the United States before being brought by her family to Montreal at the age of seven. Eaton worked in various office positions before becoming a journalist and short fiction writer. Aware from childhood of racial prejudice, she became involved in speaking and writing on behalf of the Chinese community in the various cities in which she worked. Working first for Montreal newspapers and periodicals, she also lived and worked for a time in various American cities, including San Francisco and Seattle. When she died in Montreal, the Chinese community erected a monument to her memory.

Under her pseudonym "Sui Sin Far" ("Water Fragrant Flower"), Eaton published stories and essays about Chinese and Eurasians in Canadian and American cities, about cross-cultural encounters and attempts by Chinese immigrants to adapt to western culture. Her writings appeared in such widely read Canadian and American periodicals as the *Canadian Dominion Illustrated*, *Century*, *Independent* and *Good Housekeeping*. In 1912, McClurg (Chicago) published a selection of her stories, *Mrs. Spring Fragrance*.

Eaton's ideological position, expressed in essays such as "Leaves from the Mental Portfolio of an Eurasian," *Independent* 66 (21 January 1909), and "Chinese Workmen in America," *Independent* 75 (31 July 1913), is equally evident in her fiction, in which she dramatizes political, social and family problems of Chinese immigrants coping with an alien language, religion and culture, and attacks racial prejudice and bureaucracy. Eaton's fiction most often directs attention to the women of this visible minority, living in a society strongly prejudiced against their race and continuing to be involved in a patriarchal Chinese culture which sees the wife as inferior and subordinate. Her stories deal primarily with the relationship between a woman and her husband, lover, or child, in which the home is the centre of meaningful activity and female friendship is important.

In "Mrs. Spring Fragrance," the protagonist contrasts with many of Eaton's central women characters who have difficulty adjusting to western culture: her husband can say proudly of Mrs. Spring Fragrance, only five years after her arrival in North America, "There are no more American words for her learning." The witty, intelligent protagonist is an ironic observer and commentator on east–west cross-cultural encounters. Mrs. Spring Fragrance appears also in "The Inferior Woman."

In other stories Eaton presents her themes more sombrely. In stories such as "The Wavering Image," she speaks bitterly and movingly of the situation of women who are, like her, Eurasian. In feminist and ethnic terms, Eaton's most provocative story, "One White Woman Who Married a Chinese," shows why a woman prefers her second husband, Chinese, to her first husband, occidental, and ironically points to the disparity between speech and action of those who purport to be feminist and liberal.

༄

Suggested Reading

Eaton, Edith. *Mrs. Spring Fragrance* (Chicago: McClurg, 1912).

McMullen, Lorraine. "Double Colonization: Femininity and Ethnicity in the Writings of Edith Eaton," in *Canada: Cross/Cultures* 2, ed. Geoffrey Davis (Amsterdam: Rodopi, 1989), pp. 141–151.

Solberg, S. E. "Sui Sin Far/Edith Eaton: First Chinese-American Fictionist," MELUS 8 (Spring 1981): 27–39.

MRS. SPRING FRAGRANCE

Edith Eaton (Sui Sin Far)

I

When Mrs. Spring Fragrance first arrived in Seattle, she was unacquainted with even one word of the American language. Five years later her husband, speaking of her, said: "There are no more American words for her learning." And everyone who knew Mrs. Spring Fragrance agreed with Mr. Spring Fragrance.

Mr. Spring Fragrance, whose business name was Sing Yook, was a young curio merchant. Though conservatively Chinese in many respects, he was at the same time what is called by the Westerners, "Americanized." Mrs. Spring Fragrance was even more "Americanized."

Next door to the Spring Fragrances lived the Chin Yuens. Mrs. Chin Yuen was much older than Mrs. Spring Fragrance; but she had a daughter of eighteen with whom Mrs. Spring Fragrance was on terms of great friendship. The daughter was a pretty girl whose Chinese name was Mai Gwi Far (a rose) and whose American name was Laura. Nearly everybody called her Laura, even her parents and Chinese friends. Laura had a sweetheart, a youth named Kai Tzu. Kai Tzu, who was American-born, and as ruddy and stalwart as any young Westerner, was noted amongst baseball players as one of the finest pitchers on the Coast. He could also sing, "Drink to me only with thine eyes," to Laura's piano accompaniment.

Now the only person who knew that Kai Tzu loved

Laura and that Laura loved Kai Tzu, was Mrs. Spring Fragrance. The reason for this was that, although the Chin Yuen parents lived in a house furnished in American style, and wore American clothes, yet they religiously observed many Chinese customs, and their ideals of life were the ideals of their Chinese forefathers. Therefore, they had betrothed their daughter, Laura, at the age of fifteen, to the eldest son of the Chinese Government schoolteacher in San Francisco. The time for the consummation of the betrothal was approaching.

Laura was with Mrs. Spring Fragrance and Mrs. Spring Fragrance was trying to cheer her.

"I had such a pretty walk today," said she. "I crossed the banks above the beach and came back by the long road. In the green grass the daffodils were blowing, in the cottage gardens the currant bushes were flowering, and in the air was the perfume of the wallflower. I wished, Laura, that you were with me."

Laura burst into tears. "That is the walk," she sobbed, "Kai Tzu and I so love; but never, ah, never, can we take it together again."

"Now, Little Sister," comforted Mrs. Spring Fragrance "you really must not grieve like that. Is there not a beautiful American poem written by a noble American named Tennyson, which says:

"'Tis better to have loved and lost,
Than never to have loved at all?"

Mrs. Spring Fragrance was unaware that Mr. Spring Fragrance, having returned from the city, tired with the day's business, had thrown himself down on the bamboo settee on the veranda, and that although his eyes were engaged in scanning the pages of the *Chinese World*, his ears could not help receiving the words which were borne to him through the open window.

"'Tis better to have loved and lost,
Than never to have loved at all?"

repeated Mr. Spring Fragrance. Not wishing to hear more of the secret talk of women, he arose and sauntered around the veranda to the other side of the house. Two pigeons circled around his head. He felt in his pocket for a li-chi which he usually carried for their pecking. His fingers touched a little box. It contained a jadestone pendant, which Mrs. Spring Fragrance had particularly admired the last time she was down town. It was the fifth anniversary of Mr. and Mrs. Spring Fragrance's wedding day.

Mr. Spring Fragrance pressed the little box down into the depths of his pocket.

A young man came out of the back door of the house at Mr. Spring Fragrance's left. The Chin Yuen house was at his right.

"Good evening," said the young man. "Good evening," returned Mr. Spring Fragrance. He stepped down from his porch and went and leaned over the railing which separated this yard from the yard in which stood the young man.

"Will you please tell me," said Mr. Spring Fragrance, "the meaning of two lines of an American verse which I have heard?"

"Certainly," returned the young man with a genial smile. He was a star student at the University of Washington, and had not the slightest doubt that he could explain the meaning of all things in the universe.

"Well," said Mr. Spring Fragrance, "it is this:

" 'Tis better to have loved and lost,
Than never to have loved at all?"

"Ah!" responded the young man with an air of profound wisdom. "That, Mr. Spring Fragrance, means that it is a good thing to love anyway — even if we can't get what we love, or, as the poet tells us, lose what we love. Of course, one needs experience to feel the truth of this teaching."

The young man smiled pensively and reminiscently. More than a dozen young maidens "loved and lost" were passing before his mind's eye.

"The truth of the teaching!" echoed Mr. Spring Fragrance, a little testily. "There is no truth in it whatever. It is disobedient to reason. Is it not better to have what you do not love than to love what you do not have?"

"That depends," answered the young man, "upon temperament."

"I thank you. Good evening," said Mr. Spring Fragrance. He turned away to muse upon the unwisdom of the American way of looking at things.

Meanwhile, inside the house, Laura was refusing to be comforted.

"Ah, no! no!" cried she. "If I had not gone to school with Kai Tzu, nor talked nor walked with him, nor played the accompaniments to his songs, then I might consider with complacency, or at least without horror, my approaching marriage with the son of Man You. But as it is — oh, as it is — !"

The girl rocked herself to and fro in heart-felt grief.

Mrs. Spring Fragrance knelt down beside her, and clasping her arms around her neck, cried in sympathy:

"Little Sister, oh, Little Sister! Dry your tears — do not despair. A moon has yet to pass before the marriage can take place. Who knows what the stars may have to say to one another during its passing? A little bird has whispered to me — "

For a long time Mrs. Spring Fragrance talked. For a long time Laura listened. When the girl arose to go, there was a bright light in her eyes.

II

Mrs. Spring Fragrance, in San Francisco on a visit to her cousin, the wife of the herb doctor of Clay Street, was having a good time. She was invited everywhere that the wife of an honorable Chinese merchant could go. There was much to see and hear, including more than a dozen babies who had been born in the families of her friends since she last visited the city of the Golden Gate. Mrs. Spring Fragrance loved babies. She had had two herself, but both had been transplanted into the spirit land before the completion of even one moon. There were also many dinners and theatre-parties given in her honor. It was at one of the theatre-parties that Mrs. Spring Fragrance met

Ah Oi, a young girl who had the reputation of being the prettiest Chinese girl in San Francisco, and the naughtiest. In spite of gossip, however, Mrs. Spring Fragrance took a great fancy to Ah Oi and invited her to a tête-à-tête picnic on the following day. This invitation Ah Oi joyfully accepted. She was a sort of bird girl and never felt so happy as when out in the park or woods.

On the day after the picnic Mrs. Spring Fragrance wrote to Laura Chin Yuen thus:

MY PRECIOUS LAURA, — May the bamboo ever wave. Next week I accompany Ah Oi to the beauteous town of San José. There will we be met by the son of the Illustrious Teacher, and in a little Mission, presided over by a benevolent American priest, the little Ah Oi and the son of the Illustrious Teacher will be joined together in love and harmony — two pieces of music made to complete one another.

The Son of the Illustrious Teacher, having been through an American Hall of Learning, is well able to provide for his orphan bride and fears not the displeasure of his parents, now that he is assured that your grief at his loss will not be inconsolable. He wishes me to waft to you and to Kai Tzu — and the little Ah Oi joins with him — ten thousand rainbow wishes for your happiness.

My respects to your honorable parents, and to yourself, the heart of your loving friend,

JADE SPRING FRAGRANCE

To Mr. Spring Fragrance, Mrs. Spring Fragrance also indited a letter:

GREAT AND HONORED MAN, — Greeting from your plum blossom,[1] who is desirous of hiding herself from the sun of your presence for a week of seven days more. My honorable cousin is preparing for the Fifth Moon Festival, and wishes me to compound for the occasion some American "fudge," for which delectable sweet, made by my clumsy hands, you have sometimes shown a slight prejudice. I am enjoying a most agreeable visit, and American friends, as also our own, strive benevolently for the accomplishment of my pleasure. Mrs. Samuel Smith, an American lady, known to my cousin, asked for my accompaniment to a magniloquent lecture the other evening. The subject was "America, the Protector of China!" It was most exhilarating, and the effect of so much expression of benevolence leads me to beg of you to forget to remember that the barber charges you one dollar for a shave while he humbly submits to the American man a bill of fifteen cents. And murmur no more because your honored elder brother, on a visit to this country, is detained under the roof-tree of this great Government instead of under your own humble roof. Console him with the reflection that he is protected under the wing of the Eagle, the Emblem of Liberty. What is the loss of ten hundred years or ten thousand times ten dollars compared with the happiness of knowing oneself so securely sheltered? All of this I have learned from Mrs. Samuel Smith, who is as brilliant and great of mind as one of your own superior sex.

For me it is sufficient to know that the Golden Gate Park is most enchanting, and the seals on the rock at the Cliff House extremely entertaining and amiable. There is

---

[1] The plum blossom is the Chinese flower of virtue. It has been adopted by the Japanese, just in the same way as they have adopted the Chinese national flower, the chrysanthemum. [Author's note]

much feasting and merry-making under the lanterns in honor of your Stupid Thorn.

I have purchased for your smoking a pipe with an amber mouth. It is said to be very sweet to the lips and to emit a cloud of smoke fit for the gods to inhale.

Awaiting, by the wonderful wire of the telegram message, your gracious permission to remain for the celebration of the Fifth Moon Festival and the making of American "fudge," I continue for ten thousand times ten thousand years,

Your ever loving and obedient woman,

JADE[2]

P.S. Forget not to care for the cat, the birds, and the flowers. Do not eat too quickly nor fan too vigorously now that the weather is warming.

Mrs. Spring Fragrance smiled as she folded this last epistle. Even if he were old-fashioned, there was never a husband so good and kind as hers. Only on one occasion since their marriage had he slighted her wishes. That was when, on the last anniversary of their wedding, she had signified a desire for a certain jadestone pendant, and he had failed to satisfy that desire.

But Mrs. Spring Fragrance, being of a happy nature, and disposed to look upon the bright side of things, did not allow her mind to dwell upon the jadestone pendant. Instead, she gazed complacently down upon her bejeweled fingers and folded in with her letter to Mr. Spring Fragrance a bright little sheaf of condensed love.

---

[2] In Chinese culture, jade symbolizes virtue, including purity and sincerity.

III

Mr. Spring Fragrance sat on his doorstep. He had been reading two letters, one from Mrs. Spring Fragrance, and the other from an elderly bachelor cousin in San Francisco. The one from the elderly bachelor cousin was a business letter, but contained the following postscript:

> Tsen Hing, the son of the Government school-master, seems to be much in the company of your young wife. He is a good-looking youth, and pardon me, my dear cousin; but if women are allowed to stray at will from under their husbands' mulberry roofs, what is to prevent them from becoming butterflies?

"Sing Foon is old and cynical," said Mr. Spring Fragrance to himself. "Why should I pay any attention to him? This is America, where a man may speak to a woman, and a woman listen, without any thought of evil."

He destroyed his cousin's letter and re-read his wife's. Then he became very thoughtful. Was the making of American fudge sufficient reason for a wife to wish to remain a week longer in a city where her husband was not?

The young man who lived in the next house came out to water the lawn.

"Good evening," said he. "Any news from Mrs. Spring Fragrance?"

"She is having a very good time," returned Mr. Spring Fragrance.

"Glad to hear it. I think you told me she was to return the end of this week."

"I have changed my mind about her," said Mr. Spring Fragrance. "I am bidding her remain a week longer, as I wish to give a smoking party during her absence. I hope I may have the pleasure of your company."

"I shall be delighted," returned the young fellow. "But, Mr. Spring Fragrance, don't invite any other white fellows. If you do not I shall be able to get in a scoop. You know, I'm a sort of honorary reporter for the *Gleaner*."

"Very well," absently answered Mr. Spring Fragrance.

"Of course, your friend the Consul will be present. I

EDITH EATON

shall call it 'A high-class Chinese stag party!'"

In spite of his melancholy mood, Mr. Spring Fragrance smiled.

"Everything is 'high-class' in America," he observed.

"Sure!" cheerfully assented the young man. "Haven't you ever heard that all Americans are princes and princesses, and just as soon as a foreigner puts his foot upon our shores, he also becomes of the nobility — I mean, the royal family."

"What about my brother in the Detention Pen?" dryly inquired Mr. Spring Fragrance.

"Now, you've got me," said the young man, rubbing his head. "Well, that is a shame — 'a beastly shame,' as the Englishman says. But understand, old fellow, we that are real Americans are up against that — even more than you. It is against our principles."

"I offer the real Americans my consolations that they should be compelled to do that which is against their principles."

"Oh, well, it will all come right some day. We're not a bad sort, you know. Think of the indemnity money returned to the Dragon by Uncle Sam."

Mr. Spring Fragrance puffed his pipe in silence for some moments. More than politics was troubling his mind.

At last he spoke. "Love," said he, slowly and distinctly, "comes before the wedding in this country, does it not?"

"Yes, certainly."

Young Carman knew Mr. Spring Fragrance well enough to receive with calmness his most astounding queries.

"Presuming," continued Mr. Spring Fragrance — "presuming that some friend of your father's, living — presuming — in England — has a daughter that he arranges with your father to be your wife. Presuming that you have never seen that daughter, but that you marry her, knowing her not. Presuming that she marries you, knowing you not. — After she marries you and knows you, will that woman love you?"

"Emphatically, no," answered the young man.

"That is the way it would be in America — that the woman who marries the man like that — would not love him?"

"Yes, that is the way it would be in America. Love, in this country, must be free, or it is not love at all."

"In China, it is different!" mused Mr. Spring Fragrance.

"Oh, yes, I have no doubt that in China it is different."

"But the love is in the heart all the same," went on Mr. Spring Fragrance.

"Yes, all the same. Everybody falls in love some time or another. Some" — pensively — "many times."

Mr. Spring Fragrance arose.

"I must go down town," said he.

As he walked down the street he recalled the remark of a business acquaintance who had met his wife and had had some conversation with her: "She is just like an American woman."

He had felt somewhat flattered when this remark had been made. He looked upon it as a compliment to his wife's cleverness; but it rankled in his mind as he entered the telegraph office. If his wife was becoming as an American woman, would it not be possible for her to love as an American woman — a man to whom she was not married? There also floated in his memory the verse which his wife had quoted to the daughter of Chin Yuen. When the telegraph clerk handed him a blank, he wrote this message:

"Remain as you wish, but remember that ' 'Tis better to have loved and lost, than never to have loved at all.'"

When Mrs. Spring Fragrance received this message, her laughter tinkled like falling water. How droll! How delightful! Here was her husband quoting American poetry in a telegram. Perhaps he had been reading her American poetry books since she had left him! She hoped so. They would lead him to understand her sympathy for her dear Laura and Kai Tzu. She need no longer keep from him their secret. How joyful! It had been such a hardship to refrain from confiding in him before. But discreetness had been most necessary, seeing that Mr. Spring Fragrance entertained as old-fashioned notions concerning marriage as did the Chin Yuen parents. Strange that that should be so, since he had fallen in love with her picture before *ever* he had seen her, just as she had fallen in love with his! And when the marriage veil was lifted and each beheld the other for the first time in the flesh, there had been no disillusion — no lessening of the respect and affection, which those who had brought about the marriage had inspired in each young heart.

Mrs. Spring Fragrance began to wish she could fall asleep and wake to find the week flown, and she in her own little home pouring tea for Mr. Spring Fragrance.

IV

Mr. Spring Fragrance was walking to business with Mr. Chin Yuen. As they walked they talked.

"Yes," said Mr. Chin Yuen, "the old order is passing away, and the new order is taking its place, even with us who are Chinese. I have finally consented to give my daughter in marriage to young Kai Tzu."

Mr. Spring Fragrance expressed surprise. He had understood that the marriage between his neighbor's daughter and the San Francisco school-teacher's son was all arranged.

"So 'twas," answered Mr. Chin Yuen; "but it seems the young renegade, without consultation or advice, has placed his affections upon some untrustworthy female, and is so under her influence that he refuses to fulfil his parents' promise to me for him."

"So!" said Mr. Spring Fragrance. The shadow on his brow deepened.

"But," said Mr. Chin Yuen, with affable resignation, "it is all ordained by Heaven. Our daughter, as the wife of Kai Tzu, for whom she has long had a loving feeling, will not now be compelled to dwell with a mother-in-law and where her own mother is not. For that, we are thankful, as she is our only one and the conditions of life in this

Western country are not as in China. Moreover, Kai Tzu, though not so much of a scholar as the teacher's son, has a keen eye for business and that, in America, is certainly much more desirable than scholarship. What do you think?"

"Eh! What!" exclaimed Mr. Spring Fragrance. The latter part of his companion's remarks had been lost upon him.

That day the shadow which had been following Mr. Spring Fragrance ever since he had heard his wife quote, "'Tis better to have loved," etc., became so heavy and deep that he quite lost himself within it.

At home in the evening he fed the cat, the bird, and the flowers. Then, seating himself in a carved black chair — a present from his wife on his last birthday — he took out his pipe and smoked. The cat jumped into his lap. He stroked it softly and tenderly. It had been much fondled by Mrs. Spring Fragrance, and Mr. Spring Fragrance was under the impression that it missed her. "Poor thing!" said he. "I suppose you want her back!" When he arose to go to bed he placed the animal carefully on the floor, and thus apostrophized it:

"O Wise and Silent One, your mistress returns to you, but her heart she leaves behind her, with the Tommies in San Francisco."

The Wise and Silent One made no reply. He was not a jealous cat.

Mr. Spring Fragrance slept not that night; the next morning he ate not. Three days and three nights without sleep and food went by.

There was a springlike freshness in the air on the day that Mrs. Spring Fragrance came home. The skies overhead were as blue as Puget Sound stretching its gleaming length toward the mighty Pacific, and all the beautiful green world seemed to be throbbing with springing life.

Mrs. Spring Fragrance was never so radiant.

"Oh," she cried light-heartedly, "is it not lovely to see the sun shining so clear, and everything so bright to welcome me?"

Mr. Spring Fragrance made no response. It was the morning after the fourth sleepless night.

Mrs. Spring Fragrance noticed his silence, also his grave face.

"Everything — everyone is glad to see me but you," she declared, half seriously, half jestingly.

Mr. Spring Fragrance set down her valise. They had just entered the house.

"If my wife is glad to see me," he quietly replied, "I also am glad to see her!"

Summoning their servant boy, he bade him look after Mrs. Spring Fragrance's comfort.

"I must be at the store in half an hour," said he, looking at his watch. "There is some very important business requiring attention."

"What is the business?" inquired Mrs. Spring Fragrance, her lip quivering with disappointment.

"I cannot just explain to you," answered her husband.

Mrs. Spring Fragrance looked up into his face with honest and earnest eyes. There was something in his manner, in the tone of her husband's voice, which touched her.

"Yen," said she, "you do not look well. You are not well. What is it?"

Something arose in Mr. Spring Fragrance's throat which prevented him from replying.

"O darling one! O sweetest one!" cried a girl's joyous voice. Laura Chin Yuen ran into the room and threw her arms around Mrs. Spring Fragrance's neck.

"I spied you from the window," said Laura, "and I couldn't rest until I told you. We are to be married next week, Kai Tzu and I. And all through you, all through you — the sweetest jade jewel in the world!"

Mr. Spring Fragrance passed out of the room.

"So the son of the Government teacher and little Happy Love are already married," Laura went on, relieving Mrs. Spring Fragrance of her cloak, her hat, and her folding fan.

Mr. Spring Fragrance paused upon the doorstep.

"Sit down, Little Sister, and I will tell you all about

it," said Mrs. Spring Fragrance, forgetting her husband for a moment.

When Laura Chin Yuen had danced away, Mr. Spring Fragrance came in and hung up his hat.

"You got back very soon," said Mrs. Spring Fragrance, covertly wiping away the tears which had begun to fall as soon as she thought herself alone.

"I did not go," answered Mr. Spring Fragrance. "I have been listening to you and Laura."

"But if the business is very important, do not you think you should attend to it?" anxiously queried Mrs. Spring Fragrance.

"It is not important to me now," returned Mr. Spring Fragrance. "I would prefer to hear again about Ah Oi and Man You and Laura and Kai Tzu."

"How lovely of you to say that!" exclaimed Mrs. Spring Fragrance, who was easily made happy. And she began to chat away to her husband in the friendliest and wifeliest fashion possible. When she had finished she asked him if he were not glad to hear that those who loved as did the young lovers whose secrets she had been keeping, were to be united; and he replied that indeed he was; that he would like every man to be as happy with a wife as he himself had ever been and ever would be.

"You did not always talk like that," said Mrs. Spring Fragrance slyly. "You must have been reading my American poetry books!"

"American poetry!" ejaculated Mr. Spring Fragrance almost fiercely, "American poetry is detestable, *abhorrable*!"

"Why! why!" exclaimed Mrs. Spring Fragrance, more and more surprised.

But the only explanation which Mr. Spring Fragrance vouchsafed was a jadestone pendant.

～

Hampton 24 (Jan. 1910): 139–141.

EDITH EATON

Nellie McClung (1873–1951)

THE LIVE WIRE (1910)

Nellie McClung was, like L. M. Montgomery, one of Canada's most popular writers during the period 1900–1920. Pearlie Watson, whom we encounter as a girl of twelve in "The Live Wire," was McClung's most important female hero and the central character of three of her best-selling books — *Sowing Seeds in Danny* (1908), *The Second Chance* (1910) and *Purple Springs* (1922). As is the case with Montgomery's Anne of Green Gables, Pearl is initially disadvantaged but triumphs over obstacles through intelligence, imagination and "spunk." Like Anne, she goes on from early adventures to become a teacher and marries a doctor (the Dr. Clay of this story) who values her brains as well as her beauty. Unlike Anne, however, Pearl Watson becomes active in the struggle for temperance, female suffrage and women's rights.

In her political activism and her disdain for traditional "good old boy" pork barrel politics, Pearl Watson was in fact an alter ego for her creator, Helen ("Nellie") Letitia Mooney McClung. Born on a farm in Grey County, Western Ontario, to a large, lively Scots-Irish family, Nellie became a child of the prairie in 1880, when her family moved to a homestead in the Souris Valley, Manitoba. Her parents struggled to achieve self-sufficiency for themselves and their six children. The domestic responsibilities of the young Nellie and the initial lack of a local school were such that she was unable to attend school until the age of ten, but she went on to graduate from Winnipeg Normal School in 1889 at the age of sixteen. She taught at several country schools in Manitoba and in 1896 married pharmacist Wesley McClung, the son of a woman whose Women's Christian Temperance Union activism Nellie admired and emulated.

Encouraged by her mother-in-law and others, Nellie, while raising five children, began to write fiction that expressed both her political and social activism and the world of her upbringing. After moving to Winnipeg in 1911, she played a leading role in the struggle that led to the 1916 enfranchisement of women in Manitoba. She continued such literary and political work in Alberta, her home after 1914. She sat as a Liberal — an independent and eloquent one — in the Alberta Legislature from 1921 to 1925. With police magistrate and fellow writer Emily Murphy ("Janey Canuck"), she was one of the five well-known women who pursued the landmark "Persons Case" to the British Privy Council, thereby winning for Canadian women in 1929 the right to be recognized as legal "persons" under the British North America Act, a judgement that opened senatorial and other legislative appointments to women. After the McClungs retired to Vancouver Island in 1935, she continued to publish and to play a role in public life, in part through the CBC Board of Governors (1936–1942), the Canadian Authors' Association and the League of Nations, where she was a delegate at the session of 1938. She published her autobiography in two volumes: *Clearing in the West* (1936) and *The Stream Runs Fast* (1945).

"The Live Wire" embodies both McClung's gift for rendering the life of the small-town West and her ability to embed her political and social ideas in comic fiction. She holds the male political world up to ridicule, gives us vivid characterization, valorizes female spirit, and uses skilful, colourful dialogue. This story, like the 1912 story "The Elusive Vote," has anti-liquor sentiment as a sub-theme. "The Live Wire" (1906) was revised and published in a book of stories, *Sowing Seeds in Danny* (1908), which sold over 100,000 copies. An irrepressible and charismatic maternal feminist who stoutly declared she wanted to "clean up" society, Nellie McClung was a fiction writer determined to both amuse and instruct. The results appealed to thousands of readers.

❧

Suggested Reading
Gorham, Deborah. "Canadian Feminism in the 1920s: The Case of Nellie McClung," *Journal of Canadian Studies* 12, 4 (1977): 58–68.

McClung, Nellie. *Sowing Seeds in Danny* (Toronto: Briggs, 1908).

———. *The Black Creek Stopping-House and Other Stories* (Toronto: Briggs, 1912).

Savage, Candace, ed. *Our Nell: A Scrapbook Biography of Nellie L. McClung* (Saskatoon: Prairie, 1979).

THE LIVE WIRE

Nellie McClung

"Who is this young gentleman or lady?" Dr. Clay asked of Pearlie Watson one day when he met her wheeling a carriage in which was a very fat baby.

"This is the Czar of all the Rooshias," Pearl answered gravely, "and I'm his bodyguard."

The doctor's face showed no surprise as he stepped back to get a better look at the Czar.

"See the green plush on his kerridge!" Pearl said proudly, "and every stitch he has on is handmade, and was did for him, too, and he's fed every four hours, rain or shine, hit or miss!"

"Think of that!" the doctor exclaimed with emphasis, "and yet some people tell us the Czar has a hard time."

Pearl drew a step nearer, moving the carriage up and down rapidly to appease the wrath of the Czar, who was expressing his disapproval of the delay in a very lumpy cry.

"I'm just 'tendin', ye know, about him being the Czar," she said confidentially. "Ye see I mind him everyday, and that's the way I play. Maudie Ducker said one day I never had no time to play cos we wuz so pore, and that started me. It's a lovely game."

The doctor nodded. He knew something of 'tendin' games, too.

"I have to taste everythin' he eats for fear of Paris green in it," she said, speaking now in the official voice of the bodyguard. "I have to stand betune him and the howlin' mob thirstin' for his gore!"

"I believe he howls more than the mob," the doctor said smiling.

"He's afraid we're plottin'," Pearl whispered. "Can't trust no one. But he ain't howlin'; that's his natcheral voice when he's talkin' Rooshian. He don't know one English word, only 'goo,' but he'll say it every time. See now. How is um pecious luvvy-duvvy? See the pitty manny! Pull um baby toofin.'"

The Czar, secure in his toothlessness, was not at all alarmed at this threat, and rippled his fat face into dimples, triumphantly bringing forth a whole succession of "goos."

"Ain't he a peach?" Pearlie said with pride. "Some kids won't show off worth a cent when you want them to, but he'll say 'goo' if you even nudge him. His mother thinks 'goo' is an awfully childish word, and she's at him all the time to say 'daddy-dinger,' but he don't seem to take to it. Say, Doctor," Pearlie's face was troubled, "what do you think of his looks? Hasn't he a fine little nub of a nose? Do you see anything about him to make his mother cry?"

The doctor looked critically at the Czar, who returned his gaze with stolid indifference.

"I never saw a more perfect nub on any nose," he answered honestly. "He's a fine big boy, and his mother should be proud of him."

"There now, what did I tell you?" Pearlie cried delightedly, nodding her head at an imaginary audience. "That's what I do be sayin' to his mother, but she's so tuk up with pictures of pretty kids with big eyes and curly hair, she don't seem to get used to the Czar here. She says his nose is so different, and his voice is not what she wanted. He does cry lumpy I know. You see, the kid in the book she's readin' could say 'Daddy-dinger' long before it was as old as the Czar is. He can't pat-a-cake, or wave a bye-bye, or this-little-toe-went-to-market, or nuthin'. I never told her what Danny could do when he was this age, but I'm tryin' hard to get him to say 'Daddy-dinger,' she has her heart so set on it. I must go now."

The doctor lifted his hat, and the imperial carriage rolled on.

Pearl had gone a short distance when she remembered something.

"I'll let you know if he says it, Doctor," she shouted.

"All right, Pearl, thank you," he smiled back.

When Pearl turned the next corner she met Maudie Ducker. Maudie had on a new plaid dress with velvet trimming.

"Is that your Sunday dress?" she asked, looking critically at Pearl's faded little brown wincey.

"My, no!" Pearl answered cheerfully — the family honour had to be sustained — "This is just my morning dress. I wear my blue satting in the afternoon and on Sundays, my purple velvet with the watter-pleat and basque-yoke of tartaric plaid, garnished with lace."

"Yours is a nice little plain dress — that stuff fades tho' — Ma lined a quilt for the boys' bed with it, and it faded grey!"

Maudie Ducker was a "perfect little lady." Her mother often said so. The number of days that Maudie could wear an apron without its showing one stain, was simply wonderful! Maudie had two dolls with which she never played. She could not bear to touch a baby because it might put a sticky little finger on her pinafore.

When Maudie made inquiries as to Pearl's Sabbathday attire, her motives were kinder than Pearl thought.

Maudie's mother was giving her a party. Hitherto the guests on such occasions had been selected with great care, and with respect to social standing, blue china, and correct enunciation. This time they were selected with still greater care, but with respect to their father's politics. All Conservatives and undecided voters' children were invited. The fight-to-a-finish-for-the-Grand-Old-Party Reformers were not invited.

Algernon Evans (otherwise known as the Czar of all the Rooshias), only son of J. H. Evans, editor of the *Millford Mercury*, could not be overlooked. Hence the necessity of inviting Pearl Watson, his bodyguard.

Millford had two weekly newspapers, one Conservative in its tendencies, the other one Reform. Between them there existed a feud long-standing, unquenchable, constant. It went with the subscription list, the printing press, and the good-will of the former owner when the paper changed hands. It blazed in the editorials, it even coloured the local news.

McSorley, the Liberal editor, being an Irishman, was not without humour; but Evans, the other one, revelled in it. He was like the little boys who stick pins in frogs, not that they bear the frogs any ill-will, but for the fun of seeing them jump. He would sit smiling over his political editorials with utmost good humour — sometimes throwing himself back in his chair and laughing like a light-hearted boy, and then those who heard him knew that the knife was turned in some one.

One day, Mr. James Ducker, lately retired farmer, sometimes insurance agent, read in the Winnipeg *Telegram* that his former friend, the Hon. Thomas Snider, had chaperoned an Elk party to St. Paul. Mr. Ducker had but a hazy idea of the duties of a chaperon, but he liked the sound of it, and it set him thinking. He remembered when Tom Snider had entered politics a few years ago, with a decayed reputation, a strong and growing thirst for alcoholic stimulants and about four dollars in cash. Now he rode in a private car, had a suite of rooms at the Empire, and the papers often spoke of him as "mine host Snider."

Mr. Ducker turned over the paper and read in another column that the genial Thomas had replied in a very able manner to the toast, "Our Guests," at the Elks' banquet at Ryan's, St. Paul. Whereupon Mr. Ducker became wrapped in deep thought, and it was during this passive period that he distinctly heard his country's call. The call came in these words: "If Tom Snider can do it, why can't I?"

The idea took hold of him. He began to brush his hair artfully over the bald spot. He made strange faces at his mirror, wondering which view of his countenance would be best to have photographed for his handbills.

He saw himself like Cincinnatus of old, called from the plough to the Senate, but he told himself that there couldn't have been as good a thing in it then as there is now, or Cincinnatus would not have come back to the steers!

Mr. Ducker's social qualities developed amazingly. He courted his neighbours assiduously, stopping to have protracted conversations with men whom he had known but slightly. Every name on the voters' list began to have a new significance.

There was one man whom he feared — that was Evans, editor of the Conservative paper. Sometimes, when his fancy painted for him a gay and alluring picture of carrying "the proud old Conservative banner — that has suffered defeat, but, thank God, never disgrace!" (quotation from speech he was preparing) "in the face of the foe," he would inadvertently think of Evans, and it gave him gooseflesh!

Mr. Ducker had lived in and around Millford for some time, and so had Evans. Evans had a most treacherous memory — you could not depend on him to forget anything.

When Evans was friendly with him his hopes ran high, but when he caught Evans looking at him with a boyish smile twinkling in his eyes his vision of chaperoning an Elk party to St. Paul became very shadowy indeed!

Mr. Ducker tried diplomacy. He withdrew his insurance ad. from McSorley's paper, and doubled his space in Evans', paying in advance. He watched the train for visitors and reported them to Evans. He wrote breezy little local briefs in his own light cow-like way for Evans' paper.

Mr. Ducker was very hopeful. A friend in Winnipeg had already a house in view for them, and Mrs. Ducker had decided what church they would attend and what day she would receive, and many other important matters that it is well to have off one's mind and not leave to the last. Maudie Ducker had been taken into the secret, and she began to feel sorry for other little girls whose papas were content to let their families live always in such a poky little place as Millford. Maudie also began to dream dreams of sweeping in upon the Millford people in flowing robes and sparkling diamonds. Wilford only, of the Ducker family, was in darkness. His mother said he was too young to appreciate the Change.

The approach of Nomination Day hastened the date of Maudie's party. Mrs. Ducker told Maudie that they must invite the Czar and Pearlie Watson, though of course she didn't say the Czar — she said Algernon Evans and that little Watson girl. Maudie objected on account of Pearl's scanty wardrobe and the Czar's moist little hands, but Mrs. Ducker, knowing that the Czar's father was their long suit, stood firm.

Mr. Ducker had said to her that very morning, rubbing his hands and speaking in the voice of a conspirator, "We must leave no stone unturned, my dear; this is the time of seed-sowing. We must pull every wire." The Czar was a wire, therefore they proceeded to pull him. They did not know that he was a live wire until later.

Pearl's delight at being asked to a real party was good to see. Maudie need not have worried about her appearing at the feast without a festal robe, for the dress that Camilla had made her for the musical recital was just waiting for an occasion to air its loveliness. Anything that was needed to complete her wardrobe was supplied by her kind-hearted mistress, the Czar's mother.

But Mrs. Evans stood looking wistfully after her only son, as Pearl wheeled him gaily down the walk that bright afternoon. He was beautifully dressed in the finest of mull and Valenciennes. His carriage was elegant. Pearl, in her neat hat and dress, was a pretty little nurse-girl. But Mrs. Evans' sweet face was troubled. She was thinking of the Mellin's Food Baby she had so coveted, and Algernon was — so different, and his nose was — strange, too, and she had massaged it so carefully, and when, oh! when would he say "Daddy-dinger"?

Algernon was not envious of the Mellin's Food Baby that afternoon, nor worried about his nose either, as he bumped up and down in his carriage in glad good humour, and delivered full-sized gurgling "goos" at every person he met, even throwing them along the street in the prodigality of his heart, as he waved his fat hands and thumped his heavy little heels.

Pearl held her head high and felt very much like the bodyguard as she lifted the weighty ruler to the ground inside the Ducker gate; Mrs. Ducker ran down the steps and kissed the Czar ostentatiously, and as she carried him into the house, she poured out such a volume of admiring epithets that Pearl followed in dazed bewilderment, wondering why she had not heard of all this before.

Two little girls in very fluffy short skirts sat demurely in the hammock, keeping their dresses clean, and wondering if there would be ice cream within doors. Maudie worried out "Mary's Pet Waltz" on the piano to a dozen or more patient little listeners. On the lawn several little girls played croquet. There were no boys at the party. Wilford was going to entertain the boys, that is the Conservative boys, the next day. Wilford stood at the gate disconsolately. He had been left without a station at his own request. Down at the tracks a freight train shunted and shuddered. Not a boy was in sight, and Wilford knew why. The farmers were loading cattle cars.

Pearl went around to the side lawn where the little girls were playing croquet, holding the Czar's hand tightly.

"What are you playin', girls?" she asked.

They told her.

"Can you play it?" Mildred Bates asked.

"I guess I can," Pearl said modestly. "I am always too busy for games like that."

"Maudie Ducker says you never get time to play," Blanche White said with sincere pity in her voice.

"Maudie Ducker is away off there," Pearl answered with dignity. "I have lots of fun, and don't you forget it, and it isn't this frowsy standin'-round-doin'-nothin', that you kids call fun, either."

"Tell us about it, Pearl," they cried, flocking round her. Pearl's stories had a charm for them.

"Well," Pearl said, taking the Czar on her knee as she sat on the grass. "Ye know I wash Mrs. Evans' dishes for her, and lovely ones they are, too, all pink and gold with dinky little ivy leaves crawlin' out over the edges of the cups; I play I am at the seashore and the tide is comin' in o'er and o'er the sand, and round and round the land, as far as eye can see. I put all the dishes into the big dish-pan, and I pertend the tide is risin' on them, tho' it's just me pourin' on the water. The cups are the boys and the saucers are the girls, and the butter-chips are the babies. Then I rush in to save them, but not until they cry 'Lord save us, we perish!' Of course I yell it for them, good and loud, too, you bet; people don't just squawk at a time like that — it often scares Mrs. Evans even yet. I save the babies first. I slush them around to clean them, but they never notice that, and then I stand them up high and dry in the drip-pan. Then I go in after the girls and the boys, and I save the mothers and fathers, too, that's the plates, and I rub them all well so's they won't ketch cold, and I get them all packed off to bed in the china cabinet, every man-jack o' them singin', 'Are we yet alive and see each other's face.' Mrs. Evans sings it for them when she's there, and they soon forget they were so near death's door. Then I get the vegetable dishes and the bowls and silverware, and all that, and I pertend that's an excursion, and they're all drunk, not a sober man on board. The capt'n commands them to make merry, and they're singing 'We won't go home till mornin', when crash! a cry bursts from every soul on board. They have struck upon a rock and are goin' down! Water pours in at the gunnel (that's just me with more water and soap, you know), but I ain't sorry for them, they're old enough to know that wine is a mocker, and strong drink is ragin'. But you bet they get sober prit' quick when the swellin' waters burst over them, and come rushin' upon deck with pale faces, and I've often seen a big white bowl — he's the capt'in — whirl round and round, dizzy-like, and say "Woe is me!" and sink to the bottom. Mrs. Evans told me that's what he says. Anyway, I do save them all at last, when they see what whiskey's doin' for them. I rub them all and send them home. The steel knives they're the worst of all, but tho' they're black and stained with sin, they are still our brothers. So I give them the Gold Cure — that's the bath-brick, and they make a fresh start."

"That's a lovely game," Lily White said rapturously.

"When I sweep the floor," Pearl went on, "I pertend I am the Army of the Lord that comes to clear the way from dust and sin, and let the King of Glory in. Under the stove the hordes of sin are awful thick — they love darkness rather than light, because their deeds are evil. But I say the 'Sword of the Lord and of Gideon!' and let her have it! Sometimes I pertend I'm the woman that lost the piece of silver, and I sweep the house diligently till I find it, and once Mrs. Evans did put ten cents under the door mat just for fun, for me to find, and I never know when she's goin' to do something like that for me."

Here Maudie Ducker, who had joined the group on the lawn, and was listening in dull wonder, cried, "O, here's Pa and Mr. Evans; they are going to take our picture!"

The little girls, roused out of the spell that Pearl's games had woven around them, immediately began to group themselves under the trees, and to arrange their little skirts and frills.

The Czar had toddled on his uncertain little fat legs around to the back door, for he had caught sight of a red-head that he knew and liked very much. It belonged to Mary McSorley, the eldest of the McSorley family, who had brought over to Mrs. Ducker an extra two quarts of milk which Mrs. Ducker had ordered for the occasion.

Mary sat on the back step until Mrs. Ducker should find time to empty her pitcher. Mary was strictly an outsider. Mary's father was a Reformer. His paper was in opposition to dear Mr. Evans' paper. Mary was never well dressed, partly accounted for by the fact that the stork had visited the McSorley home so frequently. Therefore, for all these reasons, any one sufficient in itself, Mary sat on the back step, a rank outsider.

The Czar, who knew nothing of these things, began to "goo" when he saw Mary. She reached out her arms, and he stumbled into them. Mary fell to kissing his bald head. She felt more at home with a baby in her arms.

NELLIE McCLUNG

It was at this unfortunate moment that Mr. Ducker and Mr. Evans came around the rear of the house. Mr. Evans was beginning to think rather more favourably of Mr. Ducker as the prospective Conservative member. Poor old goat, there are plenty worse (he was thinking); he has no brains, but heaven help us! what would a man of brains do with that bunch in Winnipeg? Brainy men make the trouble. The Grits made that mistake once — just once — and see what trouble they got into!

Mr. Ducker had adroitly drawn the conversation to a discussion of children. He knew that Mr. Evans' weak point was his little son Algernon.

"That's a clever looking little fellow of yours, Evans," he had remarked carelessly as they came up the street. (Mr. Ducker had never seen the Czar closely). "My wife was just saying that he has a remarkable forehead for a little fellow."

"He has," the other man said smiling, not at all displeased. "It runs clear down to his neck."

"He can hardly help being clever if there's anything in heredity," Mr. Ducker went on with infinite tact, feeling his private car drawing nearer and nearer.

Then the Evil Genius of the house of Ducker awoke from his slumber, sat up, took notice, and smiled. The house that the friend in Winnipeg had selected fell into irreparable ruin. Poor Maudie's diamonds vanished at a touch! Mr. Ducker's dream of carrying the grand old Conservative banner in the face of the foe, ceased to be a dream and became a nightmare!

They turned the corner and came upon Mary McSorley, who sat upon the back-step with the Czar in her arms. Mary's face was hidden as she kissed the Czar's fat neck, and in the general babel of voices within and without she did not hear them coming.

"Speaking about heredity," Mr. Ducker said suavely, speaking in a low voice, and looking at whom he supposed to be the latest McSorley, "it looks as if there must be something in it over there. Isn't that McSorley over again? Low forehead, pug nose, bulldog tendencies." Mr. Ducker was something of a phrenologist, and went merrily on to his own destruction.

"Now, the girl is rather pleasant looking, and some of the others are not bad at all, but this one is surely a regular little Mickey. Now, Evans, I believe a person would be safe in saying that that child will not grow up a Presbyterian, what do you think?"

Mr. Evans was the Worshipful Grand Master of the Loyal Orange Lodge, and well up in the Black, and Mr. Ducker was sure that this remark would appeal to him. It did.

"Ignatius McSorley will never be dead while this little fellow lives," Mr. Ducker continued, laughing gaily and rubbing his hands.

The Czar looked up and saw his father. Perhaps he saw the hurt in his father's face and longed to heal him of it, or perhaps the time had come when he should forever break the goo-fetters that had lain upon his speech. He wriggled off Mary's knee, and toddling uncertainly across the grass, held out his dimpled arms with a glad cry of "Daddy-dinger!"

∽

That evening while Mrs. Ducker and Maudie were busy fanning Mr. Ducker and putting wet towels on his head, Mr. Evans sat down to write.

"Some more of that tiresome election stuff, John?" his pretty wife asked, as she proudly rocked the emancipated Czar to sleep.

"Yes, dear, it is election stuff," he answered, as he kissed her tenderly, "but it is not a bit tiresome."

Several times during the evening and far into the night, she heard him laugh — his happy, boyish laugh. James Ducker did not get the nomination.

∽

Canadian Magazine 27, 2 (June 1906): 123–128; revised and included in *Sowing Seeds in Danny* (Toronto: Briggs, 1908), 87–111.

Mazo de la Roche (1879–1961)

CANADIAN IDA AND ENGLISH NELL (1911)

Mazo de la Roche is remembered today as an author who came to prominence in the twenties with the enduringly popular *Jalna* books, the first of which won the $10,000 Atlantic Little, Brown Prize in 1927. But she had in fact been publishing fiction since 1902. She was born Mazo Louise Roche in Newmarket, Ontario, the daughter of Alberta Lundy and William Richmond Roche, a rather quixotic businessman and salesman. Mazo grew up in Newmarket, Galt and Toronto; by 1894 Carolyn (Caroline) Clement, her beloved first cousin and lifelong companion, had come to live with the family. In 1911, her father settled his family on "Rochedale," a farm near Bronte, Mazo de la Roche's home until she was fifteen. The deaths of her father in 1915 and her mother in 1920 strengthened the bond between Mazo and her cousin. In the early twenties, the two acquired a summer cottage at Clarkson (near Oakville) and became friendly with the family of the young poet Dorothy Livesay. With fame, de la Roche travelled, and she and Clement lived mostly in England in the decade 1929–1939, raising a son and daughter whom de la Roche had adopted in 1931. In 1939, the family returned to Canada to a succession of imposing homes in and around Toronto. Mazo de la Roche published her account of her life, *Ringing the Changes*, in 1957, four years before her death.

Mazo de la Roche published her first short story in 1902 in *Munsey's Magazine*, but for the next nine years her literary output was limited by nervous debility and writer's block. In 1922, she published the well-received *Explorers of the Dawn*, a book of stories, but she still had to struggle to earn a living. Her cousin's civil service job was their mainstay. With the prize for her novel *Jalna* in 1927 came prosperity and a cornucopia of sequels to *Jalna* — fifteen in all, plus a play and a posthumous television series. These novels skilfully and dramatically combine realism and romance with strong characterization to create a myth of anglophile Upper Canadian gentry on a comfortable country estate.

By contrast, "Canadian Ida and English Nell," an early story, has as backdrop a crude and bustling Canadian town of tanneries and hostelries, not unlike the Newmarket or Galt the young "Maisie" Roche knew. (Roche's father had briefly owned a hotel in Acton, Ontario.) However, in an ironic inversion of the usual settlement pattern, Nell and her Albert return to England. There are also ironic inversions of fictional norms: Nell's ingenuity and determination enable her to reclaim a husband neither faithful nor tender but rather brutal and devious. Albert's insistence that he loves Nell "cruel well" underlies the themes of male force and dominance and the lavishing of womanly virtues of loyalty and domesticity on an unworthy male. Both the new country, and Ida, the red-haired "baggage" who is its chief exemplum, are presented starkly. Even the oafish Albert scorns the joylessness of the Canadian village: "The song is froze in their 'earts wiv the cold, an' the dawnce dried up in their bones wiv the work." Mazo de la Roche was sufficiently taken by this story to expand some of its elements for her comic novel *Delight* (1926).

ᔭ

Suggested Reading
de la Roche, Mazo. *Delight* (New York: Macmillan, 1926).
———. *Selected Stories of Mazo de la Roche*, ed. Douglas Daymond (Ottawa: University of Ottawa Press, 1971).
Hambleton, Ronald. *Mazo de la Roche of Jalna* (New York: Hawthorne, 1966).

CANADIAN IDA AND ENGLISH NELL

Mazo de la Roche

The small, eager face of the girl peering through the rain-splashed window of the railway carriage and her tense grip on her little belongings showed her an unaccustomed traveler, though her weary eyes and wrinkled dress suggested that the journey had been long. When the brakeman, swinging down the aisle, pronounced with stentorian precision, "Acford! Acfor-r-d W-est!" she rose with nervous haste, and, clutching her bundles a little closer, hurried to the door, where she clung, swaying, while the other passengers craned their necks to see the traveler who was so keen to be at her journey's end.

Her dress showed her to be English, a working girl one would say; but she carried her small dark head with more spirit than most of these, and a Welsh mother had given her a pair of fine blue eyes.

With a final jolt the train drew up, and in a moment more the girl had stumbled down the wet steps and was on the station platform. She threw back her head and drew a deep breath of joy, for at last! at last! she breathed the very air that Albert breathed.

Very muggy air it was on this November morning, and heavily freighted with the smell of the tanneries, to which Acford owed its being. But to the girl it was as wine and brought a flush to her cheek, for this was Canada, this was Acford, and yonder was a freight car being loaded with hides which Albert himself might have handled! She sniffed joyously and did not feel the rain that drenched her hair.

A yellow 'bus stood at the platform's edge, and the driver, lounging on a wheel, eyed her sarcastically.

"A fine morning it is for star-gazing," he said.

"I see a 'ole ship o' stars," answered the girl.

The man considered this a moment but could make nothing of it, so he asked:

"Are you the new girl for the Acford House?"

"Is that where Albert boards — Albert Masters? If it is, w'y, I'm for there all right!" She laughed, happily.

"Albert Masters?" repeated the driver. "Ah, one of them little Cockney fellers! Sure! He boards there, or did. What's he to you?"

"Oh — a friend," she said, still smiling. "And I think I'll get in if you don't mind. I'm awful wet."

"And I'm awful dry," said the man, "so that's a good reason for both of us to hike for the Acford."

He mounted his seat and by loosening the door strap made it possible for her to enter and occupy one of the moist leather seats, where scattered crumbs of cake told tales of an infant passenger.

The 'bus pitched fearfully and the seat was so slippery that one of her bundles was constantly on the floor, and she was obliged to brace her feet on the opposite seat to maintain her own balance.

She had glimpses of yellow frame shops, with now and then a new brick building, but the street was deserted. "My word," she thought, "after London, this is like a cemingtary!" Then, with a thrill came the thought of Albert and his joy at seeing her. Surely he could not be vexed with her for following him. It had been a long, long year; she had earned the passage money herself, and ten pounds to the good to set up housekeeping, and his savings added to that!

"Gone to sleep in there?" asked the driver, pushing his head in at the door. "We're here, because we're here, because we're here — ."

"And I'm better here than there," laughed the girl, clambering out. "Wot's the price?"

"Nixie, when you've got a pair of eyes like them," he

answered. "You tell Albert I said that. I ain't afraid of any Cockney!"

The Acford House had a deep stone porch, leading to a low hallway, pleasant with the smell of ale. The sound of men's laughter came through a shutter-like door.

The 'bus driver tapped on this and called, "Bill!"

The door swung open and a young man appeared, shirt-sleeved, with a cigar between his teeth.

"Say, Billy," said the driver, "this young lady wants to see Albert Masters. He boards here, don't he?"

"Not now," replied Bill, "but he'll be in for a nip at noon, sure. What's he to you?"

His eyes were bold and the teeth that gripped the cigar very white, so the girl dropped her lids and said, demurely,

"Oh, a forty-second cousin, if you like."

Billy laughed and took her traveling bag.

"Well, you just come up to the ladies' parlor with me and I'll pinch Albert for you all right."

He led the way upstairs. The 'bus driver looked yearningly after them, then slowly disappeared into the bar.

Bill gave her a seat by the window and balanced himself on the edge of a table opposite as though for a chat, but from below came the ceaseless banging of a bell and cries of "Bill! Bill!" Then a scuffling sound and some one yelling, "Chuck him out!"

Bill flung angrily downstairs, the girl looking after him for a moment with shy admiration, before she settled herself contentedly in the chair to watch for Albert.

It was a quarter to twelve by the clock on the mantelpiece. In fifteen minutes more the tannery would close for the dinner hour. She rubbed a clear space on the misty pane and looked out. On the opposite corner of the street was a tailor shop. She could see the tailor sitting cross-legged, stitching placidly. No youthful bliss awaited him in fifteen minutes! In a window across the way a baker's wares were temptingly displayed — rows of shiny buns and jam tarts. She was very hungry, but — what a meal when Albert came!

At five minutes to twelve a whistle blew shrilly, and a flock of little children, the smallest of the school, scampered down the street, hurrying home out of the wet. "Dear little things!" thought the girl. Perhaps some day she and Albert would send a little kid to school.

A great bell clanged and, with a start, she perceived that the hands of the clock pointed to twelve. She ran to the mirror to tuck some stray locks beneath her hat. How sallow her face looked after the seasickness, and how blue below the eyes! Her little white hat, too, was soiled and mussed. She rubbed her cheeks to give them a color, and twitched a fold of the pink silk handkerchief about her throat into view.

The front door banged. Softly she crept half way down the stairs and leaned over the rail. A dozen men had entered and were pushing toward the bar. The smell of hides rose from them. Albert was not among them. The last one, a yellow-mustached Scot, saw her, and caught at her skirt with, "Coom along an' hae a drap, my lass!" But she shrank back.

Again the door banged. Three Englishmen, mere boys, passed in chanting a London music-hall song. It was coarse, but it brought the tears to her eyes. Would Albert never come?

As the bar filled the noise increased, and other men entering saw her and some called to her.

Again the door opened and closed, more gently this time, and a man entered alone. She knew the step before the thickset figure appeared. She leaned toward him and held out her arms.

"Albert! Oh, Albert!"

He stopped with a jerk of the head as though struck, then he saw her and his face went white.

"Gawd Orlmighty, 'elp me!" he gasped. "Nell!"

She reached down and caught his face between her hands and kissed him.

"W'y, Albert," she whispered, "ain't you glad to see me?"

He freed himself and pointed fiercely up the stairs.

"Out o' sight," he said, hoarsely; "get up there quick or they'll see you!"

With a fearful look at the bar door he ran stealthily up the steps behind her, and the girl, stumbling ahead of him, sobbed now in dread. He closed the parlor door behind them, locked it, then turned to face her with an accusing frown.

He had round, childish eyes, with a slight cast in one, and wide-spaced teeth which gave his smile an almost infantile look of candor, but they were set now in a desperate effort at self-control.

"Well," he growled, "you 'ave made a bally mess o' things! You 'ave."

"Oh, Albert," she wailed, "I thought you wanted me! You said the money was the only hindrance — and I earned it all myself — honest, too — and I've ten pound left for furnishing — and — . Oh, Albert, don't you love me no more?"

"Blarst the money!" he said. "Wot the 'ell do I care for your ten pound? And you promised to obey me, and now you comes over 'ere, as chipper as you please, arter me a-tellin' you perticlar to stop 'ome! You're a nice, dootiful wife, now, ain't yer?"

As he called her wife his face softened. He came and put his arms about her trembling form.

"Aw, Nellie," he said hoarsely, "I'm in a 'orrible fix and I orta be arskin' your forgiveness instead of runnin' on yer. Don't you cry, ducky! I do love yer, but — but — . I s'y, Nell, daon't you look at me thet w'y. I cawn't tell you — ." His voice broke and he hid his face on her shoulder.

"Go on, Albert," she said gently. "I'll try an' bear it."

"Oh, it's orful!" he moaned. "I didn't go for to do it — but she just chivied me inter it an' — an' — I married 'er six months ago!"

He raised his eyes to look into hers, but the sight of her white agony made him hide them again.

"Oh, Gawd!" he whined, "I wish I'd never seen 'er ugly red 'ead, I do!"

"Red 'ead," she repeated dully. "I cawn't 'ardly

believe it. Wot did you s'y 'er nime was?"

"Ida."

"Canadian?"

"Yus. And a baggage she are, too."

Of a sudden Nell pushed him from her.

"Oh, you — you — brute," she cried fiercely, "an' me eatin' my 'eart out in old London for you!"

"That's orl very well *in* old London." He wagged his head resentfully. "But it's another story *'ere*! Wot wiv the bloomin' climate, an' the stink of the vats allus in a feller's nose, an' 'is 'eart cryin' out for 'ome, 'e ain't responsible for wot 'e does! — An' — an' I thought I'd find a w'y out of it, I did!"

Nell threw up her chin defiantly.

"She ain't your legal wife, any'ow."

But Albert shook his head dolefully.

"You daon't understand a little bit, old girl. W'y, if I tried to cut loose, she'd 'ave the lor o' me, an' I'd get a term for bigamy, an' you'd be disgriced. Oh, I couldn't bear ter 'ave *you* disgriced in this bloomin' country! But a thought *'as* come to me." He took her in his arms again and rubbed his cheek on hers. "Lord! I'd clean forgot wot a little beauty you was, Nellic!" (No need to rub her cheeks for color now, and her eyes — how blazing!) "I allus loved a black-haired lass — well, I was sayin' as 'ow it come to me that if you'd tell you were my *cousin* —— ."

She laughed bitterly.

"Yes. I told the 'bus man that — for a joke!"

"You did? Good! Now, we shall s'y, old girl, that you're my little cousin, wot 'eard there were a kitchen girl wanted 'ere. You can easily get the job an' earn good money. I'll see you every day, an' then, some-ow, we'll find a w'y out of this fix. But just keep dark for the present, won't yer? I cawn't stand a row."

"You coward!"

"Call me orl the nimes you will, Nell. It's yer right to do it. But I cawn't bear to see you disgriced. Aw, Nellie!"

Two tears rolled down his cheeks.

Then the poor girl, being very tender for him,

promised, with a sinking heart, not to disclose their real relationship until Albert should "find a w'y."

So it came that the eager passenger of the Westbound train found herself at her journey's end more lonely than when she had been in old London dreaming of a little home with Albert in far Acford.

II

Albert made all the arrangements for his sad-eyed little cousin, even to the wage, the largeness of which amazed Nell, though, with Cockney shrewdness, she concealed her surprise. She was handed over to the cook, Mrs. Sye, a Surrey woman, whose husband, Old Tommy, was the porter and of much less importance than she. There were two other maids, both Canadians: Edith, the dining-room girl, who had once, for a night, been on the stage in vaudeville, and who ever since had worn the most beautiful boots and rolled her eyes amazingly; the other was the chambermaid, little brown-eyed Annie, who, Nell soon discovered, loved the shirt-sleeved young man, Bill.

They were all very kind to her, and Old Tommy stood so long questioning her, with a bucket of water in each hand, that his wife had to order him about his business.

There came a great rush at dinner time. Nell was set to fill dishes with cabbage, stewed tomatoes, and potatoes, the three for each order. At first she was much confused between the cook's excited face and Edith's rushing out, calling:

"One on beef, rare! — Two on pork! — Beef, on a side! — Soup and fish for a traveler!"

But she tried to imitate Annie's coolness, and served so well that when it was all over Mrs. Sye, mopping her face, said that it took an English girl to get onto the racket without any fuss, whereupon Edith and Annie gave their heads a toss.

When they had eaten their own meal — in spite of her trouble the soup tasted good — great stacks of dishes must be washed; and that over, she was set to scrub the dining-room, and later she had an hour in her bedroom, but not alone. She was to share a room with Edith and Annie, and they lounged on their bed, watching her unpack and teasing each other about Bill and a boarder named Sandy.

They told her about Ida, whose place she was to fill.

"The way she ran after your cousin Albert was a fright," said Annie. "Every noon hour, no matter how we was driven in the kitchen, she must mop the upstairs hall, so as to meet him. She used to carry hot water to his room for his shave, too. Didn't she, Ede?"

"Sure," affirmed Edith, who was easing her feet after two hours of the beautiful boots. "And often, when I had the tables set, she'd slide into the dining-room and lay a serviette at his plate. The tannery boarders ain't allowed serviettes, you know, Miss Masters."

At the name Nell dropped her head lower over a drawer she was filling. Then Annie changed the subject.

"Look here, Ede," she said sternly. "Bill says that if you don't quit shutting the dining-room door when he's eating he'll complain to the boss. How do you s'pose he can mind the bar through a shut door?"

The discussion thus started lasted till Mrs. Sye called up the back-stairs:

"Come along, girls, do! There's five early teas on!" Which sent them all scurrying to the kitchen.

At last the day was over. Nell, crouching on the foot of her narrow iron bed, watched Edith and Annie dress for an evening party. She had never seen hair so wonderfully done, and how fresh they seemed and full of spirits, while her whole body ached; but oh, it was nothing to the ache in her heart!

When they had gone, and she was left in the solitude she craved, she made her few preparations for the night and crept to the friendly shelter of the sheets, and there the dry sobs shook her as she raged against Ida, and, after a while, her pillow grew wet as she moaned his name.

Another day came, and many others like it. Nell worked so hard that she won the approval of the whole kitchen. The hard work was her only solace — the hard work and the short meetings with Albert, snatched at noon, or beside the great range at night, while she nursed Birdie, the cook's little child, in her tired arms. She thought that perhaps the sight of her with a child would touch him.

With the same object in view she gave him her first month's wage to keep for her.

Young Albert pocketed the money, well satisfied, and urged her to bide her time in silence till he should be able to "find a w'y."

She had a fear that some day Ida would come to the hotel to see her. Ida did come. She happened to be dressing a doll for little Birdie when she became conscious that the girl's chatter in the dining-room was augmented by a new voice, laughing immoderately. At the same moment Annie appeared through the swing-door.

"Say, Nellie," she began eagerly, "Ida's in here and she's coming out directly to see you. She wants us girls to —— ."

With a white face Nell pushed the clinging child from her and, with an imploring look at Annie, fled up the stairs to her own room.

Annie came running after her, and, kneeling beside the bed where Nellie had thrown herself, she put her arms about her warmly and whispered:

"Oh, Nellie, I believe you're just heartbroken over some man — that makes you act so queer. I'm fond of Bill, you know, and sometimes he's awful mean to me!"

But before the month was out Annie's friendship had given place to jealousy, and her round cheeks had grown a trifle paler, for Bill, being "awful mean to her," had turned his fickle eyes on Nell. At first his attentions were but casual, such as untying her apron-strings when he came to the kitchen to fill his sugar basin; but after a little they became more marked. He would fetch her a glass of porter when she swept, and once, of a Jewish peddler, he bought her a blue silk tie.

And when Annie saw this her round eyes grew so wistful that Nell resolved to put an end to his familiarity.

Next morning, armed with this resolution and a mop, she was washing the oilcloth-covered floor of the reading-room when Bill entered, cigar between his teeth, and set down a foaming glass of lager on the table near her.

Without raising her eyes she plied the mop with redoubled vigor.

"What's the matter with you, Nell?" he asked in surprise. "Got a grouch this morning?"

"No, but I don't want any of your beer," she retorted, swishing the mop perilously near his patent-leather boots.

Bill moved a little closer.

"Now you just splash one drop of that dirty mess on my boots and you're going to get into trouble, see?"

Nell's blue eyes were mischievous. With a deft turn of her wrist she sent a spray of soapy water over the immaculate shoes, and was preparing another, when Bill, uttering a growl of pretended rage, sprang across the watery space that divided them and caught her in his arms.

She would have struck him, but at that moment Albert appeared in the doorway, his jaw hanging in mute astonishment. She fixed her eyes on him and waited.

Bill took his cigar from between his teeth, grinned down at her for a moment, then kissed her on the mouth. Still Albert did not strike him.

Bill, following her gaze, saw Albert, and, with a wink at him, released her, then rattled down the stairs in response to the ever-ringing bell of insistent thirst.

Albert came so close to her that she could feel his breath on her face, but the blow she longed for did not fall. Instead —

"Nell," with a nervous little laugh, "if Bill Goldham was to marry you it would be a damned good thing for both on us, old girl."

She gave him a long, long look, then, without a word, she raised her pail and mop and carried them to the kitchen.

That night, for the first time since she had come to Acford, her pillow was not wet with tears.

The end of January came, that time of hopeless and enduring cold. The very stench of the tanneries was frozen out. Dearly would Nell have liked to creep into bed with the two others, for warmth, but dared not because of Annie.

"One would think you two girls was starved," complained Mrs. Sye, "you look so pasty, and never a word to throw to a dog, either of you!"

"Women is kittle kattle," said Old Tommy from his corner, "an' no one knows it better nor me. Two wives I've 'ad and beant afeared on any woman; but I grant ye they're fair mysterious, an' if a man body but 'ad the time, they'd make a pretty bit o' study."

"If men bodies would study their Bibles more and women less, it 'd be a far better world," said Mrs. Sye, thumping her dough.

They were all in the kitchen together. Annie and Edith polishing silver, Nell at the ironing board, Mrs. Sye baking scones for tea, and her husband in the corner nursing little Birdie.

Tommy opened his mouth for a scathing reply, but gaped in silence as the swingdoor flew open and Ida, red-haired and radiant, appeared in the aperture.

"Lord, what a heat!" she laughed, showing her even, white teeth. "I'm glad I'm out of this in my own home, with a little parlor cook-stove, and just us two to do for!"

Her eyes fell on Nell and to her she came rather awkwardly, holding out her hand.

"Seems a pity we couldn't be friends," she said. "And you Albert's only relation in this country."

Nell straightened herself, still clutching her iron.

"Don't you offer your friendship to me —— ." Her voice quivered. "Don't you dare do it!"

"Come now, girls. No nasty words!" interposed the cook.

"Let 'em 'ave at it, mother," said Old Tommy chuckling.

"This ain't no street fight!" Nell flashed at him. "I ain't goin' to pull anybody's 'air. But don't you let 'er offer me 'er friendship, that's all!"

"*I* wouldn't be *seen* scrapping with the likes of *her*!" cried Ida, also addressing Old Tommy. "But I must say it's a hard way to be treated, just when I'm off to my own cousin's funeral." She seated herself, with an injured air, and raised her hands to her large black hat. "*Is* my hat on straight, girls?"

"Sure!" said Edith, adding soothingly, "It's a regular beauty, and so genteel!"

Mrs. Sye asked: "Which cousin is that, Ida? Lottie?"

"No, Irene. The one learning dressmaking at Bayside. It was double pomonia. They're having the large hearse down from Milford. My married sister and I are going to drive over in McLean's cutter and stop the night. I thought I'd just drop in and tell you, expecting, of course, to find *everyone* agreeable." With an air of melancholy she adjusted a gold bangle on her plump wrist. (Oh, the scorn in Nell's blue eyes, and the way she spat on her hissing iron and wished that it were Ida!)

Mrs. Sye brought her a cup of tea and a scone, which she nibbled with little fingers curled.

"Where will Albert get his tea?" asked Annie.

"Oh, there's potatoes to fry and apple sauce," Ida replied carelessly. "For breakfast he'll just have to forage. I may be back by noon to-morrow." Then she added, in a mincing tone, while drawing on her long gloves, "I think it is extremely probable that I shall return to-morrow."

"Fool!" Nellie shot after her as her nodding plumes departed. "To show off to me!"

The ironing was done now; the ironingboard stood upright in its corner; with scarlet cheeks the little ironer stole past Birdie and her dolls, up the back-stairs, and threw herself face downward on her bed.

All her bitterness toward Albert had melted since Ida's visit. How could a poor boy hold out against such a red-haired tyrant? She had forced him to marry her, and now by force she held him. Well, wit had overcome force before now, and when the wit was fed by love —— . Oh, God, give him back to me!

She feigned sleep and heard Mrs. Sye bid the girls let her lie as the work was light that night. Noiselessly she slipped to her feet and removed her working dress. She would not cheapen Albert by her rags! She bathed and put on fresh white undergarments and her blue Sunday frock. Her thick black hair she coiled in many smooth braids and on them perched her little white hat. Then, with her purse in the pocket of her long gray coat, and with never a look behind, English Nell fared forth to claim her own.

III

The great green door snapped behind her, her nostrils curled to draw in the crisp Canadian air. Her step was light. Now the little town, which had always seemed so alien to her, spread itself in friendliness. Evening already poised with violet wings above the roofs, but every upward-curling spire of smoke was pink.

Oil lamps burned in some of the windows, and where the blinds were up she saw the little bobbing heads of children. The mothers were preparing the evening meal. Her man, too — her man — oh, he should have his supper!

She stopped at the shop where, inside, frozen halves of beef hung from the ceiling, and there were displayed deep platters heaped with sausages. She bought three pounds of these and a chunk of cheese.

Again outside she almost ran, and she loved the way the cold bit her cheeks. Over the railway track, behind some dwarfed apple trees, stood Albert's house, a rough-cast cottage.

The front door was locked, but the back door yielded, whining on its hinges. The room was dark and very cold. A cat, that had been crouching on the stove hearth, scurried noiselessly into a corner. She closed the door and stood motionless a moment, alone, in Albert's house — and *hers*!

Cautiously she shuffled across the floor and touched the table, where she laid her parcels. She lifted the stove lid and discovered a few embers flickering like a forlorn hope. When stirred by the poker a tiny flame shot up and gave her from the gloom the main objects of the poor room. A scarlet shawl dangling from a nail showed in the light like blood.

Nell lighted the oil lamp with a wisp of burning paper and set about her preparations without delay, for she knew that in a few minutes the great town bell would strike the hour that freed the factory hands, and made every man a master in his home.

The thought fired her. She had learned much of cleanliness and neatness from Annie, and now she flew so fast from table to stove, and from stove to cupboard, that the cat, which had crept back in feline curiosity, eyed her in wonder, and mewed to sniff the sausages.

Love can make a kitchen glow. The lamp was trimmed — the table scrubbed — the pot of potatoes began to boil; and the sausages, smeared with drippings, fumed in the oven. The blinds had been drawn, and somehow the red shawl had come to the floor, where the cat found it and made a bed.

The lamplight glistened now on a table spread for two; mounds of buttered toast and slabs of cheese; and two chairs, hobnobbing with an expectant air.

A step crunched on the frozen path, some one kicked the snow from his feet before entering. The town bell must have rung unheeded in her hurry — Lord, how her heart beat! She hid her head in the cupboard.

Albert entered.

For a second there was silence as he blinked in the light, then he demanded with sarcasm:

"Well, an' wot's the matter wiv *you*, Missis Orstrich?"

No answer.

"Might I arsk wot brung *you* 'ome so bright an' hearly, I dunno?"

Silence.

"So, you've turned narsty again, 'ave yer?" And he added, in a complaining voice:

"If you 'ad *some* men you'd get a good smack on the jor!"

She faced him.

Albert's mouth widened in an astonished, even a frightened, grin. The eye with a cast turned from her as though to wink at some bystander and remark, "*Ain't* she a corker!"

"Nell!" he broke out. "Nellie, old girl, *'ow did you dare*? Lor', but you're a plucky 'un! An' supper for the two on us! Aw, Nellie, you loves me yet, doan't yer?" He closed his arms about her waist. "Give us a good 'un now!"

"Not arf a one," she refused, putting her hand over his mouth. "Wait till we've 'ad supper."

"My eye! I thought you were Ida, sure, an' w'en I *saw* it were *you* —— ." He rocked her ecstatically in his arms.

"Wash up a bit now, Albert. Make 'aste, or the saursages will be overdone."

"Saursages!" He clicked his tongue. "I s'y, this *is* a little bit of orl right, Nellie! Whot does *she* give me for supper, can you guess? 'Otted-hup pertaters an' apple saurce! Apple saurce an' *'er saurce*, that's wot *I* get." (He was mumbling through the towel now as he rubbed his ruddy face.) "These 'ere Colonials is orl right in their plice, but — they cawn't appreciate a Londoner as another Londoner can, you lay your Davey on that!"

The platter was set before him now, a steaming mound of mashed potatoes, garnished with sausages — not a mean half dozen, mind you, but four-and-twenty fat ones, bubbling with grease as though they would fain burst into song like four-and-twenty blackbirds.

Albert's mouth was so full that he could not speak, but he reached across the table now and then to slap her playfully on the wrist, and anon he would shake with silent laughter.

As for Nell, she did not laugh much, but when she smiled a determined-looking dimple dented her left cheek in a way that boded ill for Ida.

When he had done eating she drew him on to talk of Ida, and he said, while feeling luxuriously in his pocket for a "fag":

"She 'as 'er good points, you know, an' one o' them is 'er dear old father. 'E's a well-orf farmer, got a 'undred acres a mile out o' town, an' just two dortars, so I suspect that w'en 'e pops orf, Albert Masters, Hesquire, will become a landed proprietor. An' w'en that 'appy d'y comes — no more tannery for this 'ere bloke!"

Nell smiled, but the dimple looked almost wicked.

The "fag" was between his teeth now, and he stretched out his hand for a match.

"Give us a light, girl, an' come sit on my knee. That were a mighty refined bit o' eatin' you gave me, an' now I wants that kiss."

She gave the cat the platter to lick and then slid to his knee, and held the blazing match to the cigarette. He eyed her keenly while he puffed.

"Wot's come over you to-night, anyw'y? You look so chipper an' somethin' besides — I cawn't tell wot."

"I'm just thinkin' it is like a bit of old times, dearie." Her shoulders shook a little.

Albert snuggled his cheek to hers.

"Now, don't you tyke on, young 'un, *becars* I'm goin' to look arter you in spite of 'er, an' anyw'y, don't let's begin worryin' right on top o' them saursages." He could feel her trembling, and he said to comfort her:

"Aw, do you mind the old 'op-pickin' d'ys in Kent, w'ere we first met? Those were the times! Do y' mind the warm, soft evenin's, an' the nights w'en the pickers dawnced an' sang arf the night through, an' we ——— . Aw, Gawd, let's ferget it!"

"No, no! Go on!"

"Will you ever ferget the nights in old London at the music 'alls, drinkin' beer, an' the crowd of us goin' 'ome in the starlight singin' the songs we'd 'eard?"

"They don't do much singin' an' dawncin' in this country, Albert."

"Naow," he sneered. "The song is froze in their 'earts wiv the cold, an' the dawnce dried up in their bones wiv the work. Wot's the use?"

"I remember. Talk some more."

"Then there were the Bank 'Olerd'ys at 'Amstead 'Eath — lord! Do y' mind the menageries an' the cock-shies, an' the pianerorgans, an' wasn't I waxy neither w'en I caught you a-dawncin' the mazurker wiv a Jackey?"

"Jackies allus dawnce better'n Tommies, someway."

"That's becars they 'ave the 'ole deck to practice on.

Then there were the swing boats, an' the movin' pictures, an' the shootin' at bottles for chocolate an' fags! An' arter it was orl over there was our own little room wiv some 'errings an' a bit o' greens to our supper. An' onct you 'ad a *hyercinth* an' — it bloomed."

His voice had grown pensive. For a moment there was silence in the room, save for a soft rasping of the cat's tongue on the platter.

"It seems to me to-night wot I can smell that hyercinth on your hair, Nell, an' as sure's fate there's a bit on it got inter your eyes — sort o' purple, they are."

She sat up straight and looked him in the eyes.

"Awbert," she said, using the old pet name, "do you mind the time you struck me that blow? And I lay in a swound a long time, an' — an' there was blood —— ."

He drew her passionately to him.

"D-don't, Nellie, d-don't! I want to ferget wot a brute beast I've been to you!"

"It were just onct, Awbert, an' you were sorry arterwards!"

"I loved you more than ever! I'll never lay a finger on yer again, s'elp me! But *w'y* do you want to tark abart it, darlin'?"

Suddenly she freed herself from him and rose to her feet.

"Becars, I want you to think of it *just once more*. I'll tell you now wot I 'aven't before — this is our last supper together. I came to-night to s'y farewell, Albert — no, no, it's no use tryin' to 'old me — I'm leavin' for 'ome to-night!"

He had caught her dress and dragged her to him. She held her arms tensely at her sides.

"You're just tormentin' me, Nellie!" he cried. "S'y you are! You cawn't go 'ome wivout *me* — an' I'm tied fast! *Oh, Gawd, these women*! S'y it's only a bluff, girl!"

She hit his shoulder with her clenched hand.

"Wot do you tike me for, anyw'y? Do you fawncy I shall drudge my life out at the hotel, wiv *'er* flauntin' 'er plumes in my fice? Do you think I'll be jeered at by the other servants for my starved looks wiv *'er* a-gettin' fat on *you*? Do you think — Oh! 'ave you no 'eart? — that I'll wet my pillow wiv my tears every night, an' 'er red 'ead w'ere mine should be?" Her voice panted through the hot little room like a live thing struggling to get free. Her hands were on her heart.

"Oh, shime, I say, to the mother that bore you!"

He fell to his knees at her feet and twined his arms about her.

"Aw, Nellie, don't look at me like that! I'm broke! I'm broke! Just give me a chawnce an' I'll desert 'er. I swear it! That's wot I've been wantin' to s'y orl the time, but you drownded me out!"

The sight of his round boy's eyes, wet with tears, moved her to the tenderness always so ready for him. And she knew she was the victor. She said:

"Albert, are you sure that you *want* to leave 'er for always an' come wiv me, for keeps? Are you *sure*?"

"Wot's come over you to mistrust me so?" he sobbed. "Arter orl I've done for you! W'y, I married you on the square, didn't I? I'm glad on it, too," he hastened to add, "an' I'll foller you to the hend o' the hearth, if you'll let me!"

She smiled a bit sadly.

"It's becars you're just a man that it's 'ard for you to understand everythink I feel. But — I love you — cruel well ——. So, we'll begin again, my dearie."

She took him back to her heart then, unreservedly, as the tree takes back the truant bird.

They had not much time in which to make their simple preparation. Albert, all agog now, rushed about the tiny bedroom cramming his belongings in a traveling bag.

And Nell, left to herself, whipped out the rapier of her woman's wit and gave poor Ida her *coup de grâce*. She cleared one end of the white pine table and wrote on it with a charred stick. In fierce black characters she wrote the words — oh! to be there when the cast-off read —

IDA, CANADIAN IDA,
I HAVE COME AND
TOOK MY OWN.
ENGLISH NELL.

With the eye of an artist she regarded her master-piece. As she pinned on the jaunty white hat she even broke into a bit of song:

Oh, it's 'ome, 'ome, 'ome!
And it's never more to roam
From our fathers' little sea-girt isle!
Don't you 'ear the billers, roll,
And the stoker shovellin' coal,
And our 'earts beatin' out the miles?
Oh, it's 'ome, 'ome, 'ome —— .

"Hello, Awbert, you ready?"

Albert, closely buttoned in his Sunday togs, waited, bag in hand. And, lest he should give one last regretful look about the room, she quickly turned out the light and pulled him to the open door, where the moon shone down.

"Look, Awbert," she cooed, turning his face up to it, "over your left shoulder — the new moon — wish on it!"

Albert rose to the occasion.

"I wish," he said solemnly, "that we may see the next new moon shine on Britanier's breast!"

They stood gazing up in silence. The cat, which had followed them, rubbed her sides against Nell's skirt and purred loudly.

At last with a sigh they withdrew their gaze and, giving each a hand to Albert's bag, hurried down the white street, stretched like a stainless new path before them, to the station.

When they reached the tracks she stopped him, pressing his arm closely and looked into his face.

"Tell me," she said — "tell truly now, wot was it that made you come wiv me? Wot *one thing touched you*?"

"I think," he hazarded, his brow puckered in thought, "I *think* as it were the saursages."

"No," she insisted, her blue eyes on the stars, "no, it *weren't that*, Awbert. It were rememberin' that *blow*!"

༄

MacFadden Fiction Lovers' Magazine (June 1911): 279–289.

Ethelwyn Wetherald (1857–1940)

JEALOUSY (1912)

Ethelwyn Wetherald, poet, fiction writer and journalist, was
born in Rockwood (near Guelph) on 26 April 1857. She was
one of eleven children of Jemima Harris Balls and William
Wetherald, founder and principal of Rockwood Academy
and later a Quaker minister. Ethelwyn Wetherald was educated at home, at the Friends' Boarding School in Union
Springs, New York, and at Pickering College, Ontario. In
1864, her father became superintendent of Haverford
College, near Philadelphia. A few years later, the family
moved to a farm near Fenwick in the Niagara and, except for
short work sojourns elsewhere, "The Tall Evergreens"
remained Wetherald's cherished home until her death on
9 March 1940.

      Between 1887 and 1889, Ethelwyn Wetherald first
came to prominence as a regular contributor to the Toronto
Globe, under the pseudonym "Bel Thistlethwaite," her pater-
nal grandmother's maiden name; she was also contributing
poetry and essays on Canadian literary women to the *Week*.
From 1890 to 1893, on the invitation of John Cameron, its
editor, she worked for the London *Advertiser*. In addition, she
was at the same time sub-editor — responsible for most editorials, book reviews and poetry selections — of Cameron's
mildly feminist monthly, *Wives and Daughters*, edited by
Cameron's wife. In the nineties Wetherald was a major contributor of poetry to *The Youth's Companion* (Boston), edited
by her friend and mentor E. W. Thomson, who admired her
talent and "zest for life." In the winter of 1895–96, she was
assistant to the editor of the *Ladies Home Journal* and held a
similar position for nearly a year at *The World's Best Literature*.
The first of her five books of poetry, *The House of the Trees and
Other Poems*, appeared in 1895. The 1931 *Lyrics and Sonnets*
contains the poems — chiefly well-crafted lyrics on love,
death and nature — she wished to preserve.

      "Jealousy" suggests that the tone of Wetherald's fic-
tion is more astringent than that of her poetry, an impression

borne out by another story, "Lovers' Quarrel" (1912). "Jealousy" deals dramatically with the dark side of the powerful Victorian/Edwardian domestic ideal which cast the wife in the role of the self-sacrificing, unworldly "angel of the house." As wife and mother, sequestered in domesticity and ignorance through no fault of her own, Laura Emmett is the victim of both internalized self-effacement and her husband's "benevolent" condescension and insensitivity. The other possible role for a woman, that of the single, intellectual "new woman," is embodied in her cousin Cora Braithwaite who is "incapable of self-sacrifice." The story's opening description of Laura's husband, heavily laced with narrative irony, highlights the two women's unrelieved preoccupation with their male interlocutor. Even in death, moreover, Professor Emmett is the focus of his wife's attention, as she seeks desperately to affirm and experience his proprietorship. That his dead body is a symbolic counterpart to her subjugated mind is underlined by the story's closing words: "My husband never seemed so near to me as now." Male hegemony in love also surfaces in Wetherald's poem "Under the King" (1895):

> How can I at his lifeless face
> Aim any sharp or bitter jest,
> Since roguish destiny did place
> That tender target in my breast?
>
> Nay, let me be sincere and strong;
> I cannot rid me of my chains,
> I cannot to myself belong,
> My King is dead — his soul still reigns.

∾

Suggested Reading

Hale, Katherine. "Ethelwyn Wetherald," *Leading Canadian Poets*, ed. W. P. Percival (Toronto: Ryerson, 1948).

Wetherald, Ethelwyn. "Lovers' Quarrel," *Canadian Magazine* 39 (June 1912): 163–167.

———. *Lyrics and Sonnets*, ed. John Garvin (Toronto: Nelson, 1931).

Jealousy

Ethelwyn Wetherald

Professor Emmett's brow was surprisingly low for a pedagogue, and he had other points of beauty apparent not only to his wife, who adored him, but to his fellow-teachers in the academy. One of these assistants, Miss Braithwaite, boarded in his house, being a distant connection of Mrs. Emmett's. She had come to their city from Chicago, and Professor Emmett's first impression of her was that she spelled Culture with a larger C than any other person he had yet chanced to encounter, and he anticipated with an almost boyish love of mischief the pleasure it would give him to scratch the polished surface of her intellectual pretences.

It was Theocritus who first made them really acquainted. Emmett was passing through the class-room one day while she was instructing the "literature class," and he overheard some opinions of hers on the Syracusan poet which he knew were her own and not borrowed, and which implied an acquaintance born of long and close association. Apparently she had grown up with the poet as with a brother or father. That he could ever have supposed her shallow now began to puzzle him, until he reflected that a clever woman will often assume superficiality for the sake of pleasing the superficial people with whom she is inevitably brought into contact.

It is quite possible that this adaptability, added to an appearance of critical and fastidious reserve, was a part of

Miss Braithwaite's novelty for Francis Emmett. He was fond of refined, graceful and sympathetic women, and he had found them extremely easy to get on brotherly terms with. His theory was that women value brotherliness above all other manly qualities; and in the scanty social hours snatched from the gormandising of books he plied them with this quality in a superfluous degree. He made not the slightest attempt to conceal his moods from them — sparkling, sullen, sad, jovial, boisterous; spiritually speaking they took him as they found him.

The only mood in which the women of his acquaintance discovered him to be entirely insufferable was the one in which, having been carelessly set on fire by statements contravening his pet literary theories, he would crackle and snap, blaze and roar for hours together, to the imminent deadly boredom of his enforced listeners. That slightly vacant look which, among the refined and sympathetic, is the only permissible sign of inward torpor, was visible on every face when he paused for breath. His wife's face was no exception; but how was it possible for the inexpressiveness of unawakened intellect to mar a cheek of such pure and perfect roundness and lips as sweet as raspberries? "She is too young to think," was his inward defence of her mental shortcomings when he married her. That was twelve years ago; and now as he looked at her and their children he said with the forgivable irrelevance of a married lover, "She has made my home a paradise."

The newcomer into this Eden was neither angel nor serpent. She was a woman of the artificial world, as incapable of self-sacrifice, of deep feeling and real passion as warm water in a sunny window is incapable of boiling. Her enthusiasms, prettily expressed by aid of handclasps, superlatives of the less familiar adjectives, and exclamations, were quite as genuine in their way as the outflowing lava of a volcanic nature. Miss Braithwaite, indeed, had a poor opinion of outflowings, volcanic or otherwise, which transcended the limits of good form.

To poor Laura Emmett, who supposed Lucretius to

ETHELWYN WETHERALD

have been a woman,[1] and who mentally supplied the missing aitch in Ben Jonson's name, imagining its omission due to a British irregularity in the matter of aitches, the long evenings of literary chit chat between her husband and cousin were naturally not very interesting. It struck her as distinctly odd that any cause for animated discussion should arise out of the opinions of any critic upon any author, or out of a comparison between a given critic's opinions and the opinions of a number of his contemporaries. After the critics and the critics of the critics had been disposed of it was necessary to get a full hearing of the views of Francis Emmett and Cora Braithwaite, together with quotations, partially remembered, but frequently patched out by excursions to the library, from this pathetic chapter and that incomparable passage. And then they considered the probable sources of the author's inspiration, the people he wrote for, his relatives, his discouragements, and everything that was the author's.

At the close of so much conversation it was only to be expected that Francis should stretch out his long legs, put out his arm until it rested caressingly on the back of his wife's chair, and inquire cheerily, "Got any lemons, Lollie? My throat's as dry as an ash-barrel." When it was discovered that there were none, he kicked off his slippers, pulled on his shoes, and went after some. In his absence Cora's talk lapsed so naturally and unaffectedly into discourse on bibs, baby-bottles and croup cures, together with spontaneous reminiscences as to the smart sayings of little Jacky Emmett, that Laura's generous heart warmed to her, and they all joined in pleasant talk over the lemonade.

After a dozen of these evening talks on literary subjects, Laura assured herself frequently that she liked Cora and was glad she lived with them. She made the evenings so agreeable to Francis, who, prior to her coming, had

----

[1] Lucretius: Latin poet and philosopher of the earlier part of the 1st century A.D., author of the poetic treatise *De rerum natura* ("On the Nature of Things").

occasionally been dull in the hours before bed-time, semi-occasionally a little cross, and often a self-made prisoner in the library with a book that his wife did not wish or have time to share. On Saturdays he was away with his boys to the woods or the lake; or when it rained he read to them by the hour. With the exception of two or three congenial associates he had no love for his fellow-men. Once, when his wife, with an urgency for which she herself could not account, induced him to attend a political meeting, he groaned through the preparations and left her with a kiss of magnanimous forgiveness. But in twenty minutes he came blithely back again.

"The place was crowded with roaring monsters and smelt to heaven, so I came back to you," was his serene explanation, as he faced Cora under the library lamp. "And to you, too," he quickly added as he became aware that his wife was in the room.

The two ladies had united in a search for "John Halifax, Gentleman," which Cora now declared her intention to read aloud to Laura.

"Oh, very well," said Francis, without enthusiasm, "read ahead."

He sat down, with a face of dreary vacancy. To this Cora paid not the slightest attention, being resolved for one night at least to lift from her own spirit the conscious heaviness of her cousin's downcast face. It was now Francis's turn to look dull and absent, and to make irrelevant remarks. It seemed to him that there was an expression of almost malicious pleasure in the hand with which Cora turned page after page. Laura, who in her husband's absence would have enjoyed the narrative, suddenly turned to him, exclaiming:

"This isn't fair; I am getting all the pleasure. Francis, please bring a book of your choosing for you or Cora to read aloud."

He arose with alacrity, and was soon reading for the twentieth time "The Bible in Spain," which Laura supposed to be a religious work, until bursts of laughter, interspersed with such exclamations as, "Isn't Borrow a droll rogue?" and "Oh, the delicious rascal!" harassed her with doubts.[2]

These impromptu literary evenings were often varied with argument, in which Cora stoutly maintained her position, and brought to its defence numberless quotations and the well-considered fruits of wide reading. In these disputes she was cool even when her opponent grew heated, and even when she was manifestly worsted in battle. She laughed the easy, unforced laugh of pure pleasure when a ridiculous light was thrown upon her own convictions. She had certainly an acute sense of humour.

Laura, whose heart burned and froze in consecutive moments of emotion, and who, if she had disputed any subject with her husband as many minutes as Cora had hours, must infallibly have lapsed into hopeless and humiliating tears — Laura looked on this elegant nonchalance with envious wonder. Did the secret of happiness come only to people whose cheeks never crimsoned, whose pulse never galloped, whose hands never trembled, whose hearts never broke?

In an empty hour before bedtime she went up to her room and tried to face the thing out. From below came the sound of voices talking on and on. There were the familiar inflections used by her husband in argument, in narration, in earnest exposition, in the picturesque derision infallibly accompanied by Cora's continuous applausive laughter. There was the pause in which her apt question or comment or quotation acted as a spur to a mind already at its best. In this grand rush of fancies, theories, facts, citations, and reminiscences Cora felt the keen zest of a horsewoman on a mettlesome charger. His tirelessness would have kept him talking all night, but as the clock struck ten she was careful to assume the weariness she did not feel, and this

---

[2] *The Bible in Spain*: a vivid travel narrative of Spain at a period of civil war by George Henry Borrow (1803–1881), which recounts his adventures as a distributor of Bibles for the British and Foreign Bible Society, 1835–1840.

brought him at once to his feet. She rose also, and apropos of her fatigue he told her the latest funny thing about the stupid boy in his class who was held never to be really awake till broad noon. She retaliated with an even better anecdote about the oversmart boy in her class; and these, with sundry repartees and much laughter, kept them in lively communication up to the head of the stairway, where, with a cheerful good-night, they separated.

Laura gave herself a violent little shake, and, hastily pulling out a bureau drawer, pretended to be searching for something in it when her husband entered. He came beamingly forward and put his arm around her. She forced herself to face him with a smile.

"Why did you run away from us?" he asked with tender reproach. His words stung her to sudden anger.

"Us!" she exclaimed. "Us! So you and Cora are the 'Us' of this house?"

"You force us to be so," he said gently. "Why did you come up here to sit alone?"

She began inwardly to appeal to her own love for him to save herself from saying something terrible to him. She leaned against him and drew his arm closer around her.

"It's because I'm so ignorant, Francis," she said. "I either sit in stupid stillness or else ask absurd questions. And it shames me so to hear you say, 'Why, I've just told you it was nothing of the sort, or how could it be when something was something else?' I don't know. But I always feel belittled and cheapened someway when I try to take part in your talks; and when I don't, it is so much more lonesome to be with you than to be alone."

"Poor Lollie!"

"And then you don't need me."

"Don't need you! Child, what are you talking about? I need you always when I am in the house. When I don't see you it is as though the bottom had fallen out of everything. You make the reason and the meaning of my existence — don't you understand? You are my life, my heart, my love." He held her with passionate closeness. "Cora gets no more of me than I would gladly give to a dozen of

286   ETHELWYN WETHERALD

my big boys at school if they would only listen to me and knew enough to ask the sort of questions that egg me on. Now are you going to give me another cold storage smile?"

She laughed happily against his breast.

"There isn't an atom of sentiment between us," he continued. "Why you jealous little girl, I've been supposing all along that you were proud of my conversational prowess, and that you were happy in the thought that while she was picking up stray scraps of ore the whole mine belonged to you."

"I'll never be a simpleton again," said Laura.

Afterwards, for many successive evenings, she endeavoured to take an interested part in the talks, with such resultant fatigue as might come to a shrub that aspired to be a vine. She had a sense of strain, as of one who has stood too long on tiptoe. In her innermost heart she longed for the old evenings before Cora came, when Francis asked her about the children and the events of the neighbourhood, and had yawned a little before going off to the library. If she was glad that he was happy, as she constantly assured herself, her gladness did not suffice to lighten her spirit. She began to form the habit of returning monosyllabic replies to the others, in response to their infrequent attempts to include her in the conversation; and the time came speedily again when she was glad to escape to her own room from the unbearable solitude of three.

Again her husband came to her with reproachful eyes and tender inquiry. She flung herself to his breast in a passion of sobbing. He protested that he loved her dearly — dearly; that his love had not abated one jot from that of their marriage day.

"Yes, I know — I know," she said. "But I wish that your love was given to Cora and your liking to me."

"What!" he cried, as a suspicion of her sanity crossed his mind.

"Then I should get four hours' attention from you in a day instead of four minutes."

"Four minutes?"

"Yes. You give me four kisses a day, leaving the house

and returning; and each kiss, with the accompanying kind word and look, occupies about a minute. But you talk to Cora from six to ten every night."

"You know I've tried to talk to you," he began, and then a sense of his prodigious selfishness mastered him. "Laura," he said, with sudden determination, "Cora shall find another boarding-place, and I will be your friend as well as your lover."

For a moment her gladness enveloped her like a flame, and then the woman's inveterate altruism asserted itself.

"But you will be dull. You will miss the stimulus of her companionship."

"No matter."

"My interests and my prattle will bore you to tears."

"No matter — no matter."

"If you try to instruct me — to enlarge my knowledge — it will be adding another pupil to those who have already wearied you. And I have no taste for books."

"No matter. It is my business to make you happy."

He looked large and splendid in the glow of premeditated self-sacrifice.

"Oh, you grand fellow," she cried, "do you think I will let you give up a perfectly innocent pleasure to suit my narrow, selfish, whimpering nature? No! It's my business to make you happy."

"You are a noble girl."

"No, I'm simply coming to my senses." She smiled up archly at him, and he marvelled at the ease with which a man can secure his own way by a timely expression of his willingness to sacrifice it.

For several weeks Laura maintained an even serenity of demeanour. Her face was inflexibly pleasant, her eyes wide and full of courageous light, her smile heroic. She had marked out for herself an almost impossible line of duty, and she did not swerve to the extent of admitting to herself that she was committing slow suicide. Even her husband did not guess what she was suffering until an attack of pneumonia prisoned him in bed. This sickness broke her self-imposed calm and filled her heart with an anguish of <u>relief</u>.

"Ah, dearest," she said to him when he was no longer able to speak, "this pain is like the happiness of Heaven compared with the old pain — the old, undying pain of feeling a devil of jealousy in the heart. It is such a humiliating thing to be eaten alive by a devil. But it is all past now. You are with me alone, and I can talk to you out of my heart. Such a sore heart — such a tortured heart. And oh, darling, <u>the blessed relief of having you sick and suffering and all my own</u>. The doctor says you will die, and your death is the only thing that can take me out of hell — that can free me from the devil. Cora will forget you; she will find others to talk to. And I will remember only that with you in Heaven our love is perfect — nothing can come between us; while with you on earth there was always the hell of my own selfishness between."

When Cora entered the room Laura was kneeling at the bedside, with her dead husband in her arms. She looked up with her natural, effortless, luminous smile.

"It is a lovely thing to die," she said. "My husband never seemed so near to me as now."

~

Canadian Magazine 38 (April 1912): 505–509.

Jean N. McIlwraith (1859–1938)

THE ASSIMILATION OF CHRISTINA (1913)

Jean Newton McIlwraith, writer of fiction, literary criticism and biography, was born in Hamilton, Ontario, in 1859, one of seven children of Scottish immigrants Mary Park and Thomas McIlwraith, early Canadian ornithologist. She was educated at Hamilton Ladies' College and took the correspondence program in modern literature offered by Queen Margaret College, Glasgow University. She nursed her mother through the long illness that ended in her death in February 1901. From 1902, Jean McIlwraith worked for publishers in New York City, becoming head reader for Doubleday, Page and Co., a position from which she retired around 1919, returning to Canada to devote more time to her own writing. On 17 November 1938, she died in Burlington, Ontario, her home from 1922.

Jean McIlwraith's first short story appeared in *Harper's Bazaar* in 1890; articles and stories for *Harper's*, *Atlantic*, *Cornhill* and other magazines followed. She published books on Shakespeare and Wordsworth and a Canadian history for young people, and wrote a highly praised biography of an early governor of Quebec, *Sir Frederick Haldimand* (1904), for the landmark "Makers of Canada" historical series. She published many well-documented historical novels. Her lively historical fiction contributed to the popularity of the form. *The Curious Career of Roderick Campbell* (1901) recounts the story of three Scottish families who immigrate to Canada.

McIlwraith was interested in women, and in how women fared in life and love. In her first novel, *The Making of Mary* (1895), published under the pseudonym "Jean Forsyth," an older woman admonishes a bumptious young orphan in search of a husband that "If once you were able to support yourself, you'd think very differently about marrying anybody that turned up, just for the sake of a home."

The historical point of departure for McIlwraith's story "The Assimilation of Christina" lay in the large influx of immigrant domestics (often British) at this time: young women emigrated, often under the auspices of immigration societies, to work as maids, housekeepers and "home helps." In this story, which shows her skill in dialogue, McIlwraith turns to a depiction of mental adjustment to the new world, rather than the physical act of immigration. In the valorization of the native Indian, and in the sturdy Burnsian reminder to the reader (and the heroine) of the affinities between servant and native (each wrongly undervalued by their society), the plot unfolds. Water takes on symbolic value: Christina is not simply assimilated to the true spirit of the new land, she is immersed in it, to emerge changed in consciousness. In this arcadian Canada, a newly christened Christina, now Wah-sah-yah-ben-oqua, spurns raw, urban "semi-civilization" in favour of the "untrammelled" Ojibway "world of nature."

༄

Suggested Reading

Barber, Marilyn. "The Women Ontario Welcomed: Immigrant Domestics for Ontario Homes, 1870–1930," *Ontario History* 72 (Sept. 1980): 148–172.

McIlwraith, Jean. *The Making of Mary* (New York: Cassell, 1895).

———. *The Curious Career of Roderick Campbell* (Boston: Houghton, 1901).

Wilson, Elizabeth. "Beloved Friend," *Saturday Night*, 17 Dec. 1938: 28.

THE ASSIMILATION OF CHRISTINA

Jean N. McIlwraith

When Miss Maitland made up her mind to go to her island in the middle of June in order to have her cottage in readiness for the influx of nephews and nieces expected by the Fourth of July, she decided to take with her Christina, the maid servant who had come out from Scotland the preceding spring.

"She thinks we're all uncivilised over here. I'll show her the real thing," said the mistress to herself, having in mind the log hut upon the island wherein dwelt the family of Ojibway Indians who protected her summer home from autumn marauders. "It's a good idea, too, to get Christina away from the baker, the mill man, and all the other men who come about the house in town. She's pretty and she's homesick, so she might easily be won; but I don't intend to have her snapped up just as soon as I get her trained into my ways."

"Is all America as flat as this?" Christina asked Miss Maitland, when they were on the steamer northward bound from Penetanguishene.

"Oh, no, but there aren't any mountains about here, only bare reefs and wooded islands, thirty thousand of them!"

"Indeed!" said Christina, and at once began to count them. She lost her reckoning as the day wore on, for the number mounted up with bewildering rapidity. There were all sorts and sizes and shapes of islands, smoothly water-worn, twisted into grotesque forms by volcanic action, some thickly wooded, others entirely bare, or carrying only grasses and shrubs in the cracks.

"This is the original granite, Christina," said Miss Maitland, "the first rock that hardened on top of the fire inside the earth. We are at the very oldest part of America."

"It doesna look so new as the town," replied the girl with a heart-felt sigh. She had been dreaming that this was Loch Katrine and that behind the next headland Ben Lomond would presently come in sight.

There was not a sign of human habitation, when all at once the steamer whistled four times.

"That means the captain is not going into our harbour, but expects a boat out for us. He might have gone in," continued Miss Maitland, testily, "considering he has women to land, but I suppose he's late, as usual. I hope the Indians are on the look-out."

Apparently they were. A rowboat with two men in it rounded the point of the island just in front and pulled far ahead of the steamer, which slackened speed so as not to sweep past them. One of the Indians grasped the bow fender with a boat hook and held on, while the other received Miss Maitland's hand baggage and then Miss Maitland herself.

Long experience had made the elderly lady an expert at embarking and disembarking between steamer and rowboat, but with Christina it was different. She stood irresolute at the gangway, looking down in abject terror at the "sma' boat," the like of which she had never ventured into in all her four and twenty years. The stalwart young Ojibway who was holding up an encouraging hand to her only alarmed her the more.

"Come, be quick, Christina," said Miss Maitland, impatiently. "The captain won't wait."

"I canna, I'm so feared," quavered the girl.

"Where's our rope ladder?" asked the porter at her back, but the purser said:

"There's really no danger, Miss. Sit down at the edge

of the gangway, if you like, and then you can slip in quite easily."

Christina was sure she would — into the water.

"Hurry up there!"

The stentorian call from the front of the wheelhouse made the girl cast a hurried glance backward into the haven of the lower deck. Why, oh, why, had she ever left the firm soil of her ain countree? But the smiles of stewards and deck hands fired her Scottish blood. She turned her back upon them all to look down upon the fearsome North American Indian. He was not laughing at her, that was certain. His perfectly calm face so nerved her that she gave a mad leap fairly into his arms.

Joe was surprised, but, true to his race, betrayed no emotion. It was not customary for Miss Maitland's nieces to disembark in that fashion; but neither was it customary for them to have hair like burnished copper, cheeks the colour of a sunset sky, nor eyes like the dome above or the water beneath upon a sunny day. This girl did not talk like those either. She had a softer, lower-toned voice more nearly akin to his own.

Joe wished that his father, the old man in the bow, would not persist in rowing so hard. For his own part he would fain double the distance to the shore. *Wah-sah-yah-ben-oqua*, that was the proper name for her. Being interpreted it meant Daylight. Perhaps she had come like dawn to the island.

Christina was a grand house cleaner. Miss Maitland had never before drawn such a prize in the domestic lottery. Through the long June days, while the tiny wren was chortling in its joy at the corner of the cottage, and the insistent egotistical refrain "Phoebe! Phoebe! Phoebe!" was ringing out near by, the Scotch lassie scoured, scrubbed, swept, shook rugs, and beat pillows with a fierce energy that astounded the solemn young Indian who sat on the nearest boulder to watch her. He did not rest content with watching. The day after her arrival he took the beating stick out of her hand to wield it with a strength born of many winters' work in the lumber camps. That he should thus demean himself was a surprising circumstance to the maid from Scotland, where the lords of creation think it beneath their dignity to do anything about the house. Joe's command of English seemed limited, but he came round quite naturally to lend a hand in whatever she was doing, from cleaning windows to mopping floors. To see a swarthy savage, who, judging by his features, ought to be in war paint and feathers, deftly handling wire screens and shouting through a megaphone, were anachronisms which the girl fully appreciated. He had his reward when the first free evening came.

"I want you to take Christina out in your canoe," said Miss Maitland. "The sooner she gets over her silly fear of the water the better. Show her some of the islands round about."

To go out in a wee boat, alone with a red Indian, was a terrible thought to the lassie. Joe noticed her faltering footsteps as she came down the slanting rock toward him, but that she should be afraid of him did not enter his mind. None of Miss Maitland's other nieces had been. They had ever treated him as if he were scarcely a man at all, merely one of the lower animals whom they could, metaphorically, pat upon the back and make use of with scant ceremony. He motioned Christina to put her foot in the centre of the canoe, her hand upon his shoulder, while he held the boat to the landing-place. Once seated, the girl set off into wonderland. The setting sun claimed one-half of the sky with its violet, crimson, and gold, and silhouetted against it were the trees of intervening islands, resting in a red sea. The other half of the sky was possessed by the cold, pale moon, swimming in a fathomless sea of azure.

"What way are all the tall trees bent to the east?" she asked.

"Wind," Joe replied.

"What way is there such a wheen o' bare poles stickin' up abune the fresh green trees?"

"Bush fires."

But when the girl proceeded to question him about the curious formation of the rocks, the Indian shook his

JEAN N. MCILWRAITH

head. Geological knowledge was beyond him, though he knew the whereabouts of every submerged reef that had to be avoided, and Christina was drawn on from being afraid when she did not see bottom to being afraid only when she did.

Joe knew where the bass were likely to bite at sundown, and night after night the girl was carefully landed upon one rock or another to try her luck with a bamboo fishing pole. The Ojibway sat patiently by, baiting her hooks and killing all that she caught. If fortune proved unkind, she would see a light far out on the bay, when the late darkness fell, indicating that her faithful friend was spearing fish for her, which he would bring over in the morning, skinned and boned, ready to be cooked for breakfast.

Christina lived in a dream those days, the centre of her own romance. All the tales of red Indians that had been told to warn her against seeking her fortune in America circled about this tall young brave with the eagle face, who was so gentle, so timid even, in his approaches to herself, though there was an expression gaining force in his eyes which she could not ignore. Miss Maitland smiled, as she watched what was going on.

"Never before did I get so much work out of those lazy Indians," she said to herself.

How could any young girl with a heart in her bosom keep on thinking about a man's dark skin or his broken English when night after night he took her out into the world of nature where he belonged? Motor-men, plumbers, electric light men, with their cheap slang and clumsy gallantries were part of the semi-civilisation that had kept up the heartache for old Scotland. Here, at last, was the free, untrammeled America of her dreams. To be no hireling, but to fish and hunt directly for his living — that seemed the fitting way for a man to live. Joe did not wait for other folk to do things for him; everything that had to be done he could do for himself. He built and repaired his own boats. It was he who had moved over from the mainland and set up on the island the log cabin which his parents occupied. Joe was the only one remaining to them out of a large family, and the old man told with pride how the boy had brought home his first deer on his shoulder when only thirteen. Family affection seemed to be quite as strong among the Ojibways as among the Scotch. There was nothing of the "I'm-as-good-as-you-are" attitude toward parents and others in authority which had fair affronted this Scottish peasant while in town.

By the end of the first week, the house was well in order, the company had not yet come, Miss Maitland took long sleeps in the afternoon; what was to hinder Christina going sailing with Joe? The boat was large enough for her to feel safe in it, but not too large to be rowed home should the wind fail at sunset. Away out into the open sailed these two young people, saying little, but feeling in sympathy with each other and with the wavelets dancing in the sunshine all about them. As the dinghy leaped forward like a live thing, Christina's red hair blew in curly rings about her neck and face, now thickly freckled, for she had long since discarded a hat. The look of adoration deepened daily in Joe's black eyes. What were the dark-haired, dusky-skinned women of his own race in comparison with this gloriously tinted stranger from over seas? He thought of her continually as he laboured at his old-fashioned plowing and planting on the mainland. She was ever talking of how these things were done in Scotland. Perhaps one day he would learn.

Already he had drawn from their hiding-place his treasured hoard of books, being secretly proud of his scholarship, though he disdained to display it before his kinsfolk who valued only those virtues that bespoke the primitive man — hunting, fishing, the like. He could both read and write in English, but was diffident about speaking it, though he had understood perfectly all that was said to him until this braw lass, with her Scottish dialect, had been landed on the island. What did she mean by being "sair forfoughten" for example? He could find no such words in his dictionary, nor could he there discover the meaning of "scunner" or "swither."

JEAN N. McILWRAITH

"Joe's spoiling you, Christina," said her mistress, one day. "How will it be when you go back to town and have to put up with a policeman and a letter carrier for beaux?"

"Black men dinna count," replied the girl with a toss of her head, but she reddened through her sunburn, for Joe was at the door. He turned away in silence.

"Take care," said Miss Maitland. "These Ojibways are not the descendants of slaves from Africa. They used to own all this part of the country. We are the land thieves."

Christina missed Joe sorely for the four long days that he avoided the house. Only then did she realise how much he had been doing for her. The weather had turned very warm, the cottage was crammed with guests, and the amount of work was appalling to one not yet acclimatised.

"Get the old squaw to help you wash up the dinner dishes, Christina," said Miss Maitland one evening when she noticed how languid her maid was looking.

"I wadna see her in my road, mem," was the tart reply.

A startling crash at her back announced that Joe had just flung down upon the hearth the armful of logs he was carrying. Now he was stalking out of the door with the air of a brave upon the warpath. That this idol he had been worshipping should despise himself was bitter enough, but that she should turn up her already tip-tilted nose at his poor old mother was an insult not to be endured.

He remembered now how Christina had held up her skirts the few times she had come into his father's shanty. The expression of her face as she looked round had been the first thing to make the young man feel that the place was dirty and untidy. He had been trying to clean up of late, but she would probably never enter the door again to see what improvement he had made. He had even tried to get his mother to don the spotless white cap which Christina said had belonged to her own mother. It was evidently the proper thing for women of her age to wear, but the old squaw had used it for making cottage cheese. This girl was not of their own race nor of their own kind. He would forget her. He would sail over to Christian Island next Sunday and see the Johnson family. They had a pretty daughter who had smiled upon him last summer; this year he had never gone near her. The red locks had made him forget the raven.

The gay party of young people had gone off on a fishing picnic and had taken Miss Maitland with them. Christina was left behind in peace to get through a very large ironing, and the day was one of August's warmest. The water was like glass, the leaves without motion. Everything in nature seemed poised, breathless, as if waiting the onrush of the relentless winter. With the neck of her dress turned in and her sleeves rolled up to the elbows, Christina toiled away at her task. Surely plainer underwear might have done for these fine young ladies in this out-of-the-way place.

"The simple life they talk about," sighed the girl, "there isn't ane o' them what lives it — but Joe." Again she sighed. Joe had been seen by moonlight the night before, paddling a dusky maid in his canoe.

"He's no' carin' to learn the meanin's o' ony mair Scots words."

Apparently he already knew how to use some, for just as a tear sizzled on the hot iron there was his dark head at the window.

"What way you no go fishin'?" he asked.

"I wasna invited," replied Christina, whisking her back toward him as she wiped her eyes on her apron.

"Have they scunner at you?"

"Na, na, Joe!" cried the girl, dimpling and smiling. "It's no my place to gang aboot wi' the gentry, bein' but a servant, ye ken."

"Not me!" The young man threw back his head in aboriginal pride.

Christina laughed outright.

" 'A man's a man for a' that.'"

Joe did not quite understand. Was she jeering at him again? "Black men dinna count."

"No, indeed, Joe, you mistake me." She put her iron on the range and leaned her elbow on the window sill, looking up through the wire screen at the dark face without.

JEAN N. MCILWRAITH

"I'm no better than a black slavey myself since a' they fine folk came about, but it's a gran' thing for me to have this guid place and mair pay than ever I got in Scotland."

"Huh! Your own home better."

"Indeed it was not, Joe. My mother had nine o' a family, and seven o' them lasses. We had a' to turn out and work afore we kent what hame was."

"I mean," said Joe, with great deliberation, "I will make for you here a home of your own, over on the mainland. There is my farm and you can be my wife."

"Squaw!" retorted the girl with heightened colour, and the tall Indian left the window without another word.

Christina attacked her ironing viciously. "Gey like me to be thinkin' o' sic a thing," she said to herself, but she continued to think about it, and the more she thought the more amazed was she at the presumption of that wild Indian dreaming she could ever marry him, even if he were more intelligent and manly than any white man of her acquaintance.

"Christina! Christina! The boat has whistled four times, so she's not coming in. Run down to Joe with the milk can and tell him to row out with it." Christina hesitated. "Quick! Quick! You know the captain gets cross if we haven't a boat out there on time."

The girl ran till out of sight of her mistress, but her pace grew slower and slower as she drew near the youth sawing logs into lengths that would be split and brought to the back door after dark, ready for her fire in the morning.

"Joe!" He lifted his head and silently regarded her. He saw the can in her hand and knew well what was wanted, but waited for her to tell him. "Miss Maitland says will ye no gang out to meet the boat. Nane o' the ither men are aboot."

"So black man do." He went on with his sawing.

"She will be blamin' me if ye winna gang."

Joe kept on sawing. "I'm no nigger," he said at last.

"She kens that fine, Joe. She tellt me hersel' ye were ane o' the first folk o' America." The Indian looked sharply at her. Was she making game of him? Christina seated herself upon the end of the log to steady it for him, as she had often done before.

"Old man not here — can't go alone," he said shortly.

"If that's all, Joe, I can gang wi' ye. Ye mind how brawly ye hae taught me to row."

The young man lifted his head from his sawing and looked her squarely in the face. Christina's blue eyes faltered for a moment, and when they met his own there was mirth as well as woe in them.

"My mother do better." He took up another log.

"Ay, that she wad, Joe. She's far smarter nor me. But she's thrang wi' her washin'. I was in the shanty enow mysel'."

"You not afraid?"

"I wad gang wi' ye onywhere, Joe, onywhere."

He led the way stolidly to the boat. She was beguiling him, this fair lass, but not easily would he let himself get into the toils again.

Scot and Ojibway rowed with all their strength, but they were late, and the captain had given up expecting them. He did not slacken speed soon enough and the steamer had still considerable way on when Christina, as Joe directed, stood up in the bow of the rowboat and caught the front fender, while the mate at the gangway took secure hold of their craft with a boat hook. Joe let his oars drag to free his hands for delivering up the empty milk can and receiving the full one, as well as whatever else might be coming.

But the steamer was still moving ahead too fast for the safety of the small boat pinned to its side. The bow was drawn under water. Joe heard a frightened gasp — that was all — but he saw Christina's pink gingham skirt spreading out around her like a balloon. She was sinking.

The boat was swamping, her foothold gone — where was Joe? Her one hope of rescue died, as his head disappeared beneath the water. But what was this coming up below her? A strong hand was at the back of her neck, raising her face above the surface. The one word "Still!" in her ear calmed her struggles. Had she ever doubted that

Joe could take care of her?

He was in no hurry to reach the nearest island. The milk pail might sink to the bottom of the bay and the boat be split into kindling by the paddle wheel for aught he cared, as he very leisurely drew *Wah-sah-yah-ben-oqua* out of harm's way.

"All right, Joe?" sang out the mate from the gangway.

"All right!" was the response. The sensation among the passengers was at an end, though several of them suggested that the captain linger to let them watch the handsome young Indian swimming to the rock with the red-headed girl. Christina lay upon it where he left her, drenched, half conscious, till the thought came to her, "This is no like a brave squaw. He will be thinkin' lightly o' me."

Trembling with nervousness, she tottered to her feet and began to wring the water out of her skirts. Where was Joe? The black head of him had been visible a moment since, above the water, making toward the spot where the boat had gone down. Surely he had not been daft enough to dive after it. If so, he was keeping below as long as one of those loons he had bade her watch, guessing all the while where it would come up. The girl shaded her eyes with her hand and gazed along the track of the setting sun, but there was naught to be seen but a ripple of golden waves.

"He's owre guid a swimmer to be droont," she said to herself, "but whaur is he?"

The short twilight of early September would speedily deepen into darkness. What if she should be left alone all night upon her islet? This was certainly not one of those upon which pigs had been placed to eat up the rattlesnakes. The reptiles were swarming all about her, she felt sure. At midnight they would come out of their holes and devour her bodily. But her keenest alarm was not for herself. What had become of that braw laddie who had but now saved her life? Had he swam away off to the island and left her there alone to repent of her sins? A just punishment, truly, for having lightlied him! But he must know how wet and cold and frightened she was. It was not like Joe to have left her thus forlorn. Perhaps he was even now drying himself at the shanty stove, and laughing at the fright he was giving her. Well, he should find out she had a spirit equal to his own, even if she were not so good a swimmer.

The water seemed shallow between the back of her islet and the next one. If she waded through it she would probably find a shallow channel between that and the next again. Before it was dark she might work her way near enough to Miss Maitland's island for her shouting to be heard. One of the nephews would surely come to the rescue. That dour savage, Joe, should see that she was not in any way dependent on him.

After the chilly evening air, the water felt warm as she slipped into it. Her foothold was firm to the next island, much larger than the one she had left. Indeed, it proved to be a peninsula, and there was still easier wading to the next island, and the next again. But Miss Maitland's home did not appear to be drawing any nearer. The Union Jack had been hauled down at sunset and there was no other indicator to the site of the cottage. All the islands looked alike to Christina, even by daylight.

She shouted herself hoarse, but who was there to hear? Her mistress would be seated snugly at the side of the blazing fire of logs in the living-room, reading her novel and worrying not at all about the return of her nephews and nieces from their far-away picnic, still less about the excursion of Joe and Christina out to the steamer and back. The girl could go no farther. A swiftly running current, whose depth she could not estimate, barred her advance. She must try to get back to the rock whereon Joe had left her. It was there he would look for her and he was the only one likely to look, or to care whether she ever came back or not.

But where was that island? Darkness had crept in to bewilder her. She stumbled along in despair, swinging her arms at intervals, in a vain attempt to warm herself. Her teeth were chattering and her heart died within her as she thought of the snakes. Oh, it was a cold and cruel country, this Canada! Why had she ever left her own? The lads

Jean N. McIlwraith

there were not the sort to leave a shivering lassie all night alone upon a bare rock.

"Joe's no the ane to dae that either," she moaned. "He's droont! He's droont! And his mither — she will be blamin' me, puir auld body!"

She buried her face in her hands and cried for some minutes. When she lifted it the whole aspect of the bay had altered. The harvest moon had risen in all its glory above the horizon. Here she was, not near Miss Maitland's island, as she had imagined, but quite close to the mainland. There was no mistaking that point of rock standing out so clearly in the moonlight. Joe had taken her there to fish, many a time.

"*Wah-sah-yah-ben-oqua*! *Wah-sah-yah-ben-oqua*!"

"Joe! Joe!" she cried in response.

The canoe darted round the jutting rock, swiftly as an Indian arrow, but the Indian in it was quiet, as usual, while he wrapped the girl in a homespun blanket and lifted her into his boat. He paddled out into the moonshine before he spoke. "What way did you not stay where I put you till I go get the canoe?"

"I was feared ye'd never come back to me, Joe."

"Would you be caring?"

The girl snuggled so deeply into the blanket that only the top of her head was visible, but her voice came out of the nest.

"What was yon ye cried to me?"

"Your name — *Wah-sah-yah-ben-oqua*."

"It's a squaw name, but maybe it suits me."

The moon was high in the heavens when the pair reached home. It was so late that even the unexacting Miss Maitland was scandalised.

"Christina! Where have you been? Spearing fish?"

"No, mem. Joe's been speirin' at me — "

"What?" She looked astounded.

"He's been asking me to marry him."

"Good heavens! The impertinence of him! Why, the man can hardly talk English."

"But he kens it fine."

"Oh, I see! You did the proposing."

"I did naething o' the kind," said the girl, her Scotch dander rising. "He showed me his farm and whaur he means to build his bit hoose. It will be a gey bonny place in a year or twa. Hech, sirs! I never thocht to marry a landed propreeitor."

"But think of the long, cold winters up here, Christina."

"If I dinna marry him it will be a lang, cauld winter for me a' the rest o' my life."

༄

Canadian Magazine 41 (Oct. 1913): 607–614.

Mary Lowrey Ross (1891–1984)

An Adventure in Youth (1917)

Mary Lowrey Ross, journalist and writer, was born in
Brantford, Ontario, on 21 February 1891, the youngest of
four children of Mary Cathey, a teacher, and David Lowrey,
a doctor and real estate investor. The family moved to
Toronto when Mary Lowrey was about twelve, and her
interest in writing and the arts began to emerge at Harbord
Collegiate. At the age of sixteen, she moved with her family
to 62 Delaware Avenue, Toronto, a house that was to remain
her home for six decades. Graduating in social work from
the University of Toronto about 1913, she found the field
uncongenial and became a reporter at the Toronto *Star*,
where her colleagues included Morley Callaghan, Gregory
Clark and Ernest Hemingway. She left the paper to join
Saturday Night. Its film critic from 1931 to 1937, she also
contributed book reviews and sketches to its pages. From
1915 through the 1930s she also did freelance work for
Chatelaine, *Maclean's*, *Saturday Evening Post* and *Canadian
Home Journal*.

In 1924, Mary Lowrey married W.W.E. (Eustace)
Ross (1894–1966), geophysicist and pioneering Canadian
imagist poet. They adopted two daughters, Molly (1934)
and Nancy (1936). The couple were part of a lively circle of
literary friends that included historian Frank Underhill, and
journalist-writers like Gordon Sinclair, Pierre Berton and
Morley Callaghan, whose son Barry remembers Mary Ross
as "open and full of talk and the confident laughter of a
woman of wide experience and elegance." In 1983, Mary
Lowrey Ross moved to Brighton, Ontario, near her elder
daughter; she died on 2 November 1984.

The setting of "An Adventure in Youth" reflects
Ross's love of the landscape of "cottage country" fostered at
cottages in Muskoka and at Lake Scugog. More important-
ly, the story expresses both her developing feminism and
her awareness of the spiritual trauma of the Great War.
The existential malaise of wartime is refracted through the

elderly narrator, whose role in the courtship of a young war hero is ultimately tinged with pain and loss. Loss of illusion is a pervasive theme in the story: Miss Armitage's illusion that she is more than a stereotypical "old dear" to her pretty young friend Geraldine Ross ("For now, though I have failed my destiny as a good wife and mother, I have been promoted to the sisterhood of the rising generation") fades. Ross skews the story to melancholy by her final focus on the lonely narrator, a focus suitable to the "strained and tired" disillusionment attendant on the wartime setting. "An Adventure in Youth" crystallizes the frustration inherent in the narrow range of roles open to women of Miss Armitage's generation, restrictions described by psychologist Clara Thompson in *The Role of Women in This Culture* (1941):

> If [such a woman] made no marriage, she was doomed to a life of frustration. Not only was sexual satisfaction denied her but she felt herself a failure who must live on sufferance. . . . Not only must she suffer actual disappointment, but she had the additional burden of inferiority feelings. She had failed to achieve the goal demanded by the culture — and for women there was only one goal.

෬

Suggested Reading

Callaghan, Barry. Memoir, *Shapes and Sounds: Poems of W.W.E. Ross* (Toronto: Longman, 1968), 1–7.

Ross, Mary Lowrey. "Are Women News?" *Maclean's*, 15 March 1926: 14, 67.

———. "Educating Margaret," *Saturday Night*, 24 June 1933: 9, 16.

———. "Mrs. Pritchard and Mrs. Eberle," *Saturday Night*, 13 Oct. 1934: 3.

An Adventure in Youth

Mary Lowrey Ross

In this warm month of July it is good to be back again at Westhaven. I had been thinking about it all winter — not as it really must have been, with the snow packed to the edges of the hotel verandah and stretched across the ice to the black trees on the other side, but as I have always seen it; a tiny, red-roofed settlement on the edge of a little lake that looks like nothing so much as a big, blue saucer with a charming serrated etching of inverted pines at its rim.

That is Westhaven. From my bedroom window — the bedroom I have occupied for ten years — I can look out across the water to the pine-trees beyond. At home my window commands a view of a row of little gabled houses, all so exactly alike that it is, I believe, a daily occurrence for the owner of any one of them to find one or another of his neighbours withdrawing confusedly from his front vestibule. I think it must be that view from my winter window that makes me long for Westhaven as soon as the weather begins to warm towards spring. Westhaven is monotonous, too. But it is a very gracious monotony.

This year there are more guests than usual — a great number of pretty young girls and little children. But there is a tragic dearth of young men, tragic, alas! in a very real sense. For most of them are in France now — the boys I remember who came here summer after summer to swim and flirt and sail; and even the ones who used to play pirate in the old flat bottomed dinghy, and to shoot marbles, on rainy days, down the long hotel corridors.

To-day I met Jerry.

Her real name is Geraldine Ross, but in most of her moods, Jerry suits her best. She is tall and vigorous and young; beautiful, too, I think, with the sort of beauty one feels sure must be the gift of ancestry and not of accident. She can swim and sail like a boy, and she handles a canoe with the dexterity of a French habitant.

"It's curious, isn't it, Miss Armitage?" an elderly spinster like myself said to me as we sat on the verandah watching Jerry executing a remarkable series of "jack-knifes" at the end of the pier. "We were taught that all a woman's destiny lay in being a good wife and mother; and the modern girl seems to believe that her destiny lies entirely in being a good sport."

I smiled without replying. For my part, I love this gay young generation, that takes such good care of its muscles, and lets its manners take care of themselves.

I do not mean that its manners are not excellent. They are. And their very excellence lies in the fact that they are allowed to take care of themselves in their engaging self-unconsciousness.

Jerry came up from the pier and paused on the verandah to talk to us. She sat on the railing with the water dripping from her short skirt and bright hair, looking like a classic water-nymph in an extremely modern bathing suit. She has offered to teach me to "do jack-knifes."

Jerry and I have become very good friends.

She takes me out every morning in her canoe. Ordinarily, I have a deep-rooted distrust for that tricky craft; but in her competent hands I feel quite safe, and become so absorbed in watching the rhythmic swing of her paddle that I sometimes find myself forgetting to clutch tightly to the sides.

"I like you, Miss Armitage," she said to me this morning. "You're an awfully good sport."

I felt extraordinarily pleased. For now, though I have failed my destiny as a good wife and mother, I have been promoted to the sisterhood of the rising generation.

This morning we had a new guest. A very tall young

MARY LOWREY ROSS

man clambered out of the little motor boat which the hotel despatches to meet its guests, and came up the pebbly path to the verandah. I had a fleeting impression of rather exceptional good looks just as he disappeared through the doorway.

The impression was confirmed at dinner time. The new guest has pleasant gray eyes and an excellent profile. He is a little shy, I think. For though we are very informal and cordial with strangers at Westhaven, he had very little to say to anyone. And after dinner he disappeared immediately in the direction of the boat-house.

Jerry and I were standing on the verandah as he went by.

"Now, why isn't he in khaki?" demanded Jerry, following him with a frowning glance. She has a younger brother in Flanders, and her patriotism runs very strong.

"He probably has an excellent reason," I said. "A widowed mother — or a weak back — "

"He may have a widowed mother," she answered, eyeing his large form disapprovingly. "But he hasn't any weak back."

Plainly the new guest may expect small favor from Jerry.

Her acquaintance among the militia, I have observed, is extremely wide. Almost every week-end, a soldier on his last leave comes up to say good-bye to her. Under her competent guidance I am rapidly learning to distinguish between the various ranks. At first I recognized rank only by its leather leggings, and when it abandoned its leggings, I was altogether lost.

This morning we had an unusually full breakfast table. There were Dr. and Mrs. Edwards, and their large family (they have five little girls, ranging in age from rompers to middy blouses), one of Jerry's soldiers, who, a laggard in love, had overslept and lost his place at her table, the new guest, whose name is Allan, Miss Wilson, the other elderly spinster, and myself.

We talked about the war, of course. Dr. Edwards, who expects to go overseas with a medical unit in September, will talk of nothing else. This morning he could not be restrained from outlining the Western front on the table cloth with the handle of his spoon. He illustrated the great Somme drive with his knife and fork, and conducted a spirited infantry attack with the salt and pepper.

Mrs. Edwards took occasion to congratulate Jerry's soldier on the fact that he was in the service of his country.

"Oh, well, life's pretty uncertain anywhere," he responded, cheerfully attacking a large slice of toast.

"It is, isn't it?" said Dr. Edwards, diverted for the moment. "Almost every human being takes a chance one way or another. Some people live on the sides of volcanoes, and some don't pay any attention to the warning of their livers. And I don't suppose," he added, making the neat professional application, "that it's any more dangerous to cling to the side of potential calamity than to have a potential calamity cling to the side of you."

He returned to the subject immediately, however.

"I haven't much of an opinion of the man, especially the young man without a family, who isn't willing to take a chance these days," he said, resting his gaze absently upon young Allan.

The boy did not respond. He sat crumbling a piece of bread with restless fingers, his eyes on the window, and the water and pine trees beyond. I could not bear to look at him. I believe firmly that conscription is a democratic measure, and I can see no defense for the slacker. But the youth of to-day is faced by a very terrible alternative; and when it is publicly tried and condemned for its choice of the ignoble part, the sight is not a pleasant one.

It is sad to think that the responsibility for the whole future of the race must be thrust upon the young shoulders of a single generation.

We held a Red Cross garden party this afternoon on the grounds of the hotel.

Jerry sold ice cream. She came down about two o'clock wearing a fresh summer gown and a green wide-leafed hat that cast a pleasant shade across her eyes. And she looked so altogether delightful that it scarcely seemed

MARY LOWREY ROSS

possible she should be unaware of it. She wasn't.

Young Allan and I were talking on the front steps, and he was just about to leave for one of his solitary canoe trips. He spends very little time about the hotel. Almost every morning, immediately after breakfast, he takes his canoe and disappears; and sometimes we do not see him again until breakfast time the following morning.

He paused a moment when he saw Jerry, and then went up the steps towards her, with a crisp new bill in his hand.

"It's for the Red Cross," he said, as he handed it to her. Jerry took it without enthusiasm.

"Thank you very much," she said, and thrust it negligently into the wide pocket of her skirt.

Had it been anyone else than young Allan she would certainly have paused, exchanged a few remarks, and invited him to be present. And she would somehow have contrived to leave him with the delightful impression that the sweet perfection of her afternoon depended, to a far greater extent than he might have suspected, upon his presence. But Jerry will waste none of these courtesies upon a slacker.

He looked after her with a rather curious expression as she went across the lawn towards the big striped tent where the ice cream was being sold. And then he went slowly down the path to the boat-house.

One wonders whether in the days that are to come, it will be possible for a historian to arise great enough to grasp the significance of the tragedy through which we are living to-day.

And there are terrible moments, too, when it almost seems that it can have no significance, after all; that our unhappy old world has somehow been wrenched away from the hand of its Maker, and is passing, unguided and uncontrolled, through a meaningless agony of blood and tears.

Few of us, I think, waver for long from the creed which is, after all, the only one we dare to hold — God in His Heaven, and good — somehow — the final goal of ill. Only the good seems very obscure and far away, and the ill, enveloping and very dark, and our spiritual sight grows at times a little strained and tired.

Perhaps the great historian, seeing the situation steadily and seeing it whole, will be able to show that profit and loss are not so sadly disproportioned as we believe them to be now. And even we, looking back across the unreal horror of the last two years, may at least thank God for what they have revealed to us of the gallant spirit of youth.

To-day the casualty list was headed by the name of a boy I remember in Westhaven ten years ago. He was killed while leading his men into action in an engagement in Flanders. And side by side with the picture that rose to my mind of the gallant officer, Lieut. William Carter, charging at the head of his men into the face of destruction, came the memory of Willie Carter, a mild little boy, nicknamed Bunny for reasons all too apparent, who never used to like to go into the dark alone.

Jerry, it seemed, had known him too. Looking very white, she came out to the verandah where I was talking to young Allan.

"Bunny Carter has been killed," she said to me. "He was a friend of my brother Jim's. They were in the same company."

She stood looking away from us so that we would not see the tears in her eyes. But she could not keep them out of her voice.

"It wasn't fair for Bunny to have to go to war," she said. "He wasn't very strong. And he was so young — only eighteen when he enlisted!"

And then she faced about unexpectedly and regarded young Allan with scornful eyes.

"Why don't *you* go?" she demanded.

I saw him open his lips to say something, and close them again in a stubborn angry line. And after a moment he replied rather sullenly,

"I'll go when my turn comes."

"You slacker!" said Jerry, and went haughtily down the steps, and along the pebbly path to the shore.

I remonstrated with Jerry this morning when we were out in the canoe, but she remained obdurate.

"If he's a slacker he deserved it; and if he isn't, of course he would have denied it," she declared with the beautifully simple logic of youth.

"Not necessarily," I said, remembering the look that had crossed his face when she challenged him so unexpectedly. And I added as gently as possible, "Even so, I can't help feeling that your methods as a recruiting agent are perhaps — insufficiently diplomatic. Even a slacker has feelings."

Jerry fell back on the syllogistic form of argument.

"A slacker is a worm," she said. "And a worm can't feel. I don't see how it's possible for a slacker to have any feelings."

I had no reply for this. So we sat silent for awhile, drifting about the quiet lake with the little waves slapping against the sides of the canoe.

"Miss Armitage," said Jerry presently. "Do you remember the line from the "Battle Hymn of the Republic," about "sifting out the hearts of men before His judgment seat"? That's what is happening to-day, isn't it? There are some, like poor Bunny Carter, whom no one ever suspected of heroism; and they go away and are killed. And there are others whom one would naturally expect to be — more the soldier type. And they stay at home and let the Bunny Carters do their fighting and dying for them."

"You mean young Allan," I asked.

"Yes — young Allan," answered Jerry thoughtfully, taking up her paddle again. "I suppose if I hadn't known the sort of person he really is I might have liked him — quite well."

I have been trying to analyze the friendship between Jerry and myself.

It is a little unusual, I think. We of the older generation are separated, by a long line of years, from the experiences of youth; and youth accepts us pleasantly for what we are, and regards with secret skepticism the platitudes that argue, rather pathetically, that age is simply an attitude of mind. It respects us deeply and pities us a little, convinced of our wisdom and our tendency to rheumatism.

With Jerry it is quite different. It is possible that she may refer to me, in my absence, as "an old dear." But when she is with me she meets me frankly and simply on the basis of one and twenty. And before I realize it, the decorum of years slips away from me, and I find myself boldly scraping acquaintance again with youth.

She has asked me to go into town to the movies with her to-night.

An incredible thing has happened!

We went to the movies, Jerry and I. We paddled into town in the late dusk, and arrived there just as the lights began to glimmer down into the water.

The first play was nearly over when we entered the crowded little theatre, and we sat in a seat near the back and watched the performance of the "greatest emotional actress in America". The great emotional actress had very definite ideas about deportment, and she slapped the face of the floor-walker (the floor-walker is the villain *par excellence* of the movies, I have observed) because he remarked, with an odious leer,

"Some chicken! how about a little lunch?"

("Now, if he had only said, 'How about a little lunch — some chicken?'" said Jerry regretfully. "He wouldn't have been nearly so likely to get his face slapped.")

And we saw her entrapped at last, and watched her effect a rather ingenious escape through a dumb waiter. And after that our interest flagged a little, and we sat and talked about something else until hero and heroine faded rapturously off the screen.

But the next picture caught and held my attention from the first. It was a war picture, taken in France — very old and streaked, and belonging, I imagine, to the earlier period of the great struggle. And it showed long, patient lines of soldiers passing over a dusty country road. The silent tragedy of it caught suddenly at my throat, and the desolated landscape and the gray figures on the gray road, blurred to a mist on the screen before me. And the words of a sad little poem I had read somewhere came back to my mind:

> Oh, living pictures of the dead,
> Oh, songs without a sound —

Jerry said the pictures were probably faked.

"*C'est magnifique, mais ce n'est pas la guerre,*" she remarked knowingly.

But they were not faked. For the next picture showed the late Earl Kitchener reviewing the Canadian troops. And at the end of the line nearest the camera, standing at salute before the greatest soldier of them all, was young Allan!

Jerry made a little exclamation.

"Oh-h, it *can't* be!" she gasped.

But it was. The picture was very clear and close, and young Allan's excellent profile is not to be mistaken.

We were both a good deal startled, I think. It was almost uncanny — as though a familiar acquaintance had suddenly been presented to us in the spirit. Jerry did not utter another word until we were getting into the canoe to go home. Then she said tragically,

"And I called him a slacker!"

"He's home on leave, I suppose," I said.

"I can never look him in the face again," declared Jerry passionately; and after a moment,

"If you could see him first, Miss Armitage, and explain how I didn't understand — and how terribly sorry I am — "

I said I would, rather reluctantly. I am quite sure that she could do it a great deal more effectively herself. And we went the rest of the way home almost in silence.

I overslept this morning, and woke to the vague consciousness of a task to be performed. And then I remembered my promise to Jerry.

I should have been quite content to lie there much longer, with the yellow sunlight across my bed, and a fragrant little breeze kicking at my curtains, and a bright windowful of blue sky to look at. But I knew that if I did I should probably miss young Allan, who is seldom to be found around the hotel after nine o'clock. Life, as the industrious moralist has pointed out (in pink embroidery, on the pillow-shams of a former generation) is not Beauty but Duty.

I came down just in time to waylay him in the lower hall. And I told him about our discovery of the night before.

He looked a good deal surprised; I could not tell whether or not he was pleased. And I told him how sorry we were — especially Jerry.

"But why didn't you tell us yourself?" I asked.

He did not reply for a moment. And then he said with extraordinary abruptness,

"Did you ever go to Hell, and then come back?"

I gasped, I think. It was, perhaps, an odd question to put to a mild little elderly person who had never gone to anything more questionable than the movies in her life.

"No, I don't think I ever did," I replied.

"Well, I have," said young Allan, "and I didn't want to talk about it."

It was dramatic, perhaps. But it was terribly pathetic as well. And just for a moment I caught a glimpse into the troubled depths of the boy's mind. And I knew that the things he had seen and heard were still so real and close that he could not bring himself to think about them — the sights and sounds of death, and the hideous futile desolation of which we understand so little.

"I thought I'd like to get away by myself for awhile," he said, "I haven't any folks, you see."

I did not know what to say. I could only murmur that we were terribly sorry — especially Jerry.

"Miss Ross really didn't give me a chance to tell her," he said. "Everyone took it for granted from the first that I was a slacker. I didn't think it worth while to make explanations."

It was what I had suspected — a bit of stubborn pride carried over from his not very remote boyhood. I tried to set things clear.

"Jerry is very loyal," I said. "She has a younger brother in the trenches. We all feel it unfair that the burden of the war should rest only on the willing, like yourself."

"Of course I understand that that was how you felt about it, Miss Armitage," he said politely. "It wasn't necessary to explain."

The awful haughtiness of youth! I was reminded of that absurd poem of Lewis Carroll's:

I said it loud, I said it clear,
I went and shouted in his ear,
But he was very stiff and proud,
He said, "You needn't shout so loud!"

"Then I shall tell Jerry you forgive her," I said.

"Why certainly. There was nothing to forgive," he answered and started toward the door. There he hesitated a moment.

"I — she — ," he began, and then turned away. "Oh, there's no use now," he said, and disappeared. And a few minutes later I saw his canoe moving slowly across the lake.

I told Jerry about the interview.

"I don't blame him," she said soberly. And she added after a moment, "But what do you suppose he meant by that Ibsenesque farewell?"

I am sitting in my room in an unlovely purple kimono, a hot brick at my feet, and my hair in wire curlers — the crowning offence of *déshabillé*. And the rain is beating sadly.

And less than an hour ago —

It must have been almost eight o'clock when Jerry, who had been wandering restlessly about the verandah, came up to me as I sat knitting, and suggested going into town for the mail.

"And the morning paper," she added persuasively, seeing me hesitate.

(When Jerry wants me to go into town she always suggests the morning paper; for when one is a little withdrawn from the world the daily newspaper assumes an undreamed of value. Sometimes at home, I do little more than glance at the headlines. But in Westhaven I read everything in it — even that least inspiring of departments, the Woman's Page, and the curious lyric outbursts that have taken the place of department store advertising.)

So I consented, and she went down and brought her canoe around to the pier. And we set out just as it began to grow dusk.

It was quite dark by the time we emerged from the little land-locked harbor of Westhaven. Outside, in the open lake a chilly breeze was blowing, and the water was beginning to move and murmur restlessly. And in spite of my confidence in Jerry I felt a little shiver of fear.

We arrived in town safely however. It was too late to linger there long, and we secured the mail and the paper and hurried back to the dock.

The wind had risen alarmingly. Standing there, with that murmuring blackness before me, and the waves beating up against the dock at my feet, I felt a dreadful sinking sense of terror. There are moments when I find the business of being a good sport a little trying to my years. If there had been any other way of getting back to Westhaven to-night, I should certainly have insisted upon taking it.

The situation did not appear to trouble Jerry. She was humming softly as she lit the lantern and steadied the canoe while I got in. And she was still humming as she swung the bow about and headed toward the open lake.

I do not know how long it was before I discovered that something was wrong. I remember noticing that Jerry had stopped humming, and wondering why we were so long in making the little Westhaven harbour; and wishing, with a rising sense of fear that the terrifying sound of wind and water would begin to die away.

And then, quite suddenly, I knew that we were lost. And I knew that Jerry, paddling silently at the end of the canoe was matching her strength against the strength of the wind and the mounting water about us.

We did not seem to be going forward. We seemed to be hanging there, between heaven and earth, in an awful rocking blackness — blackness that stretched away on every side, and held no sound but that dreadful sound of wind and water.

It rained too — great drenching gusts that swept along with the increasing wind.

It was young Allan that rescued us, three miles outside the entrance to Westhaven. He had been out patrolling the lake in the little hotel launch for an hour, and he came riding toward us in answer to our frantic calls, the searchlight in the front of his boat cutting a narrow lane of brightness through the dark. And somehow we scrambled aboard.

"I heard someone say you had gone into town," he said. "I had just got in and I knew it was pretty rough out here. So I thought it might be a good idea to borrow the launch and scout around a little."

"If you hadn't," said Jerry shakily, "I'm afraid we might never have got back at all. You — you have probably saved our lives."

There was a little awkward pause. The customary line of conduct in a case of this kind, I suppose, is to seize the hand of one's rescuer and pour out broken words of gratitude. But our rescuer sat with his large unresponsive back toward us, and his hands resting firmly on the steering wheel. So I murmured, "Thank you very much," which was the only thing that occurred to me, and nothing more was said until we ran into our own little lake and the lights from the boathouse trembled faintly through the rain. Then Jerry ventured resolutely,

"I want you to know that we realize what you have done for us. I know you must feel — unfriendly toward me — "

Young Allan faced about with a half reluctant grin.

"Not exactly unfriendly," he said. "In fact I believe I've been hanging around Westhaven most of the summer simply on your account."

I left them standing under the dim light in the hotel hallway, talking in low mysterious voices, in that sudden absorbing intimacy that is possible only to youth. And I came up to my room, and got into my old purple kimono, and put my wet hair into its wire curlers.

There is a curious deadening of the spirit that can no more be reasoned away than can damp and dreary weather.

To-morrow morning the sun will be shining over the bright wet world, and a nipping breeze from the great lakes to the north will be blowing down through all the little islands. But to-night —

To-night the rain is beating sadly against my window and I have an old bleak feeling that life and the beautiful things of youth have somehow passed me by.

For Jerry came in half an hour later to say good-night. She wore a scarlet silk kimono, and her hair hung over her shoulders in two amazing yellow braids. She sat on the bed with her feet tucked under her, and regarded me with wide dreaming gray eyes.

"He has to leave on Thursday," she said, "but we — he says we will at least have to-morrow together."

She got up suddenly, thrust her muscular young arms round my neck and hugged me vigorously.

"Good-night," she said — "you old dear!"

∽

Canadian Magazine 48 (April 1917): 507–517.

J. G. Sime (1868–1958)

MUNITIONS! (1919)

Jessie Georgina Sime — an asexual "J. G. Sime" on the title page of her books and "J. Georgina Sime" to autograph seekers — was a British writer who came to Canada in 1907 on the eve of her fortieth birthday. She came into her own as a writer during her four decades of residence here. The evolving society she experienced in Montreal fascinated her, and she came to think of herself as a "near-Canadian," one focused on this country as subject matter but rooted in the social and cultural values of her English upbringing.

Georgina Sime was in fact born in Hamilton, Lanark County, Scotland, on 12 February 1868; she was brought up in London, with several intervals on the Continent. Both her mother, Jessie Wilson, and her father, James, historian and biographer, were writers in the family tradition, and Sime treasured childhood memories of such family friends as George Meredith and Thomas Hardy. She attended Queen's College School and Queen's College, London, institutions devoted to the education of women, and then trained for three years in Berlin as a singer. A brief singing career was superseded by a developing desire to write. From her pen came a column for the *Pall Mall Gazette*, book reviews for the *Athenaeum* and reader's reports for Macmillan in London (with whom her father was associated) and later for Nelson and Co. in Edinburgh. Her pen names included "Jacob Salviris." Sime initially came as a visitor to Canada, where her uncle, Sir Daniel Wilson (1816–1892), had been longtime chancellor of the University of Toronto. She landed at Quebec in 1907, and spent most of the next forty years living in Montreal, making regular trips abroad. Sime had a long and important friendship with prominent Montreal obstetrician-gynaecologist Walter William Chipman (d. 1950), whom she had met in Edinburgh.

In her adopted home Sime became known as a writer and as a lecturer on literary topics. Her fascination with Canada, urban Montreal in particular, and her feminism, which was coloured by a particular interest in working women, emerge in such works as *The Mistress of All Work* (1916), *Canada Chaps* (1917) and *Our Little Life* (1921), a novel set in a seedy section of a big city based on Montreal. The latter is the moving story of a middle-aged Irish-Canadian seamstress's love for an upper-class British immigrant, a failure in his attempt to make a new life in Canada. *In a Canadian Shack* (1937) consists of vignettes of sojourns in rural Quebec around the time of the Great War. In *Orpheus in Quebec* (1942), she assessed the promise of Canadian writing. Sime continued to publish until the 1950s. In the mid-thirties, confined for months at a time by glaucoma and other eye ailments, she cultivated an interest in dreams and the occult. With Frank C. Nicholson as a collaborator, she published a dream book, *The Land of Dreams* (1940), and later *Brave Spirits* (1952), *A Tale of Two Worlds* (1953) and *Inez and Her Angel* (1954). W. H. New tells us that she may have returned to England to live after World War II (probably in 1950), but that at her death in Wootton, England, on 13 September 1958, her permanent address was Montreal's Mount Royal Hotel, an apt symbol for her bipolar perspective.

The hardy, shrewd, worldly, nurturing lower-class women of Montreal, native and immigrant alike, held a particular appeal for Sime. *Sister Woman* (1919), from which "Munitions!" is taken, consists of twenty-eight stories told by a woman to a male companion as examples of women's multi-faceted need for self-realization and the support of men in changing a world that has been most difficult for women, most of all for imaginative, single, lower-class and/or working women. Sime's female protagonist in *Our Little Life* put it best: "It's women alone have the poor toime." The stories are set in Montreal. The narrator's perspective mirrors Sime's own — that of an independent, expatriate intellectual woman of some means, with an empathy for "sister creatures" in the spirit of the work's epigraph from Robert Burns:

> Then gently scan your brother man,
> Still gentler, sister woman.

In "Munitions!," Bertha typifies one aspect of the changes in occupation and consciousness of women precipitated by World War I. Other stories set forth the plight of the shopgirl, the seamstress, and the charwoman, and the ironies and sufferings involved in women's attempts to juggle the demands of morality, feeling and common sense. "An Irregular Union," for example, conveys the emotional ambivalence experienced by a young career woman sexually involved with her boss in a three-year relationship marked by secrecy and social tension. Sime was acutely aware that "new women" had to cope with new difficulties as well as old role models and rules of conduct.

"Munitions!" exemplifies Sime's social awareness. She uses the Canadian spring as a correlative of social change in Bertha Martin and her ilk. In its social preoccupations and its sexual frankness, both unusual for the time, the story anticipates the work of later writers like Morley Callaghan, Dorothy Livesay and Mary Quayle Innis. The fact of war threads through this story, war with its concomitant shift in women's work from a preponderance of domestic employment to factory labour, bringing greater personal freedom and exploitative working conditions. Sime eschews political dogmatism, however, a result of her belief, as she commented of Hardy's novels, that "the great sin against art" is "writing to the order of a philosophy of life instead of to the order of life itself."

༄

Suggested Reading

Campbell, Sandra. "'Gently Scan': Theme and Technique in J. G. Sime's *Sister Woman*," to be published in *Canadian Literature* (June 1992). *Sister Woman* is to be republished by Tecumseh Press in 1991, with an introduction by Campbell.

"Canadian Women in the Public Eye: Miss Sime," *Saturday Night*, 18 Feb. 1922: 9.

New, W. H. "Jessie Georgina Sime," *Dictionary of Literary Biography*, Vol. 92, ed. W. H. New, pp. 356–361.

Sime, J. G. *Our Little Life: A Novel of To-day* (New York: Stokes, 1921).

——. *In a Canadian Shack* (Toronto: Macmillan, 1937).

Munitions!

J. G. Sime

Bertha Martin sat in the street car in the early morning going to her work. Her work was munitions. She had been at it exactly five weeks.

She sat squeezed up into a corner, just holding on to her seat and no more, and all round her were women and girls also working at munitions — loud, noisy, for ever talking — extraordinarily happy. They sat there filling the car with their two compact rows, pressed together, almost in one another's laps, joking, chewing tobacco — flinging the chewed stuff about.

It wasn't in the least that they were what is technically known as "bad women." Oh no — no! If you thought that, you would mistake them utterly. They were decent women, good, self-respecting girls, for the most part "straight girls" — with a black sheep here and there, to be sure, but where aren't there black sheep here and there? And the reason they made a row and shrieked with laughter and cracked an unseemly jest or two was simply that they were turned loose. They had spent their lives caged, most of them, in shop or house, and now they were drunk with the open air and the greater freedom and the sudden liberty to do as they liked and damn whoever stopped them.

Bertha Martin looked round at her companions. She saw the all sorts that make the world. Here and there was a pretty, young, flushed face, talking — talking — trying to express something it felt inside and couldn't get out. And here and there Bertha Martin saw an older face, a face with a knowledge of the world in it and that something that comes into a woman's eyes if certain things happen to her, and never goes out of them again. And then Bertha Martin saw quite elderly women, or so they seemed to her — women of forty or so, decent bodies, working for someone besides themselves — they had it written on their faces; and she saw old women — old as working women go — fifty and more, sitting there with their long working lives behind them and their short ones in front. And now and then some woman would draw her snuff-box from her shirt-waist and it would pass up and down the line and they would all take great pinches of the brown, pungent powder and stuff it up their noses — and laugh and laugh. . . . Bertha Martin looked round the car and she couldn't believe it was she who was sitting in it.

It was the very early spring. The white March sunshine came streaming into the car, and when Bertha, squeezed sideways in her corner, looked through the window, she saw the melting snow everywhere — piles and piles of it uncleared because the men whose job it was to clear it were at the war. She saw walls of snow by the sides of the streets — they went stretching out into infinity. And the car went swinging and lurching between them, out through the city and into the country where the factory was. There were puddles and little lakes of water everywhere; winter was melting away before the birth of another spring.

Bertha looked. She looked up into the clear — into the crystal clearness of the morning sky. It was the time of the spring skies of Canada — wonderful, delicate, diaphanous skies that come every spring to the Northern Land — skies the colour of bluebells and primroses — transparent, translucent, marvellously beautiful. Bertha looked up into the haze of colour — and she smiled. And then she wondered why she smiled.

It was the very early springtime.

Just five weeks before and Bertha had been a well-trained servant in a well-kept, intensely self-respecting house — a house where no footfall was heard on the soft, long-piled rugs; where the lights were shaded and the curtains were all drawn at night; where the mistress lay late in bed and "ordered" things; where life was put to bed every night with hot bottles to its feet; where no one ever spoke of anything that mattered; where meals were paramount. There had Bertha Martin lived five long, comfortable years.

She had gone about her business capably. She had worn her uniform like any soldier — a white frock in the mornings and a cap upon her head, and her hair had been orderly, her apron accurately tied. She had been clean. There were no spring skies in sight — or else she had not looked to see them. She had got up — not too unreasonably early — had had her early morning cup of tea with the other servants, had set the dining-room breakfast, waited on it — quiet — respectful — as self-respecting as the house. And in the afternoons there she had been in her neat black gown with her cap and apron immaculate — her hair still orderly and unobtrusive — everything about her, inside and out, still self-respecting and respectful. She had "waited on table," cleaned silver, served tea, carried things everlastingly in and out, set them on tables, taken them off again, washed them, put them away, taken them out again, reset tables with them — it was a circular game with never any end to it. And she had done it well. "Martin is an excellent servant," she had heard the lady of the house say once. "I can trust her thoroughly."

One afternoon in the week she went out. At a certain hour she left the house; at another certain hour she came back again. If she was half-an-hour late she was liable to be questioned: "Why?" And when she had given her explanation then she would hear the inevitable "Don't let it occur again." And Sunday — every other Sunday — there was the half day, also at certain hours. Of course — how otherwise could a well-run house *be* well run? And down in the kitchen the maids would dispute as to whether you got out half-an-hour sooner last time and so must go half-an-hour later this — they would quarrel and squabble over the silliest little things. Their horizon was so infinitesimally small, and they were so much too comfortable — they ate so much too much and they did so far too little — what could they do but squabble? They were never all on speaking-terms at one time together. Either the old cook was taking the housemaid's part or she and the housemaid were at daggers drawn; and they all said the same things over and over and over again — to desperation.

Bertha Martin looked up at the exquisite sky — and she smiled. The sun came streaming in, and the girls and women talked and jabbered and snuffed and chewed their tobacco and spat it out. And sometimes when the car conductor put his head in at the door they greeted him with a storm of chaff — a hail of witticisms — a tornado of personalities. And the little French-Canadian, overpowered by numbers, would never even try to break a lance with them. He would smile and shrug and put his hand up to his ears and run the door back between himself and them. And the women would laugh and clap their hands and stamp with their feet and call things to him — shout. . . .

Bertha turned to the girl next her — nearly atop of her — and looked her over. She was a fragile-looking, indoors creature — saleslady was written all over her — with soft rings of fair curled hair on her temples, and a weak, smiling mouth, and little useless feet in her cheap, high-heeled pumps. She was looking intently at a great strap of a girl opposite, with a great mouth on her, out of which was reeling a broad story.

"My, ain't she the girl?" said Bertha's little neighbour; and with the woman's inevitable gesture, she put her two hands up to her hair behind, and felt, and took a hairpin out here and there and put it in again.

She turned to Bertha.

"Say, ain't she the girl alright? Did you hear?"

Bertha nodded.

The little indoors thing turned and glanced at Bertha — took her in from head to foot with one feminine look.

"You gittin' on?" she said.

"Fine!" said Bertha.

The eyes of the women met. They smiled at one another. Fellow-workers — out in the world together.

That's what their eyes said: Free! And then the little creature turned away from Bertha — bent forward eagerly. Another of the stories was coming streaming out.

"Ssh! . . . ssh!" cried some of the older women. But their voices were drowned in the sea of laughter as the climax took possession of the car. The women rocked and swayed — they clutched each other — they shrieked.

"Where's the harm?" the big strap cried.

Five weeks ago and Bertha had never heard a joke like that. Five weeks ago she would hardly have taken in the utter meaning of that climax. Now! Something in her ticked — something went beating. She smiled — not at the indecency, not at the humour. What Bertha smiled at was the sense of liberty it gave her. She could hear stories if she liked. She could *act* stories if she liked. She was earning money — good money — she was capable and strong. Yes, she was strong, not fragile like the little thing beside her, but a big, strong girl — twenty-four — a woman grown — alive.

It seemed a long, dim time ago when all of them sat round that kitchen table to their stated meals at stated hours. Good, ample, comfortable meals. Plenty of time to eat them. No trouble getting them — that was the cook's affair — just far too much to eat and too much time to eat it in. Nothing to think about. Inertia. A comfortable place. What an age ago it seemed! And yet she had expected to spend her life like that — till she married someone! She never would have thought of "giving in her notice" if it hadn't been for Nellie Ford. How well Bertha remembered it — that Sunday she met Nellie — a Nellie flushed, with shining eyes.

"I'm leaving," Nellie had said to her. "I'm leaving — for the factory!"

And Bertha had stopped, bereft of words.

"*The factory* . . . !" she had said. That day the factory had sounded like the bottomless pit. "The factory . . . !"

"Come on," Nellie had said, "come on — it's fine out there. You make good money. Give in your notice — it's the life."

And Bertha had listened helplessly, feeling the ground slipping.

"But, Nellie —— " she kept saying.

"It's the life," Nellie had kept reiterating; "it's the life, I tell you. Come on, Bert, *sure* it's the life. Come on — it's great out there. We'll room together if you'll come."

Then Nellie had told her hurriedly, brokenly, as they walked along that Sunday afternoon, all that she knew about the factory. What Agnes Dewie, that was maid to Lady Something once — what *she* said. "It was great!" That's what she said. "Liberty," said Agnes Dewie, "a room you paid for, good money, disrespect to everything, nothing above you — freedom. . . ."

Nellie had panted this out to Bertha. "Come on, come *on*, Bert," she had said; "it's time we lived."

And slowly the infection had seized on Bertha. The fever touched her blood — ran through it. Her mental temperature flew up. She was a big girl, a slow-grower, young for her years, with a girl's feelings in her woman's body. But Nellie Ford had touched the spring of life in her. After that Sunday when Bertha looked round the quiet, self-respecting house — she hated it. She hated the softness of it — the quietness — hated the very comfort. What did all these things matter? Nellie Ford had said: "It's time we *lived*. . . ."

Bertha gazed upward through the window of the car — twisted and turned so that she could look right into the morning blue. The car was clear of city life. It sped along a country road. Fields were on either side, and only now and then a solitary house. Great trees stretched out bare branches.

Then in that far-off life came the giving in of the notice. Bertha remembered the old cook's sour face — that old sour face past every hope of life and living. Could one grow to look like that? Can such things be? "You'll live to rue the day, my lady!" said the cook. And Bertha remembered how the lady at the head of things had said: "Do you realise that you'll *regret* leaving a good place like this?" And then, more acidly: "I wouldn't have believed it of you,

Martin." And as she turned to go: "If you choose to reconsider —— "

Regret! Reconsider! Never again would she hear bells and have to answer them. Never again would someone say to her: "Take tea into the library, Martin." Never again need she say: "Yes, ma'am." Think of it! Bertha smiled. The sun came streaming in on her — she smiled.

Liberty! Liberty to work the whole day long — ten hours at five and twenty cents an hour — in noise and grime and wet. Damp floors to walk on. Noise — distracting noise all round one. No room to turn or breathe. No time to stop. And then at lunch-time no ample comfortable meal — some little hurried lunch of something you brought with you. Hard work. Long hours. Discomfort. Strain. That was about the sum of it, of all that she had gained . . . but then, the sense of freedom! The joy of being done with cap and apron. The feeling that you could draw your breath — speak as you liked — wear overalls like men — curse if you wanted to.

Oh, the relief of it! The going home at night, dead-tired, to where you had your room. Your own! The poor, ill-cooked suppers — what a taste to them! The deep, dreamless sleep. And Sunday — if you ever got a Sunday off — when you could lie abed, no one to hunt you up, no one to call you names and quarrel with you. Just Nellie there.

What did it matter if you had no time to stop or think or be? What did anything matter if life went pulsing through you amidst dirt and noise and grime? The old life — that treading round with brush and dust-pan — that making yourself noiseless with a duster: "Martin, see you dust well *beneath* the bed." "Yes, ma'am." And now the factory! A new life with other women working round you — bare-armed — grimy — roughened — unrestrained. What a change! What a sense of broadening out! What . . . !

Bertha Martin smiled. She smiled so that a woman opposite smiled back at her; and then she realised that she was smiling. She felt life streaming to her very finger-tips. She felt the spring pass through her being — insistent and creative. She felt her blood speak to her — say things it never said when she was walking softly in the well-ordered house she helped to keep for five long, comfortable years. "Selfish to leave me." That was what the lady of the house had said to her. "Selfish — you're all selfish. You think of nothing but yourselves."

Well — why not? What if that were true? Let it go anyway. That half-dead life was there behind . . . and Bertha Martin looked out at the present. The car went scudding in the country road. There was the Factory — the Factory, with its coarse, strong, beckoning life — its noise — its dirt — its men.

Its men! And suddenly into Bertha Martin's cheek a wave of colour surged. Yesterday — was it yesterday? — that man had caught her strong, round arm as she was passing him — and held it.

Her breath came short. She felt a throbbing. She stopped smiling — and her eyes grew large.

It was the very early spring.

Then suddenly the flock of women rose — felt in the bosoms of their shirt-waists for their cigarettes and matches — surged to the door — talking — laughing — pushing one another — the older ones expostulating.

And, massed together in the slushy road, they stood, lighting up, passing their matches round — happy — noisy — fluttered — not knowing what to do with all the life that kept on surging up and breaking in them — waves of it — wave on wave. Willingly would they have fought their way to the Munitions Factory. If they had known the *Carmagnole* they would have danced it in the melting snow[1]. . . .

It was the spring.

ᕒ

Sister Woman (London: Grant Richards; Toronto: S. B. Gundy, 1919), 35–45.

---

[1] *Carmagnole*: A popular song and dance of the French Revolution, subsequently associated with eruptions of popular discontent.

The Canadian Short Story Library, Series 2

The revitalized Canadian Short Story Library undertakes to publish fiction of importance to a fuller appreciation of Canadian literary history and the developing Canadian tradition. Work by major writers that has fallen into obscurity will be restored to canonical significance, and short stories by writers of lapsed renown will be gathered in collections or appropriate anthologies.

John Moss
General Editor

The Canadian Short Story Library
SERIES 1

Selected Stories of Duncan Campbell Scott
Edited by Glenn Clever

Selected Stories of Raymond Knister
Edited by Michael Gnarowski

Selected Stories of E.W. Thomson
Edited by Lorraine McMullen

Waken, Lords and Ladies Gay: Selected Stories of
Desmond Pacey
Edited by Frank M. Tierney

Selected Stories of Isabella Valancy Crawford
Edited by Penny Petrone

Many Mansions: Selected Stories of Douglas O. Spettigue
Edited by Leo Simpson

The Lady and the Travelling Salesman:
Stories by Leo Simpson
Edited by Henry Imbleau

Selected Stories of Robert Barr
Edited by John Parr

Selected Stories of Ernest Thompson Seton
Edited by Patricia Morley

Selected Stories of Mazo de la Roche
Edited by Douglas Daymond

Short Stories by Thomas Murtha
Edited by William Murtha

The Race and Other Stories by Sinclair Ross
Edited by Lorraine McMullen

Selected Stories of Norman Duncan
Edited by John Coldwell Adams

SERIES 2

New Women: Short Stories by Canadian Women,
1900–1920
Edited by Sandra Campbell and Lorraine McMullen

Voyages: Short Narratives of Susanna Moodie
Edited by John Thurston